CARAUSIUS AND ALLECTUS

CARAUSIUS AND ALLECTUS

The British Usurpers

P.J. Casey

With translations of the texts
by R.S.O. Tomlin

Yale University Press
New Haven and London

Contents

List of Illustrations

Figures

Plates (Between pages 80 and 81)

(Between pages 96 and 97)

(Between pages 144 and 145)

9, 1-7 Coins of Diocletian, Constantine I, 'Carausius II', Constantius II, Constantine I, Giovanni Pesaro
a St Peter's Hill, London, foundations of Allectan date
b St Peter's Hill, London, foundations and oak piles
c Milestone of Carausius
d Portchester Castle
e Fourth-century boat from Nydam
f Mosaic of Aeneas from Low Ham villa

(Between pages 160 and 161)

g The title page of de Peyster's work on Carausius
h Engraving of the assassination of Carausius
i Boulogne in the eighteenth century
j Boulogne: the setting of the Roman fortress

INTRODUCTION

THIS BOOK BRINGS TOGETHER THE evidence from the literary, numismatic and archaeological spheres of a relatively little known yet extraordinary episode in the history of Roman Britain. For a decade the island achieved an independence which threatened the stability of the empire, brought the constitutional and administrative reforms of Diocletian into question and almost certainly delayed their full implementation. On two occasions, during these ten years, coastal areas of Gaul formed part of the separatist dominion. The urgent need to bring the revolt in Britain to an end led to the creation of a second tier of imperial rulers, designated heirs to the joint emperors. In the West Constantius Chlorus was promoted specifically to suppress the revolt. In the East Galerius was selected to deal with the encroaching threat of Persia. Constantius's success was instrumental in opening the road to power for his son Constantine, who used the province recovered by his father as the base for his own bid for imperial recognition. It was the battle-hardened army of the father which threw its support behind the son who, it can be argued, through the adoption of Christianity as the state religion shaped the world in which we still live.

The independence of Britain during the rule of Carausius and his successor Allectus was based on naval power. These rulers controlled the sea lanes of the English Channel and the North Sea and maintained what was probably the most effective naval force to exist in the Roman world after serious naval warfare ceased in the reign of Augustus. There had been previous attempts to found regimes based on naval power, notably by Demetrius Poliorcetes and Sextus Pompey, but neither of these charismatic leaders secured popular support nor did they enjoy the resources of a fertile land base, equipped with an administrative and industrial infrastructure of sufficient sophistication to support their naval forces. Indeed the absence of such resources drove them to piratical expedients in search of the wherewithal with which to maintain their forces. In the aftermath of the defeat of the rebellion strategic decisions were taken which had an impact on the north-western provinces in the fourth century and which, arguably, made them less resilient to the naval attacks mounted on them by Scots, Saxon and Pictish raiders. The abolition of a unified naval command such as that enjoyed by Carausius, and its replacement by individual fleets attached to coastal forts, reduced Roman response to seaborne raiders to a reactive strategy rather than an aggressively campaigning one. Despite rhetorical protestations to the contrary the coasts of Gaul and Britain were subject to frequent and devastating attack throughout the century following the overthrow of the British regime.

Whatever the truth behind the causes of the revolt of Carausius, and these remain obscure, it serves to highlight one of the growing contradictions in the continued existence of Rome's empire, the increased diversity of its constituent parts submerged below a thin covering of generalized *romanitas*. This diversity was recognized by Diocletian himself whose division of the empire between an eastern half, over which he retained direct control, and a western half which devolved to Maximian, effectively acknowledged the existence of a Hellenistic and a Celtic/Germanic empire. Within the context of the latter, Britain retained a distinctive character of its own which was recognized in antiquity and commented upon, with contemptuous irony, by a number of contemporary commentators. The very location of Britain placed it beyond the bounds of Ocean, the sea which encompassed the land mass of the ancient world. Despite the fact that daily commerce existed between Britain and Gaul before and after the establishment of Roman power on the Channel coast, Britain continued to be regarded as outside the bounds of the civilized world. In spite of Julius Caesar's well-publicized expeditions to Britain, in AD 43 Claudius's invasion army refused to embark on the grounds that they were being taken beyond the known world. The inhabitants themselves enjoyed a poor reputation, though Tacitus said that they were cleverer and more adaptable than the Gauls. A document of the Trajanic period, found in a fort on the northern frontier, refers to them with the demeaning epithet '*Britunnculi*' – little Britons – poor fighters who run around shaking their spears ineffectually. Generally comment is adverse: the climate dismal, the inhabitants dishonest; but the wonder of the inclusion of even distant Britain within the empire of the Roman people never diminished.

Ownership of Britain, a disappointment in terms of mineral resources, a drain on the finances of the state, populated by natives who even made poor slaves, was regarded, in a perverse way, as a measure of the *virtus* of the Roman people and their qualification to hold imperial power elsewhere. Invested with such symbolic value, Britain was not a territory to be abandoned casually, the fact of possession of Britain being too deeply embedded in imperial ideology. The recovery of the island, according to the panegyric which celebrated the reconquest in AD 296, rectified a situation which was an affront to the empire as a whole; the eternal light of *Romanitas* was restored to an island which had been benighted under the shadow of revolt. Her peoples were not to be abandoned to unlicensed savagery but once again to be enfolded in the embrace of imperial law and civilized human relationships. These blessings were restored as the result of sacrifices made on behalf of the Britons by their fellow citizens of the empire.

Despite the seriousness of the event in Roman terms, it is no surprise that the reigns of Carausius and Allectus have failed to take root in the British historical psyche. The sources are scant, the episode virtually suppressed by contemporary imperial historians and the protagonists survive as shadowy figures illuminated only by the feeble light of hostile commentators. Access to the story is made difficult by the nature of the surviving non-literary evidence, which is almost entirely numismatic. The numismatist is normally thought of by historians and archaeologists less as a contributor of primary evidence, ideas or historical synthesis and more as a classificatory specialist. A scientist in his own right, the numismatist has been marginalized in the evolution of the explication of the historical process and thus a primary source of information has been largely neglected. This factor must loom large in any consideration of the relative neglect of Carausian studies; the body of coin material is formidable, apparently confused, poorly documented in the available catalogues and contaminated, in the minds of literary scholars, by its whimsical use in the past. Overcoming these prejudices requires a clear statement of numismatic methodology, a careful weighing of the value of individual components of coin evidence in relation to other sources and, it must be bluntly stated, some small effort on the part of the reader.

Britain is rich in national heroes, some fictional some of historical reality, who enshrine national characteristics. From time to time these iconic beings find sublime expression in literature or political debate, but for the most part they exist in a hazy limbo. Nevertheless, popular heroes are powerful figures in defining national consciousness. The transmission of the specific legend is a matter of historical chance and the defining element may in itself be trivial. King Alfred's lack of culinary skill hardly constitutes his most important achievement, which must be accounted the stemming of the Norse conquest of England, whilst Boudica's revolt against Rome is a relatively unimportant episode in either British or Roman imperial history; yet, under the name Boadicea, she has a place in popular legend, a commemoration in leaden verse by Dibdin and a much photographed statue in the shade of Big Ben; the name of Tacitus, the historian who immortalized her, is known only to scholars. Carausius and Allectus have not made it to the iconic first rank but have from time to time surfaced as representatives of national aspiration or political factions. The full treatment of this aspect of the Carausian episode occupies the second half of this book. In the centuries during which insular political debate was paramount, the Carausian episode held its place in literary and historical discussion, and legendary accretions were grafted on to the bare historical framework in order to manipulate the present by recourse to a fictitious past. By contrast the academic debates of the eighteenth century accurately reflect the trivialization of classical scholarship and a downgrading of the legendary past in a period of dynamic commercial and industrial growth. When, in the nineteenth century, scholarship was again turned to social use, to intellectualize the acquisition of empire and to educate its rulers, it was to well-documented episodes of the ancient past, that were seen as being of a morally elevated nature, that the tutors of the colonial administration turned for their material, not to squalid manoeuvrings from what was perceived as a period of imperial degeneracy. Thus events which defined the insularity of Britain fell in desuetude, since they served no socially useful intellectual purpose. The revival of Carausian studies coincided with a return to insularity and a redefinition of political horizons.

In attempting to summarize current knowledge of the Carausian episode one must be only too aware of the potential for criticism. Archaeologists may find the dependence on texts, with all the problems of credibility which they throw up, to be a retreat to the practices of a former age of scholarship; an exercise in historicism of a sort which many fervently hoped had passed away from the field of Romano-British studies for ever. On the other had, classicists may find the reliance on archaeological evidence equally distasteful with, to their minds, unsupported speculation deriving from mute and ambiguous material remains. For their part numismatists may find the use of their specialism over optimistic, if not utterly jejeune. Having set up these hypothesized critical strawmen an attempt should be made to justify to them the choice of material and explain the theoretical stance from which it has been approached.

As for the choice of material itself the justification must be bluntly stated: that is that, for the present, there is no more. Like Nennius, the author has 'heaped up all that I could find'. The quality of this material is generally poor and the literary sources, specifically the panegyrics, should be approached with a caution which some might claim should verge on incredulity. The numismatic material may seem equally ambiguous to the non-specialist, but it has an ambiguity independent of the literary evidence and in its spatial distribution offers an insight into events not otherwise vouchsafed. Insofar as the coin evidence offers direct evidence for the political motives and actions of the protagonists, a path of reserve and caution has been pursued. On the other hand, where the occurrence of dated coinage in well-founded contexts is available, such as in the case of the coinage of the Rouen mint, this has been exploited to the full. The very richness of the coinage of Carausius and Allectus, the variety of known types, the multiplicity of iconographic detail and the rapidity of new discovery, imposes limitations on its use in a work which tries to strike a balance between the three branches of evidence – literary, numismatic and archaeological. A work entirely devoted to the coinage would be both unhelpful to the general reader and quite beyond the abilities of the present author. Indeed, it has been the aim of this work to demonstrate that the use of a variety of classes of evidence, no one of which is as strong as the combination of the whole, can be used to achieve a coherent picture without resort to speculation of the 'we should surely be justified in assuming that . . . ' school of history. At best we can claim that we are decoding some sort of telephone message from the past – albeit on a very poor line.

This book falls into a number of sections. Following a general sketch of Britain in the century of the revolt and a discussion of the military resources of the island, the 'accepted' version of events is stated. This is then examined in the light of recent advances in numismatic and archaeological studies in both Britain and France. A new translation of the contemporary sources is provided and these are examined in the light of the independent coin and excavation data. An attempt to view the aftermath of the revolt without accepting the constraint of a belief in an invasion of northern Britain as a concomitant of the fall of Allectus permits a re-examination of many of the accepted views which still make their appearance in the standard works on Roman Britain.

The study of Carausius and Allectus from the post-Roman period to the modern period has thrown up both the sophisticated and the bizarre manipulation of the episode for political purposes. The unedifying spectacle of British scholarship in the eighteenth century scrambling for social advantage in the wreckage of classical scholarship is offset by the touchingly patriotic use of the Carausian myth at times of savage warfare and national danger. That the myth has had no impact in the arts is evident from a study of the relevant documentation which reveals no play based on the revolt, and the sources for musical drama show that any operatic potential was not exploited. Two modern novels, *The Emperor of the Narrow Sea* by John Gloag and *The Silver Branch* by Rosemary Sutcliff, the latter a children's story, carry the theme into the last decades.

A number of people have contributed to the completion of this work, though they are not responsible for the opinions expressed or the theories put forward. Pre-eminent among these is Dr R.S.O. Tomlin whose translations of the texts form part of this book and whose profound knowledge of this period has been freely put at my disposal. Malcolm Line made available his important work on Pevensey and has allowed me to use it before publication. Drs Xavier Loriot and Helene Huvelin, my colleagues in Carausian studies in France, have put their research at my disposal and it is the former's research which is represented by the maps illustrating the spread of Carausian and Allectan coins in Gaul. I should also like to thank Dr Andrew Burnett (The British Museum), Dr Richard Reece (London University), Dr J.L. Davies (University College, Aberystwyth), Dr Kevin Greene (Newcastle University), the Librarian of the Royal Geographical Society, Tom Eden (Sothebys), Martin Schøyen (The Martin Schøyen Collection, Oslo/London); Colin Richardson, of Carlisle Museum, supplied the photograph of the Gallow's Hill milestone and Stephen Minnitt of Taunton Museum the photograph of the Low Ham mosaic. Plates a and b are © the Museum of London. Plate d is © English Heritage Photographic Library and plates i and j are © Royal Geographical Society. The plans and diagrams are the work of Yvonne Beadnall of the Department of Archaeology, Durham University, the bulk of the photographs are the work of Trevor Woods and the bibliography was typed by Julia Bowder of the same department; all responded to the author's usual confusion and demanding schedule with their normal cheerful tolerance. The Photographic Department of the British Museum supplied a number of the coin illustrations in this work. Finally, the author would like to thank Norman Shiel – though he was not consulted – whose steady publication of stimulating new discoveries has been a feature of Carausian studies for many years.

Department of Archaeology,
University of Durham

• 1 •

THE ROMAN EMPIRE
IN THE THIRD CENTURY

THE CENTURY BETWEEN THE DEATH of Commodus and the accession of Diocletian saw a transformation of the empire founded by Augustus. Although the names of institutions and offices survived, as did the old way of life in some remote areas of the empire and among some classes of society, the empire which Diocletian ruled was one that was clinging to the wreckage of the classical world.

Fundamental to this change was the worsening military situation of the empire. Confronted by militarily inferior enemies, Rome had expanded in a matter of two centuries from a middle-ranking power in the Italian peninsula to rule over a landmass which extended from Britain in the west to beyond the Euphrates in the east. In northern Europe the frontiers lay on the lines of the rivers Rhine and Danube, in Africa on the edge of the Sahara desert. In Egypt and Palestine the deserts again served as the limits of Roman settlement. Beyond the area of direct rule diplomatic activity or the threat of military intervention extended Roman influence into the territory of adjacent tribes or kingdoms.

In the east a different situation prevailed; here the Roman state confronted the Persian empire. Until the early third century the River Euphrates served to divide these imperial enemies, and areas of conflict, essentially Armenia, were ruled by nominees of Rome or, at times of military success, by candidates more sympathetic to Persian policies. After the invasion of Persia by Septimius Severus the frontier was extended beyond the Euphrates with fateful consequences.

The conquest of this vast territory had been achieved by the Roman legions, which consisted of citizen soldiers, and regiments recruited from allies or conquered peoples. On the Rhine Parthians served as frontier forces as did archers recruited in what is now Jordan, Britons were sent to the Balkans and to Egypt, and Germans were found in Britain. In these frontier districts they served the empire and received the reward of Roman citizenship on completion of their term of recruitment. The emperor Caracalla changed this situation when he gave citizenship to all free men in the empire, thus diminishing the attraction of an army career to unenfranchised provincials. Around the vast frontiers, an army protected the heartland of the empire which it never saw, a Rome whose rulers wanted nothing more than to keep the army away from the centres of political power. In the event as military crisis followed military crisis, it was political power which moved from Rome to the armies, and the capital was reduced to a symbolic seat of government, visited at infrequent intervals by rulers celebrating victories or the ceremonial aspects of imperial power.

The frontiers protected a great miscellany of peoples, unified by Roman rule while maintaining their own national characteristics. They shared whatever benefits might be derived from Roman technology and economic tolerance and were protected, to a greater or lesser extent, depending on their social standing, in their private and commercial lives by Roman law. Many of these imperial citizens were unwilling recruits to Roman hegemony and periodic revolts, such as that of Boudica in Britain and the Jews in Palestine, exemplifying the resistance which could be mobilized when government became intolerable. But revolts were normally a feature of the least Romanized parts of the empire, the bulk of which enjoyed a cultural inheritance derived from the Greek world. Here cities, once truly independent, maintained a quasi-autonomy under discreet Roman rule. A traditional culture, based on a formalized literary education, bound the provincial urban ruling classes to an ideal of public service which found expression in the provision of amenities for their native cities and charitable care for their fellow citizens. Throughout Asia Minor, Africa, Italy and the Balkans cities flourished and politically motivated benefactors employed their fortunes to provide their native towns with the adjuncts of city life, libraries, theatres, bath-houses, stadia for athletic festivals, and temples to house the benevolent gods.

In the north-western provinces of Europe, Rome attempted to graft this culture on to a very different sort of society. In the south of Gaul, and in Spain, areas which had been settled at an early date by migrants from Greece and later Italy itself, a flourishing version of Hellenistic civilization was implanted on the fringes of a deeply-rooted native population. In northern Gaul, Britain and Germany, Romanization had a more exiguous existence. The towns were built and the theatres, baths and temples provided, either by the state or by imperial coercion of the small native elite; but these arrangements were ephemeral and most of society retained its traditional values. None the less cities had to be maintained, since the functioning of the empire depended upon local communities performing essential administrative functions on behalf of the state. Among these functions were taxation, recruitment and, increasingly, the provisioning of the army.

If Roman rule offered autonomy and a formalized liberation for some and 'compulsory' autonomy for others, to those who participated what lay outside this framework hardly bore thinking about. On the other side of the frontiers was '*barbaricum*', a howling wilderness where untrammelled lawlessness and cruelty held sway, where mere impulse governed men's actions in a world of unreason. Better the benefits of the Roman peace, with all its defects, than anarchy.

In reality, the peoples of the frontier areas were complex societies in their own right and not unappreciative of the material benefits of the empire with which, as archaeology has demonstrated, they conducted a vigorous trade, providing the empire with such commodities as amber, furs, exotic animals and slaves. In return they imported finished goods, pottery, wine and silver coinage. But frontiers of themselves create problems. Given a single external political factor in their lives, quite disparate peoples find a common cause for unity of action and political sentiment. Such appears to have been the case on the German frontier and in Britain where the individual tribes, attested in first-century literary sources, appear to have been transformed into larger entities by the third century. A further factor in this transformation was the westward expansion of peoples originating in the east. Opinions are divided as to the reason for the tribal movements which were to convulse Europe in the third and fourth centuries; factors such as climatic change and population increase have been adumbrated. As a contribution to the latter factor it might be observed that population increase could be encouraged by the dampening down of inter-tribal warfare brought about by the threat of Roman intervention on behalf of allies beyond the frontier.

The first great attack on the frontiers was mounted in the reign of Marcus Aurelius (161–82) when the tribes on the Danube crossed the river to seek land within the empire. Pressured by movements from the east, they penetrated as far south as Athens and northern Italy before being defeated after years of warfare during which the Roman army came close to complete disaster on more than one occasion. In the most celebrated of these incidents the army was only extricated by a miraculous downpour of rain which obscured their retreat. Some thirty years later the emperor Caracalla fought a confederation of German tribes, the Alamanni, at the junction of the Rhine and Danube frontiers and, though the campaign was a success, he paid the tribes subsidies in gold to secure peace in Germany.

But it was the eastern frontier which was to destroy the Roman peace. Septimius Severus's campaigns in Persia destabilized the ruling Arsacid, or Parthian, dynasty, causing contempt for it among both the aristocracy and the mass of Iranians. Early in the third century the Arsacids were overthrown by the Sassanids, who sought to avenge three centuries of Roman military success in the east. Militarily efficient, they were masters of siege warfare, and riding on the crest of a national religious revival, the new Sassanian regime consolidated its position by a series of outstanding victories over Roman armies. Three Roman emperors were defeated in the field: Gordian III (238–44); Philip (244–9); and Valerian (253–60). The first of these may have died in battle, the last was taken prisoner. Forces to fight these campaigns had to be drawn from the western frontiers to which they did not return. The depletion of these defences exacerbated a worsening situation on the Rhine and Danube. Severus Alexander (222–35) was murdered for failing to maintain adequate forces to deal with the threat to Germany, and his successor, Maximinus (235–8), had to campaign hard to restore the situation.

While external threats rallied the empire to a sense of *romanitas* they also served to create a new problem at the provincial level. In order to maintain their safety the individual provinces demanded military leadership from those who would give priority to their cause. In the west the Gallic Empire represented just such a move, while in the Balkans a successful general could count on being offered, or forced to accept, imperial power by local civil and military interests. The result was civil war, the decline of the civil administration, desertion of agricultural land and the collapse of the currency. By shortly after the middle of the third century the state was in the grip of hyperinflation with the silver coinage debased to a mere token of its former worth. This apocalyptic situation came to a head in the reign of Gallienus (253–68). Faced by a collapsing Rhine–Danube frontier and an invasion of the east by the Sassanian king Shapur (241–70), Valerian led his army to defeat and himself into Persian captivity. Meantime his son, Gallienus, coped with the crisis in the west where the Franks crossed the Rhine and struck as far south as Spain. Germany, Gaul and Britain seceded from imperial rule to defend themselves under their own emperor, Postumus. Roman territory lying between the Rhine and Danube was given up, the garrisons withdrawn. In the east the defeat of Valerian exposed the richest and most cultured provinces of the empire to occupation; Antioch, the third largest city of the empire, was sacked. Occupation was averted by the intervention of the allied city of Palmyra whose forces turned back the Persian threat and assumed rule over large areas of Roman territory, nominally with imperial acquiescece. Odenathus, the Palmyrene king, was granted unprecedented titles – Leader of Romans, Victorious General, Restorer of the Whole Orient and King of Kings.

At the same time as Persia attacked previously peaceful provinces from the east, another attack was to fall on Asia Minor from the north. Hitherto the rich oriental provinces had been spared direct military threat, the areas affected having been the European provinces; nevertheless events did impinge. Already pressed by the demands made upon them by emperors and usurpers for finance to prosecute wars and to pay the army, the administrative classes of the empire may already have retrenched from their former municipal liberality. Demands for troops probably led to labour shortages on agricultural estates, while failure in warfare led to the enslavement of Roman troops in Persia rather than the acquisition of slaves, the traditional means of supplementing the work force of the empire. The depreciation of the currency inhibited trade and commerce, while the decline in disposable income abruptly curtailed spending on goods produced by craft industries. For example, by the middle of the third century privately erected inscriptions are rare in many provinces of the empire. By the end of the reign of Gallieus the civic coinage issued by scores of the cities of Asia Minor had all but ceased to exist.

Disaster fell on the cities of the eastern empire with the invasion of the Goths and their allies. Having gained control of the Kingdom of Bosporus, a Roman ally controlling the north-eastern coast of the Black Sea and the Crimea, the Goths came into possession of a navy and skilled Black Sea sailors to man it for them. In 256 and 257 Gothic naval expeditions attacked Roman cities in the eastern Black Sea region, culminating in the capture of Trebizond, on the coast of Asia Minor, and Calcedon at the mouth of the Bosporus. A foothold on the Asiatic mainland opened the way for the destruction of the inland sites of Nikomedia, Nicea, Apamea and Prusa, all opulent cities. In 267 a combined fleet of Goths and Heruls broke out of the Black Sea into the Aegean. Splitting into three groups they simultaneously attacked northern and southern Greece and the west coast of Asia Minor. Thessalonika, Athens, Corinth, Argos, Sparta and Olympia fell to the attackers. In Athens P. Herennius Dexippus, a historian and local aristocrat, recruited two thousand Athenians and inflicted serious losses on the raiders. In the south Rhodes was attacked and the temple of Diana at Ephesus, the seat of eastern government, was destroyed. The city of Side and the islands of Cyprus and Crete all suffered before the raiders turned for home.

Campaigns, led personally by Gallienus, resulted in the defeat of the Goths in northern Greece and, following his assassination, his successor, Claudius II, won outstanding victories, gaining the title 'Gothicus'. Claudius died of the plague in 270 and it was left to Aurelian (270–5) to clear the Balkans of enemy forces. Pursuing them across the Danube he inflicted a defeat which eliminated the western Goths from participation in Roman affairs for a century. But further territory had to be given up: the province of Dacia (modern Romania), which had been added to the empire by Trajan, was evacuated. A last attack by the eastern Goths in 276 and 277 was made on the provinces of Pontus, Cilicia and Galatia; on this occasion barbarian forces penetrated as far inland as Ancyra (modern Ankara) in the middle of Anatolia.

The military problems faced by Aurelian did not end with the Goths. Two great campaigns and numerous small wars occupied the reign. A German invasion of Italy, which threatened the capital itself, was defeated and the city provided with defensive walls for the first time since the kings had ruled in Rome. In the east the kingdom of Palmyra continued to exercise authority over parts of the Asiatic provinces. With the death of Odenathus his widow, Zenobia, promoted the claims of her son to imperial status and seized Egypt and further areas of the east. Two campaigns resulted in the capitulation and destruction of Palmyra and the overthrow of the separatist regime. In the west the last of the Gallic emperors, Tetricus, capitulated in face of certain defeat by Aurelian's forces. The territorial integrity of the empire had been restored.

To an extent the economic system was also restored, with an attempted reform of the inflated currency. But half a century of warfare had an irreversible impact on Roman society. No longer were emperors aristocrats, rather they were drawn from a pool of experienced army commanders of no social pretensions. No longer did the ruined urban aristocracy compete to spend their fortunes on civic amenities; cities had more need of strong walls than theatres and if the stock of accumulated monuments was sufficient they could be sacrificed to provide building materials. If the fields needed to be cultivated to feed the armies but labour was in short supply then the surviving peasantry had to be reduced to quasi-slavery to serve a compulsory attachment to the land; areas of desolation and depopulation could be reinhabited by migrating barbarians or captives.

A few areas remained largely unaffected by invasion, notably Britain and Africa; none the less they too bore the costs of recovery. Part of this cost was a strengthened pursuit of social conformity. For instance the law was applied in different ways to different social classes and religion was employed as a weapon in the war to save civilization. The fragile state was conceived to be held together by a pact between Rome and her gods and the disasters of the third century might by some be ascribed to a failure of observance. Notably blamed for this crisis were the Christian communities, especially the large ones in the east. Trajan Decius (249–51) actively pursued a policy of religious revival, endorsing the worship of deified emperors and initiating persecution of Christianity. Valerian, too, persecuted Christianity to maintain pagan orthodoxy. The policy of these emperors stemmed from the need to suppress a religion which was professedly less concerned with the 'here and now' and more with a future state of bliss. Emperors fighting for the survival of the state needed few things less than a burgeoning movement which preached a doctrine concerned with deferred gratification rather than with the present crisis, especially one which despised the gods of Rome and thus directly threatened the divine compact which was the theological basis of the state.

The success of Aurelian maintained the impetus of restoration which was to culminate in the reign of Diocletian. This process was interrupted from time to time by the perennial problem of hostile incursion. Thus Probus (276–82) was personally active on the German frontier, in Gaul and on the Danube. Further campaigns were conducted to suppress revolts in Asia Minor and it is a measure of the degree of renewal enjoyed by the empire that the luxury of revolt and military mutiny could flourish with a new vigour in the last quarter of the third century. In this regard it is a telling fact that successive emperors were concerned to carry warfare into the Persian empire itself, a policy which could not be contemplated since the reign of Valerian. Aurelian himself planned such a campaign before his murder, while Probus was on his way to the east when lynched by mutinous soldiers. Carus (282–3) pursued war with Persia with such success that he destroyed Ctesiphon, the enemy capital. Here he died, allegedly struck down by a bolt of lightning, a metereological phenomenon which cynics said had been forged in a legionary workshop.

Thus at the accession of Diocletian the Roman world had turned full circle. Internal dissent, civil war and external threats had brought the empire to the verge of destruction. The external threat had been met but the problem of random violence to the ruler had not been addressed and the threat of civil war which this engendered had not been overcome. From time to time a solution had been sought by sharing rule with other members of the imperial family: Valerian with Gallienus, Carus with his sons Carinus and Numerian; but the essential problem of the succession in a military monarchy had not been solved since military ability and political astuteness are not necessarily genetic gifts. Nor could a single ruler effectively maintain an imperial presence throughout the length and breadth of the reunified empire, though necessity forced emperors to march and countermarch from crisis to crisis.

Diocletian sought solutions to a number of problems: to restore the integrity of the frontier defences; to tax the empire efficiently in order to support the military effort; to protect the emperor himself; and to devise a system of succession which would deter would-be aspirants to the throne. The solution of the last problem was not new, in that division of power had been tried before; what was new was the complete rejection of dynastic and family ties in choosing a co-ruler and in making provision, on the same principles, of designated heirs apparent. The scheme soon broke down, mainly because two of the principals had ambitious sons who were excluded from power by these arrangements. But for the couple of decades for which the scheme operated, a relative peace was maintained in which the reconstruction of the state, the economy, army and administration could be undertaken. It must be emphasized that the peace was only relative, enemies continued to operate on the frontiers, Persia remained a persistent problem and ambitious or desperate officers, such as Carausius, still raised internal revolts. But these crises could be met by one or other of the four rulers without jeopardizing the fabric of the state.

On the other hand it can be argued that the abolition of dynastic rule actually encouraged ambitious officers to stake a claim in the ruling caste now that membership was released from the restraint of family blood-ties. Access to the emperor was made the more difficult by withdrawing the ruler from public view and by introducing rituals from the Persian monarchy which elevated the emperor from the traditional role of 'first citizen', itself a fiction, to that of an oriental ruler.

In presenting a generalized picture of the Roman empire in the third century in terms of military events and struggles for imperial power we have inevitably neglected many other aspects of life in this tumultuous period. Some of these aspects, especially the economic, have been illuminated by archaeology. Unfortunately few parts of the empire have been studied, or indeed published, with the detailed intensity of Britain.

But whatever the emphasis given, problems arise from the sources themselves with their inevitable concentration on the activities of rulers and their armies. Further, many of the ancient sources have been corrupted in transmission or are the products of incompetent historians who hung out their ignorance and prejudices like tattered banners. We must try to deduce the reaction of the unrepresented sections of society to events from other evidence, for instance from the artefacts they discarded or the coins and wealth they concealed and failed to recover, or from the failure or success of individual towns and communities to maintain their public buildings or to reconstruct them after neglect or destruction.

By these criteria Diocletian ushered in a period in which materially the Roman world flourished. Not on the scale of previous ages though. The currency system never did regain its former stability and though the cities were rebuilt it was often on a smaller scale than their original size. The armies were reconstructed and re-disciplined but they were no longer the legionary armies of the early empire. One outstanding success was the new administrative system which provided the Roman empire, for the first time, with a professional civil service which was to prove one of the most enduring institutions of the Roman world.

· 2 ·

BRITAIN

IN THE THIRD CENTURY

ARCHAEOLOGISTS TAKING THE LONG VIEW of events see the origins of observable material changes in society as being the result of complex and widespread trends. On the whole they do not look favourably on the idea that events are made by people; on the contrary, a widespread academic stance is that personalities are the product of processes and not the other way around. What this boils down to is that, in the absence of a system of interventionist religious belief, the inconsequential nature of events can be understood only within the framework of an inexplicable succession of natural causes. This philosophical stance is particularly appropriate to a science which relies for its very existence on mute and frequently unrepresentative material remains. The events with which this book is concerned are seen as part of a historical process and, it is contended, they cannot be understood unless placed in the context of their age and culture. The context is the development of Britain in the third century relative to the empire as a whole and specifically in relation to the neighbouring north-western provinces.

The conquest of Britain ground to a halt only in the early years of the third century. Until the death of Septimius Severus at York in 211, while campaigning against the tribes in the unconquered territories beyond Hadrian's Wall, the option of taking the whole of the island under Roman control had presented itself to successive rulers. When Hadrian (117–38) built his Wall across Britain and severed the tribes of the North from access to the province, it might have appeared that Rome had conceded the extremity of the island to native political interests. But his successor Antoninus Pius (138–61) immediately abandoned the newly completed Wall and advanced into Scotland, where he created the Antonine Wall across the Forth–Clyde isthmus. Strategic rigidity was not a characteristic of the administration of Roman Britain and this flexibility is further demonstrated by the decision of Pius's heir, Marcus Aurelius (161–80), to give up his adoptive father's conquests and once again occupy Hadrian's Wall. Not for long were frontier affairs left in this state, for in the first decade of the third century Septimius Severus (193–211) reverted to a policy of total conquest last pursued in the period in office of the Flavian governor Gnaeus Julius Agricola (77–83).

Severus's motives for being in Britain are obscure; one writer suggests that his campaign was as much inspired by a desire to sort out the personality defects of his sons, Caracalla and Geta, by getting them away from their vicious life style in Rome, as to remedy a serious military problem in the Roman empire's most distant province (Dio, lxxvii.11). Whatever the motives, the results of Severus's exertions failed to solve his domestic problems (Caracalla subsequently murdered his brother, stabbing him to death in their mother's arms), but did have a profound effect on the stability of the northern areas of Britain and the economic development of the province as a whole.

Perhaps most significant in the long term was the decision to divide the island into two provinces, Britannia Inferior and Britannia Superior, each with its own administration and governor. The date of this decision is disputed, the third-century historian Herodian says that the new arrangement was implemented immediately after the defeat of Albinus in 197 (Her., iii-8.2) but modern scholars have, characteristically, found this categorical statement of a contemporary historian difficult to reconcile with epigraphic evidence pointing to the division of Britain as having taken place in the reign of Caracalla, rather than in that of his father (Birley, 1981). Whenever the event, the result was the same: Britannia Inferior had its southern boundary on a line from north Wales to the Wash and within this area was stationed the bulk of the military forces in the island. At York *Legio VI Victrix* (whose commander was also governor of the province) formed the backbone of the northern army; brigaded with it were the garrisons of Hadrian's Wall and its outpost forts, comprising some twenty regiments of infantry and cavalry, while further units held selected forts in the Pennine region, where barely Romanized rural communities offered a persistent threat to military communications and the graver one of actual revolt.

The southern province, Britannia Superior, held two legions stationed at Caerleon in south Wales (*Legio II Augusta*) and Chester (*Legio XX Valeria Victrix*). As we shall see, the southern legions were probably quickly depleted by changes in the nature of the legion and by postings of detachments to elsewhere in Britain and abroad. A few troops were employed as the governor's guard, probably stationed in London, and auxiliary forts were garrisoned in north Wales (Casey & Davies, 1993). As the third century progressed more troops were stationed in the south but, on paper, the balance of forces always remained in the northern province.

The motive for the division was purely political. Severus himself had been governor of Pannonia (effectively modern Hungary) with three legions under his command. In the civil wars which brought him to the throne Severus fought with two other provincial governors of three legion provinces, Pescennius Niger of Syria and Clodius Albinus of Britain. Determined to prevent commanders of large provincial armies, such as himself, endangering the throne, Severus initiated the division of the larger provinces. In doing so he sought to remedy the situation by which a small number of powerful provincial commanders threatened imperial stability.

But the effect was catastrophic in the longer term. Instead of three commanders who were in a position to threaten revolt because they ruled three legion provinces, there were, by the end of the reign of Caracalla, as many potential threats as there were governors in provinces with two legions. The history of the third century is essentially a record of Severan political shortsightedness.

The division of Britain had a further economic effect. With the north tied to the army and the south virtually free of a military presence, two economies began to crystallize, one operating in a free market and the other circumscribed by the limited demands of a low technology army. As the century advanced and the currency was devalued, the demand of the army for goods and services in place of depreciated coin, which could not buy those goods and services on the free market, ensured that the northern economy was fixed into a rigid productive framework. The army needed basic foodstuffs, metals and organic raw materials such as hides and timber. These the northern countryside could supply without materially improving the basis on which such commodities had been produced since the late Iron Age. The absence of villas in areas of the north where the military presence was most in evidence is a graphic demonstration of this early 'North–South' economic divide.

While a distinctive character, albeit one already visible in early periods, was reinforced by the division of the island into separate administrative spheres, the position of Britain relative to its nearest provincial neighbours also underwent change in this century. At the same time these neighbours moved further and further out of the ambit of the central empire.

Archaeologists and ancient economic historians see the changes of the third century as developments characteristic of all extended empires, in which there are a number of stages in the creation and disintegration of complex imperial states. In the earliest stage, of course, comes conquest. This is a dynamic period in which expenditure is matched, or more than matched, by the acquisition of resources from the conquered territory. If, as in the case of Britain, the acquired territory is rich in raw materials or human resources the period of exploitation may be prolonged but in the long term a form of provincial autonomy will be achieved which extends into the economic sphere. The technology of the advanced core of the empire will be transferred to the peripheral areas. Building techniques, advanced metalworking, sophisticated pottery production methods and a local capital market are all available in the provinces. Thus the exchange of raw materials for finished goods with the centre of the empire becomes unnecessary. While this is detrimental to the central provinces, and, especially in the case of the Roman empire Italy, a reversal in the terms of trade is beneficial to the distant provinces. Wealth created in the provinces tended to stay there and though some of this was needed to maintain the army the stagnation of provincial armies tended to ensure that even this expenditure was recycled into the local economy. Archaeologists can trace this process through variations in the range of artefacts found on provincial sites which can be traced back to their production source. It was because of the growth of self-sufficiency that in the third century Roman London declined as a port handling imports and exports (Milne, 1985). Similarly, the decline of Italy as a recipient of provincial products can be traced in the declining fortunes of the port of Ostia which served Rome itself (Garnsey, 1983). While these tendencies can be traced on a broad scale in most provinces, or groups of provinces, they are particularly evident in Britain because they were further intensified by events in north-western Europe in the middle of the third century.

Delivering judgement on the Roman Empire, Edward Gibbon saw its golden age as being confined to a period extending from the end of the first to the third quarter of the second century:

> During a happy period of more than four-score years, the public administration was conducted by the virtue and abilities of Nerva, Trajan, Hadrian, and the two Antonines [sc. Antoninus Pius and Marcus Aurelius]. (Gibbon, 1771)

Despite this literary golden glow in which it participates, the reign of Marcus saw the first barbarian incursions across the frontiers of the western empire to a degree which threatened the heartland itself. In the reign of Marcus Aurelius (161–80) the Marcommani crossed the Danube frontier and penetrated as far south as northern Italy, where they attacked the Adriatic port city of Aquileia. The threat brought reinforcements to the area from an number of provincial armies, possibly even from Britain. For the second half of his reign Marcus made his base, and ruled the empire from the fortresses of the frontier rather than living in Rome itself. A long, slow and financially costly campaign was needed to re-establish the integrity of the frontier.

The third century saw a growing threat to the Rhine as well as the Danube frontiers. A number of serious barbarian incursions were instrumental in bringing about the rise of a succession of emperors, each proclaimed by the provincial armies, to deal with the regional problems of the frontier provinces. In the west these crises culminated in the creation of a separatist regime holding power in Germany, Gaul, parts of Spain and Britain. The Gallic Empire under its founding emperor Postumus (260–9) and his less effective successors Laelianus, Marius, Victorinus and Tetricus (271–4), demonstrated the need for effective regional leadership in times of crisis and constituted a model for the later Diocletianic system of devolved government. While fully involved in these events at the political level Britain was not directly so in a military sense (Birley, 1936). Though Gaul might be raided by land-based forces from across the frontier, Britain was safe behind her natural defence, the sea. The garrison of the island might be stripped down to supply troops for service overseas but there is no evidence of military activity in Britain, far less the sort of destruction found as far south as the Pyrenees in Gaul. Indeed it is likely that Britain gained a new industrial self-sufficiency in this period as overseas trade was disrupted by events taking place on the Continent. The pottery industry, for instance, achieved a level of market penetration for fine wares that had been previously enjoyed by imports from Gaul. On the other hand, urban development declined as towns lost their function as distributive centres for imports and British producers moved their goods directly to the rural and military markets.

None the less, Britain was not completely immune to the military events which affected its near Continental neighbour provinces and, as we shall see, provision was made on a limited scale to fortify the coasts of Britain as early as the middle of the third century. Contributing more directly to the development of the island was the economic crisis which gripped the empire in the third century and which reached its peak in the third quarter of the century.

We have already noticed a structural change in the economy of the empire in the third century, whereby the peripheral provinces grew at the expense of the central areas. But this was a gradual process and not uniform in all areas; a much more immediate problem to the state was the collapse of the currency system throughout the empire. The rapid decline of the intrinsic value of the Roman gold and silver coinage can be plotted through a series of debasements which start in the late second and accelerate in the third century (Fig.1). The reasons for this collapse are complex but a large factor was that of sustaining the pay of the army. Military pay had been fixed by Domitian at a level which, for the army of the period, cost the Roman state approximately 70,000,000 *denarii* per annum. This expenditure rose under Marcus Aurelius, who raised two new legions at an additional cost of about 2,300,000 *denarii* per annum. The cost of the Marcommanic War bankrupted the emperor's resources and Marcus was reduced to auctioning imperial property to raise cash. The continuous debasement of the silver coinage starts in this period.

An acceleration in the depreciation of the currency followed the accession of Septimius Severus, who consolidated his throne by raising the pay of the soldier so that the annual cost of a legion rose to about 2,470,000 *denarii*. His son Caracalla further raised military pay, taking to heart Severus's deathbed advice as recorded by the historian Cassius Dio: 'take care of each other, pay the soldiers and damn the rest' (Dio, lxxvii.15.2).

Following a further pay rise awarded by Caracalla (211–17), the annual cost of a legion had risen to about 3,712,000 *denarii* by the end of the reign. Meantime the standard silver coin, the *denarius*, had fallen over a period of a quarter of a century, to about 50 per cent of its former intrinsic value. Ever innovative in securing revenue, Caracalla introduced a new denomination of silver coin which effectively institutionalized debasement. The so-called *antoninianus* was struck from the same alloy as the *denarius* (i.e 50 per cent silver) but was tariffed as a 2-*denarius* piece. Its weight, however, was that of only one and a half *denarii*. Thus an effective

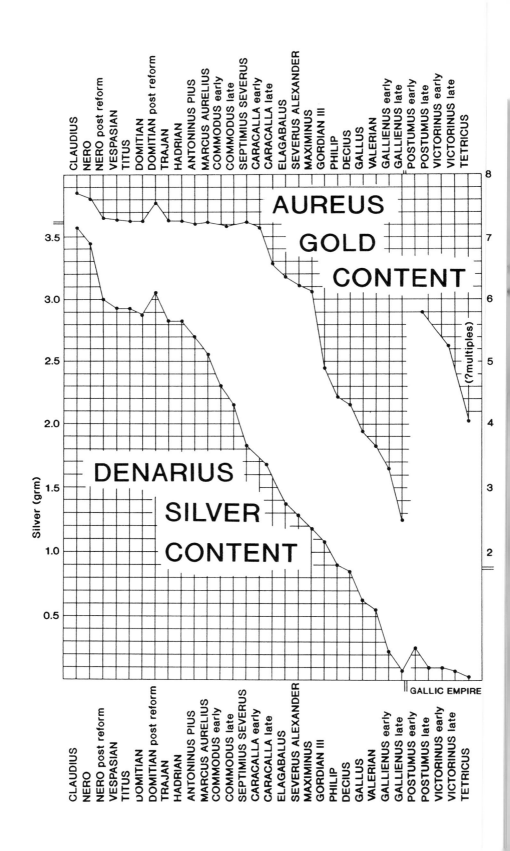

debasement of 25 per cent was achieved by circulating the new coin. Caracalla's other bold financial stroke was to give Roman citizenship to all free men in the empire, and at the same time he doubled to 10 per cent the rate of death duty charged on the wills of Roman citizens. This change was specifically designed to enhance the military treasury. Thereafter the decline of the intrinsic value of the coinage was a steady progression from the barely acceptable to the ultimately rejected. It is noticeable that every attempt was made to keep the traditional relationship between the silver coin and the gold, in this instance by lightening the weight of the *aureus* as the silver content of the *denarius* and *antoninianus* fell (Casey, 1984).

The effects of such steady and unremitting financial difficulty were felt throughout the empire. From the middle of the century the failure of the coin to keep its intrinsic value drove up prices as expressed in terms of that currency. The grip of inflation fuelled a cycle which demanded more actual coins to be circulated in order to meet the needs of commerce. More coins meant more debasement, more debasement higher prices.

In a situation of ever-increasing inflation individuals can adopt a number of strategies in order to protect their wealth. Since Roman coinage had an intrinsic value, more valuable specimens could be hoarded as they achieved a monetary premium against later, baser issues. Numerous hoards dating from the 230s to the 270s show that this was an expedient resorted to by those who could afford to immobilize their wealth. On a higher financial plane were those who could turn depreciating cash into property. It is in this period that the foundations were laid for the fortunes evidenced in Britain by luxurious villas in the fourth century. On the other hand, in hyperinflation the poor get poorer, and the evidence for rural discontent, amounting to peasant revolts, is found in the historical sources throughout the third century.

We may postulate further effects such as the decline of urban slavery, since slaves are an expensive luxury to keep in hard times and small urban craftsmen are likely to have been the first to suffer in an economic downturn. On the other hand, there might be a rise in slavery in rural areas with the growth, in real terms, of the wealth of primary producers such as farmers. The quasi-enslavement of tenant farmers to landlords may also be anticipated as well as a rapid decline in the place of the army in fuelling the provincial economic machine. The army's sharply declining purchasing power might also be accompanied by a decline in morale and self-esteem, especially since the army of Britain was inactive for most of the century. The less militarily effective an army becomes, the more likely it is to assuage its inadequacy by imposing its declining power on those it was designed to protect. The Roman army is not an exception to this observation and as it began to

The decline of the gold and silver coinage. Claudius – Gallic Empire. (After Casey, 1984.)

depend more and more on the produce of the farming sector to provide it with goods and services in lieu of cash taxes, the identification of interests between landowner and army became a feature of provincial political life.

The rise of the Gallic Empire, which lasted to within twelve years of the revolt of Carausius, brought changes to the military forces. While the Gallic provinces had to sustain themselves against both the depredations of barbarian invaders and the attacks of the central empire striving to recover lost territory, Britain suffered no military crises and it seems inherently likely that troops were deployed from Britain to the Continent. There is no direct evidence to show that units were withdrawn permanently or in their entirety, but the archaeological evidence from Hadrian's Wall suggests that garrisons were run down after the middle of the century.

Although there is a great deal of epigraphic evidence for small foreign units being posted to the northern frontier in the earlier third century, by the middle of the century recruitment into the main body of auxiliary regiments that had served long in Britain was largely from the local population (Casey & Noel, 1993). Hadrian's Wall was garrisoned by units who, although they bore exotic ethnic titles derived from their original place of recruitment, consisted of soldiers who were locals, born and bred in the civilian settlements which grew up outside the forts. A method of depleting these garrisons would be to direct recruits from the *vici* to overseas regiments rather than into their local units. This policy would both supplement the forces of areas under direct military threat and allow a rational control of the size and composition of units on the peaceful frontier in Britain.

There may have been a decline in offensive effectiveness but there is no evidence to suggest that the function of garrison troops in local policing declined. To provide a force which could deal with larger local problems a number of large forts were constructed on the main north–south roads in the hinterland of the frontier zone: these garrisons could be deployed to the frontier itself should the need arise. Little excavation has taken place in these forts which have, hitherto, been dated to the early years of the fourth century.

There is no evidence to suggest that the army of Britain was reinforced after the collapse of the Gallic Empire, though the emperor Probus (276–82) drafted an unspecified number of Burgundians to Britain 'because they would be useful to him there'. The Burgundians were prisoners captured in Gaul and their posting to a distant province might reflect a desire to isolate them, rather than a need for more troops in Britain. In the event, their usefulness did stretch to the suppression of a governor who attempted a revolt (Zos. 1. 68). By the end of the third century, however, there is evidence of defence problems arising in Britain which probably culminated in a campaign of pacification by the emperor Carinus (283–5). These problems were not ones which could be dealt with by the traditionally distributed land forces which were deployed to deal with incursions across the land frontiers of the north and to police the still unruly peoples of the northern uplands. The new threats came from overseas and called for the construction of fortifications to house coastal defence units. But these new threats were slow to be appreciated and, on the whole, the first half of the third century treated Britain well. In the second half of the century it was spared the destruction wrought on the Continent by barbarian attacks and was probably modestly enriched by the economic changes being felt detrimentally by the empire as a whole.

Looking at the second half of the third century in detail it is in the military sphere that the most information is available, though even here the situation is little understood and not much studied. After the Severan campaigns little is recorded in the very sparse surviving literary sources. The normal resource of inscriptions dries up; like the rest of the empire Britain lost what has been called the 'epigraphic habit'. Pottery studies cannot yet define closely enough the differences in techniques and fabrics which might differentiate wares made in the middle of the third century from those made at the end, or even material from the first quarter of the next century. Easily classified fabrics such as samian ware had long since ceased to be imported. Finally, in this recital of archaeological woes, it must be acknowledged that coin evidence presents very difficult problems of interpretation.

After the collapse of the currency system in the 270s reforms were initiated by the emperor Aurelian (270–5). The reformed coinage system was a complex attempt to re-establish a denominational structure similar to that which had been in use before the collapse of the system. A stable gold coinage was accompanied by base metal *sestertii* and *dupondii*, while the retariffed billon coin (silver/bronze alloy) was probably valued as a 4-*denarius* piece (Pl. 1, nos 1, 5). The issue of this coinage was recorded by the historian Zosimus who says that Aurelian 'officially issued new money after arranging for the state to buy in the debased coinage to avoid confusion in financial dealing' (Zos. 1.61). In fact, an equally cogent reason for withdrawing the old coin was that most of what was circulating in the north-western provinces bore the images and propaganda of an illegal, separatist regime which had held power in Gaul, Germany, Spain and Britain for the previous decade.

The withdrawal of the coinage appears to have been a less than completely successful operation since large numbers of Gallic Empire coins formed a component of the currency until Carausian issues achieved sufficient volume to drive them out of circulation. A further complication arises because the reformed coinage was supplied only in minute quantities to the territories of the former Gallic Empire; a profound shortage of coin resulted. This shortage was made good by the production of an informal, but apparently officially countenanced, coinage consisting of copies of the very coins the reform sought to eliminate (Pl. 1, nos. 2–4). Thus between 274 and the mid-280s there was little official coin in circulation. This is reflected in the poverty of such coins in archaeological deposits in the period running up to the revolt under review.

Bearing in mind these problems we can essay a survey of the military resources in Britain at the time of the revolt. When conquered in 43 Britain became unwilling host to an army of four legions, each consisting of approximately 5500 soldiers; there was probably an equal number of auxiliary troops organized in regiments of infantry, cavalry or a mixture of the two. This army of 44,000 troops was depleted by the permanent removal of *Legio II Adiutrix* in the reign of Domitian.

By the middle of the second century the remaining legions were permanently based in their fortresses at Caerleon, Chester and York. The disposition of the auxiliary units varied from time to time but by the middle of the third century a certain level of stability had been achieved. Wales had been largely denuded of troops, with the exception of the forts on the north coast and a small selection of stations in the rugged interior. In the Pennines occupation was still intensive and was to undergo major review in the period under discussion. The northern frontier of the province was Hadrian's Wall, with its five outpost forts screening the approaches to Roman territory down the routes from Caledonia on the eastern and western side of the island. In the south there is little evidence of garrisoning at this time with the exception of four sites. At Brancaster on the Wash (but see below p. 124) and at Reculver in Kent on the Thames estuary, forts are thought to have been built in the 240s; these forts were antecedent to a series extending from the Wash to the south coast of Wales which were erected later in the century. At Dover a fort provided accommodation for the sailors of the *Classis Britannica*, the Channel fleet; another in London housed the bodyguard of the imperial governor. At Richborough the triumphal arch erected by Domitian, to commemorate what he mistakenly thought was the completion of the conquest of Britain by the governor Gnaeus Julius Agricola, was converted into a watchtower.

The nominal strength of this army was probably similar to that of the Flavian period, but the reality was clearly different. Unfortunately the excavation of forts and the publication of the results has not reached a stage at which the density of occupation of the majority can be estimated. A few sites, however, have been examined in detail and conclusions reached which suggest that manning levels of some forts and fortresses were very low. Of the three legionary forts Caerleon, the base of *II Augusta*, has been the most thoroughly examined. The picture established here is of steady decline from the end of the second century, which complements the epigraphic evidence for parts of the unit being posted abroad, or elsewhere in Britain, and squares with the known changes in legionary formations in the third century (Casey, 1990). During this century the legions were stripped of their cavalry who were upgraded into superior units from their messenger corps status. Also removed were the new highly trained light legionary infantry, the *lanciarii*, who became independent regiments. It is possible that by the time of the Carausian revolt the muster of the legion may have been only 1000 men. If Chester and York yield the same sort of evidence we would dispose of a force of 3000 legionary troops in Britain, though the York base might have been maintained at a higher manning level because of its proximity to the frontier.

Looking in detail at a number of auxiliary forts we can see some evidence that they too were physically run down and had understrength garrisons. In Wales the fort at Caernarfon (Segontium), which was one of the north Wales stations still maintained, accommodation for a unit of 1000 men had been reduced to being sufficient for less than half that number; by the later third century nearly half the interior of the fort had been given over to industrial activity and rubbish dumping (Casey & Davies, 1993). At Birdoswald, on Hadrian's Wall, an inscription dating from the first years of the fourth century records that the commanding officer's house had decayed to a point where it was a soil-covered heap (RIB 913). At Halton Chesters, also on the Wall, the unpublished excavations suggest a very diminished occupation in the last quarter of the third century. A few miles south of the Wall a study of Lanchester suggests that the fort, which was built to hold a thousand troops, was accommodating only half that number, if not less (Casey & Noel, 1993). The fort at South Shields, designed for a garrison of 500, had been converted to a fortified grain store in the early years of the third century; gradually accommodation was reintroduced but the site never again offered housing for a unit as large as that for which it had been originally designed. Elsewhere the abandonment of the civilian settlements, or *vici*, which, stimulated by Septimius Severus's relaxation of the ban on army marriages, grew up around forts, suggests that large-scale troop movements took place in the third century. For instance at Chesterholm, just behind the Wall, the *vicus* was abandoned a year or two before AD 270 and, though the fort continued to be manned, the absence of civilians suggests movement of a significant part of the garrison troops and perhaps the accommodation of remaining civilians within the fort (Bidwell, 1985). Coin studies also suggest that *vici* were abandoned at various times in the third century over a wide area of the north (Casey, 1982).

There is thus a consistent picture of the delapidation of forts and the decline in numbers of the garrisons wherever excavation has made information available. The reasons are not far to seek. Britain avoided the disastrous barbarian attacks which characterize the history of the north-western provinces in the third century. Rather, Britain had served as a reservoir of reinforcements for the armies fighting on the Continent. Troops were withdrawn by Gallienus for his German wars and by the emperors of the Gallic Empire for their own campaigns on the Rhine and to help resist the encroachments on their territory by the central empire. A realistic estimate of the garrison of Britain at the time of the takeover by Carausius might be something under half of its nominal strength, still a formidable force if it could be concentrated at a single point. But this was not its function; this army was designed as, and refined into, a force for piecemeal disposition on local policing duties. The fact that Septimius Severus had to bring an independent campaign army with him in 209 emphasizes at what an early date the immobility of the bulk of the provincial army rendered it useless as a coherent offensive force capable of unified response to non-local events.

To whom did this army owe its loyalty? The brief answer should be to the emperor who, as supreme commander, embodied the Roman empire and the Roman people. To reinforce loyalty the state evolved a religious cult of devotion to the emperor which was celebrated by the army through communal observance. A list of the religious rites observed by the army in the first quarter of the century demonstrates with what importance this cult was regarded by the imperial authorities, with 'church parades' scheduled several times a month and the liberal provision of oxen, bulls and cows for sacrifice (Fink, 1940). Animals which, after serving the gods, served the mess tables of the appreciative soldiers. Individual emperors took a very close personal interest in the army, ostentatiously caring for the welfare of the soldiers through gifts of money and the conferment of legal privileges. The imperial image was paraded to the army on banners, and the emperor's statue was to be found in every fort, to confirm his presence in the midst of his soldiers. Honorific titles were awarded to the regiments in apotropaic ritual. For instance, the regiment at Birdoswald, the *Cohors I Aelia Dacorum*, was given the title *Gordiana* (Gordian's Own) in the reign of Gordian III (238–44); later they were similarly honoured by the Gallic emperors Postumus (260–9) and Tetricus (271–4) (RIB 1893, 1883, 1885). Possibly these honours were accompanied by monetary gifts to the soldiers after meritorious action.

The award of these unit titles and honours was ineffective; the majority of imperial names attached to regimental titles are those of emperors who were murdered by, or with the acquiescence of, their own troops – Caracalla, Severus Alexander, Gordian III, Gallienus, Probus, Aurelian and Postumus. As each emperor fell and his memory was vilified the regiments sent out fatigue parties to smash the statues and erase the now embarrassing name from the honorific inscriptions.

Table 1 demonstrates the frailty of army loyalty in the third century by listing the usurpers and mutinous commanders, each of whom was supported by a larger or smaller component of the army. Any such list must derive a great deal of its detail from the *Scriptores Historiae Augustae* (SHA), a fourth-century compilation of biographies of third-century rulers. The SHA is a notoriously difficult source and scholars pick and chose from its contents in a rather arbitrary manner, accepting what is convenient to their argument and rejecting what appears to conflict. The possibility of sheer invention and duplication of personalities in the SHA should not be discounted. Usurpers whose existence outside the SHA is in doubt are listed thus – Silbannacus(?).

Table 1   *Usurpation and revolt 218–300*

Date	Name	Place	Ruler
218	Elagabalus	Syria	Macrinus
218/22	Seleucus	Syria	Elagabalus
	Uranius	"	"
	Gellius Maximus	"	"
	Verus	"	"
222/35	Taurinus	?	Sev. Alexander
	Maximinus Thrax	Germany	"
235/8	Magnus	Germany	Maximinus
	Quartinus	"	"
	Gordian I/II	Africa	"
	Balbinus/Pupienus	Italy	"
238/44	M. Annius Sabinianus	Africa	Gordian III
	M. Iulius Philippus	Persia	"
244/49	T. Cl. Pacatianus	Pannonia	Philip
	Iotapianus	Syria	"
	Marcus	"	"
	M. Silbannacus (?)	Germany	"
	Sponsianus (?)	?Pannonia	"
	Trajan Decius	Pannonia	"
249/51	T. Iulius Priscus	Thrace	Trajan Decius
	Iul. Valens Licinianus	Italy	"
253	Uranius Antoninus	Syria	Treb. Gallus
	M. Aem. Aemilianus	Moesia	"
	P. Lic. Valerianus	Germany	Aemilian
253/59	Mareades	Syria	Valerian
260/68	Ingenuus	Pannonia	Gallienus
	P. Cornelius Regalianus	Illyricum	"
	T. Fulvius Macrianus	Persia	"
	T. Fulvius Macrianus, jun.	"	"
	T. Fulvius Quietus	"	"
	C. Piso Frugi (?)	Thessaly	"
	Valens	Macedonia	"
	Ballista	Syria	"
	Mussius Aemilianus	Egypt	"
	Memor	Egypt	"
	M. Aelius Aureolus	Italy	"
	Trebellianus	Isaura	"
	Celsus (?)	?Africa	"
	Saturninus	?	"
	Postumus	Germany	"

Date	Name	Place	Ruler
270/75	Domitianus	?Illyricum	Aurelian
	Urbanus	?	"
	Septimius	Dalmatia	"
	Firmus	Syria	"
276/82	Bonosus/Proculus	Germany	Probus
	C. Iul. Saturninus	Syria	"
283/84	M. Aurelius Iulianus	Pannonia	Carinus
	Sabinius Iulianus	Italy	"
	Diocles (M. Aur.	"	"
	Diocletianus)	"	
284/305	Domitius Domitianus	Egypt	Diocletian/ Maximian
	Aurelius Achilleus	Egypt	"
	Eugenius	Syria	"
	Iulianus	Italy	"
	Carausius	Gaul/Britain	"

In the discussion above we have seen that the bulk of the troops were stationed in the north or in the upland areas of the Pennines and Wales. By contrast, clustered in the lowland areas of the Midlands and the south was the overwhelming majority of towns and substantial rural settlements. A number of these towns had defences in the shape of earthwork ramparts erected, for unknown reason, in the late second or early third centuries. A few high-status centres such as London, St Albans (Verulamium), Colchester, Lincoln and Gloucester boasted stone walls, but more for symbolic reasons than for military. None of these towns normally held garrison troops with the exception of London which housed the provincial governor's guard. A few soldiers may have been allocated to the supervision of taxation, customs duty or the acquisition of military supplies; they did not constitute a force which could, or would, defend the ramparts of a fortified town.

Like the forts and fortresses, the towns appear to have been, if not in decay, at least at a low stage of their development. Large inner city areas of London had ceased to be used for housing and deposits characteristic of decay, or horticultural use, overlay what had in the second century been attractive residences furnished with mosaic floors (Perring, 1991). Investment in urban amenities diminished as money lost its value and craftsmanship declined for lack of patronage. The once proud symbols of self-government, the municipal basilicas, were in decay. At Silchester the building in which the local political elite had managed the affairs of their town and its rural community was sublet for metalworking (Fulford, 1985). Parts of the basilica at London, the largest building in the Roman world north of the Alps, was dismantled, the porticoes demolished and metalworking hearths were installed; where once the commercial affairs of the province were conducted the very fixtures and fittings were reduced to reusable metal (Milne, 1992).

This survey is drawn from a small sample and necessarily presents a dystopian view, but the picture given by excavation is ratified by other evidence which suggests that Britain was neither militarily nor economically dynamic. A depressed level of commercial activity is suggested by the volume of low-value coinage in circulation in comparison to gold. Finds of third-century gold coinage in Britain are insignificant when compared to those from Gaul. If this accurately reflects the volume of high-value money circulating in Gaul, despite its political and military problems, then Britain is shown to be of secondary economic status (Brenot, 1992). Dated private building activity is also rare and the use of decorative mosaics virtually unknown in the period (Smith, 1969).

If the symbols of quasi-autonomous administration disappear it may be conjectured that a more authoritarian system dominated affairs and that the hand of central government was felt more directly. Laws drafted in the next century imply that this trend was recognized to be a mistake and attempts were made to reverse the trend and maintain the institutions of local government against the will of the participants, who were expected to pay the expenses of urban magistracies. Any centralizing tendencies were regretted as throwing a financial burden on the state. The tribal structure which had formed the basis of regional self-government was probably attenuated after a century and a half of imperial control to a point where it was a nugatory element in the political framework of the provinces. When the island was further divided into four provinces in the next century no cognisance seems to have been taken of tribal boundaries. In any event, a steady process of homogenization had taken place in the population; the influence of the military recruitment of non-British auxiliaries led to the creation of a large non-indigenous population in the military zone. The deportation of foreign populations to Britain is recorded on two occasions, and for all we know there may have been more. The first of these deportations, in the reign of Marcus Aurelius, was of 5500 Sarmatian cavalry from the Danube region who were settled in the region of Ribchester, in Lancashire (Richmond, 1945). The second deportation was that of an unknown number of Burgundians and Vandals by the emperor Probus. Earlier, in the third century, a number of German units were sent to Hadrian's Wall where they were brigaded with loyal auxiliary units in their forts. These units may have been made up of captives taken in the German wars of Caracalla or Maximinus Thrax (Casey & Noel, 1993).

Despite urban and military problems Britain remained economically strong in the sense that its agricultural industry was unimpaired; neither the invasions of barbarians nor the peasant revolts which characterize the history of Gaul and Germany had impinged upon Britain. The island was self-sufficient in foodstuffs, and imports of Mediterranean products, as evidenced by amphorae, ceased. A decline in the size of the army certainly led to an increase in agricultural surpluses. There is evidence that by the next century this surplus was being exported to northern Europe. Industries also expanded to the detriment of foreign imports, with domestically produced pottery achieving mass-production levels in some centres and overseas fabrics being virtually absent from excavated assemblages. By the time that the emperor Diocletian promulgated his Edict of Maximum Prices in 301, the price of British textiles was quoted in the official government price index posted in the markets of towns of the farthest eastern provinces (Giacchero, 1974).

· 3 ·

THE DATE AND DURATION

OF THE REVOLT

THERE IS CONFUSION IN BOTH the ancient sources and in modern histories as to the date at which Carausius came to power; there is no less confusion as to when he met his death and was succeeded by Allectus. Further there are adherents to two different dates for the defeat of Allectus by Constantius.

A number of apparently contradictory ancient sources exist from which dates have been calculated, and modern scholars have accepted or rejected these dates without discussion of the reason for their choice of one or another. All the contemporary, or near-contemporary, sources agree that the inception of the revolt should be placed in either 286 or 287. The three main modern contributors to Carausian numismatic studies differ among themselves over the choice of either of the ancient dates.

Webb, in his earliest work, unequivocally states that 'The history of the short-lived British empire which was founded by Carausius in 287 ... terminated on the death of Allectus in 296' (Webb, 1906). This opinion was carried through to Webb's volume of *Roman Imperial Coinage*, which covers the issues of the usurpers (Webb, 1933). This date was also accepted by Shiel, with a compression of the dates of issue of mintmarked coins (Shiel, 1977). By contrast R.A.G. Carson's date of 286 has received wide acceptance, especially as it is linked to a coherent scheme of dates attached to the various sequential mintmarks which are a feature of the coins of the London and Colchester mints (Carson, 1959).

Carson based his choice of year on the only ancient source with a calendar date, St Jerome's translation and continuation of the *Chronicle of Eusebius*. In Carson's words, 'Jerome's account limits it [i.e. the accession of Carausius] to Diocletian's third year, i.e. between 17 September 286 and 17 September 287. Since good reason can be shown for placing the fall of Carausius in the latter part of 293, if we accept the duration of the reign as the stated seven years, we can guess that the reign of Carausius began in the last three months of 286.'

But this statement does not square with the manuscript tradition of Jerome's *Chronicle* in which, in the earliest surviving copy, dating to the fifth century AD, the revolt is placed not in the entries for the third but in those for the fourth year of Diocletian (Helm, 1984). Here it is stated that 'Carusius [sic] sumpta purpura Brittanias occupavit.' ('Carausius assumed

39

the purple and occupied [the provinces of] Britain.') On a revision of Carson's system of reckoning the regnal years, this places the event between 17 September 287 and 16 September 288.

Although few would dispute St Jerome's sanctity there are certainly some who would dispute his chronological consistency. For instance, further confusion is added to the issue because Jerome equates Diocletian's fourth year with the start of the 267th Olympiad, which ran from 289 to 293. The reason for this confusion is clear. Jerome allocated Diocletian a reign of twenty years whereas in reality the emperor had twenty-two regnal years from his accession on 20 November 284 (not 17 September, as stated by Carson) to his abdication on 11 May 305. In common with other chroniclers of the late Roman period, Jerome ignored two of Diocletian's regnal years by subsuming those which were less than a significant part of a calendar year into the nearest full year. Since regnal years could be calculated from the date of accession to the end of the year and from the beginning of the last year to the date of death or, this case, resignation, the regnal years of Diocletian can be read as follows (Jones & Casey, 1988).

Table 2

Regnal Year		
I	Nov–Dec	284
II	Jan–Dec	285
III	"	286
IIII	"	287
V	"	288
VI	"	289
VII	"	290
VIII	"	291
IX	"	292
X	"	293
XI	"	294
XII	"	295
XIII	"	296
XIV	"	297
XV	"	298
XVI	"	299
XVII	"	300
XVIII	"	301
XIX	"	302
XX	"	303
XXI	"	304
XXII	Jan–Sept	305

In this framework the accession of Carausius should fall at some time in 287 on the corrected Jerome reckoning.

Before accepting this date, with the concomitant revision of Carson's widely accepted dating scheme based on a mintmark sequence starting in 286, we should examine the collateral evidence for the date of the revolt. There are a number of lines of approach. Firstly, we can examine the generalized accounts of the period to see whether they offer any relative dates. Secondly, we can look at the numismatic evidence, especially that associated with the celebration of the suppression of the revolt, to see whether it is possible to reference backwards from dated events.

The accounts of Aurelius Victor and Eutropius are at odds with each other. Aurelius Victor says: 'He [i.e. Carausius] was overthrown six years later, by the treachery of someone called Allectus', whereas Eutropius states that: 'After seven years his own ally Allectus killed him, and himself held the British provinces for three years.' Eutropius also records that '... whilst matters were in great disorder throughout the whole of the Roman world and Carausius was raising a war in Britain, Achilleus in Egypt, the Pentapolitans harassed Africa, Narseus made war upon the East, Diocletian raised Maximianus Herculeus from the dignity of *Caesar* to that of Emperor, and made Constantius and (Galerius) Maximian Caesars...'.

In these accounts we have the choice of either a six-year reign (Victor) or a seven-year (Eutropius) reign for Carausius. The Eutropian account is duplicated by Orosius, but this has no independent evidential value, being itself derived from Eutropius or the Eutropian source.

We are also told by Eutropius that Carausius revolted before Maximian was raised to the rank of Augustus, an event which is dated to 1 April 286. The passage containing this information is a conflation of events which, in reality, occupied an extended period and were not simultaneous as the text implies. For instance, the revolt in Egypt took place in the Egyptian calendar year 287/8 (Thomas, 1976, 1977). Jerome, incidentally, dates this revolt to 292, further undermining his credibility.

Of the other occurrences conflated by Eutropius, Constantius and Galerius were promoted in 292 and the Pentapolitans, or Quinquegentianae, rose up in North Africa in the same year. Clearly the date of Carausius's insurrection must be treated as a non-specific reference and merely as part of a generalized account of events in the early years of Diocletian's reign.

Jerome does not record the death of Carausius but does give a duration for the revolt in an entry under the fifteenth year of Diocletian's reign: '*Post decem annos per Aescepliodum praetorio Brittaniae recepta.*' ('After ten years [the provinces of] Britain were recaptured by Asclepiodotus the praetorian praefect.) As we have already seen, Jerome's chronology needs to be adjusted to take into account the missing two years of the reign. In reality his fifteenth year runs from January to December 298. But even this corrected date is clearly erroneous because the defeat of Allectus was celebrated in a panegyric delivered in 297, though this date in itself is only

41

a *terminus ad quem* and not evidence that the defeat was inflicted in that year. To establish a date for the vanquishing of Allectus and the date of the death of Carausius, we need to turn to the coin evidence and then look at the literary evidence again.

Attention has already been drawn to a series of coins which allude to the events surrounding the death of Carausius, the capture of Boulogne by Constantius, the invasion of Britain and its repossession by the central empire (Burnett, 1984a). A crucial piece of evidence is the coin issued by the Colchester mint in the name of Maximian which commemorates the consulship which he held in 293. Since no coins were issued for the legitimate emperors by Allectus we can be confident that this issue was sanctioned by Carausius and that it constitutes irrefutable evidence that his reign extended beyond 1 January 293, the date at which the consulship commenced. It is usually assumed that the fall of Carausius was brought about by the loss of Boulogne, though this has been questioned (Huvelin, 1983). The panegyric which celebrates the fall of the town says that it fell by siege 'immediately' after the elevation of Constantius to the rank of Caesar on 1 March 293. We may deduce from this that Carausius fell in the spring or early summer of 293.

Were this to be accepted, the various statements of Aurelius Victor and Eutropius can be reconciled if we regard the former's claim of a six-year reign as being a statement that Carausius held power for a period of about 72 months, whereas Eutropius's seven years are regnal years, counting part of 287 as a year and January to March 293 as another regnal year.

All, then, apparently points to 287 as being the year of the revolt, but two further pieces of evidence suggest an earlier date, one as early as the middle of 286. It was then that Maximian abruptly suspended the production of gold coin at the imperial mint of Lyons (Lugdunum). There seems little reason to remove the gold stocks from the principal mint of Gaul, presumably to Rome, if there was not some threat to its security. This threat cannot have been from the Bagaudae who had already been defeated, but may have been the presence of Carausius, or his supporters, on the Continent.

There is a further piece of numismatic evidence which points to a problem in Gaul. Hoard evidence from Britain shows that the last coin issues of the Gallic mints in the names of Diocletian and Maximian to reach the island before the severance from legitimate rule, date to no later than the middle of 286. This suggests that normal connections between Britain and Gaul were interrupted at this time. Evidence of a coinage produced on the Continent very early in the reign of Carausius (below p. 90) also suggests that there was an episode which has left no record in the main literary sources. The panegyric addressed to Maximian on the eve of his attempt to reconquer Britain in 289 contains a suggestive passage: '*Vestrae, inquam, fortunae vestrae felicitas est, imperator, quodiam milites vestri ad oceanum pervenere victoria, iam caesonum in illo litore hostium sanguinem reciproci fluctus sorbuerunt.*' (It is proof of your good fortune, your success, Your

Majesty, that your soldiers have already reached the Ocean in victory, that the tides have swallowed the blood of enemies slaughtered on that shore.)

Maximian's attempt to recover Britain failed and in consequence Carausius was able to establish a considerable enclave of territory in north-western Gaul. Although written three years after the event, the passage quoted above must refer to events before the defeat of Maximian and the occupation of Gaul. It follows that in an unrecorded episode Carausius held parts of Gaul before the unsuccessful invasion of Britain in 289. This opens up a number of possibilities, the most attractive of which is that the revolt took place in Gaul in the middle of 286 but that most of the historians regarded this as a minor phase of the episode and based the computations of the reign from the date at which Carausius was established solely in Britain. Despite his chronological inconsistencies St Jerome appears to give credibility to this view when he says 'Carausius assumed the purple and occupied Britain'. The word order suggests that the occupation of Britain followed on the decision to rebel and was not the occasion for the revolt. Thereafter the Continental episode is ignored and the focus switches to Britain.

In summary, while at first sight the bulk of the documentary sources suggest a date of 287, the independent numismatic sources point towards the earlier date. The panegyric of 289, which predates all other chronological sources, implies an early phase of the revolt centred in Gaul itself which is unnoticed by the later sources.

If we turn to Allectus we find equally disparate calculations for the duration of the reign, its start and its termination. Allectus came to power as a result of the assassination of Carausius though, as has been noted, the equation of the loss of Boulogne with the death has been questioned. It is true that Carausius is not mentioned in relation to events during the siege but does this demonstrate that he was already dead and that it was Allectus who lost the regime's Continental possession? This suggestion quite overlooks the fact that no one is named in the account of the fall of Boulogne; the adversaries of the legitimate emperors are simply 'pirates' or 'robbers', not dignified with names. The ancient sources are not united on the length of Allectus's reign. Aurelius Victor states that he fell shortly (*brevi*) after the death of Carausius, while Eutropius gives him three years of power. Further inconsistencies arise when comparison is made between the accounts of the total duration of the British empire. Victor says that Carausius ruled for six years of the ten-year revolt, implying a four-year reign for Allectus. Eutropius allocates Carausius seven years, so assigning Allectus three. In a variation Orosius claims that Britain was 'recovered after ten years', possibly suggesting that Allectus survived into an eleventh year.

The coins issued by the victors after the defeat of Allectus offer some insights into the problem. These have been summarized by Burnett (Burnett, 1984b). The series of gold commemorative medals issued to celebrate the recovery of Britain is best known by the so-called Arras Medallion which depicts the Caesar, Constantius, entering London (Pl. 7, no. 4), but a number of gold pieces were issued at the same time. On the obverse of one of this series Constantius is shown in the robes of a consul, an office which he held in 296 (Pl. 7, no. 3). The medal provides a *terminus ad quem* for the recovery of the island and since the consular office was entered upon on 1 January, it follows that Britain must have been recovered in 295 or 296. It is unlikely that the medal was issued later than the date of the consulship, as a sort of retrospective award, and a date of 297 for this piece must be rejected. This is supported by the issue of coins of minor denomination whose iconography can be interpreted as celebrating an imperial victory in 296. At Trier and Lyons, coins issued in 296 bear imperial busts of military style in which the ruler is represented in armour with spear and shield. An issue of Trier, solely for Constantius, depicts a figure of Victory on the shield. The assumption of the title *Britannicus Maximus* by Diocletian and his colleagues on the completion of the war does not, of itself, offer a firm date for the end of hostilities. The earliest inscription recording the title is dated to Diocletian's thirteenth tribunician year (CL VIII. 21550). The date of the inscription depends on whether the emperor counted these years from his *dies imperii* (20 November) or from the start of the consular year (1 January) and whether, in any case, the title was taken in conjunction with this event. If Diocletian took the title with the assumption of the thirteenth tribunician power and that power dated from 20 November then Allectus's defeat and death must have preceded November 296.

Another area of numismatic evidence is found in the coinage of Roman Egypt. Here the coinage system, until it was reformed by Diocletian, was unique to the province and had no circulation elsewhere in the empire, though a few examples reached the west through travellers. For chronological purposes the products of the mint of Alexandria have the incomparable advantage over other Roman coins of bearing a date in the form of the regnal year of the issuing ruler. Studies of this coinage show that Alexandria accurately reflects, by choice of types, imperial campaigns and victories throughout the empire (Casey, 1987). If we look at the coinage of Egypt in this light a number of issues appear to allude to the activities of Constantius. Burnett draws attention to a series of coins which do not appear to have been shared by the co-Caesar, Galerius. For example, an issue of Year 3 shows Constantius spearing a fallen enemy (Pl. 1, no. 7). Another, of the same date, depicts Constantius wearing a helmet decorated with a figure of Victory and carrying a trophy over his shoulder (Pl. 1, no. 6). A third example, once again of Year 3, shows the Caesar in military dress, holding a figure of Victory on a globe, with bound captives at his feet (Pl. 1, no. 8).

Burnett's view is that these coins commemorate a victory won 'before the end of August 295', the end of the calendar year which coincides with Constantius's third year. He acknowledges that this victory might have been achieved before the reconquest of Britain over hostile forces on the Rhine, as recounted in the Panegyric of 297, but comes down firmly in favour of a British inspiration because 'no other victory is recorded for Constantius on the abundant Alexandrian coinage of the next year'. Attention may also be drawn to an issue of Maximian which depicts the emperor of the West helmeted, holding a spear and bearing a shield decorated with a flying Victory. This coin is dated to the tenth year of Maximian in the Egyptian system, 295/6.

While the evidence is tentative, the cumulative impact of the Egyptian coins and the consular gold medallion, issued in 296, is strongly in favour of an early date for the defeat of Allectus either in the first eight months of 295, or at latest, by early 296. Of these two dates the latter has the virtue of easing the problem of reconciling the coin evidence with Orosius's claim of a three-year reign for Allectus. On the other hand, Orosius may have simply been wrong. In summary, the cumulative literary and numismatic evidence points to the revolt having taken place in mid-286 and to have been suppressed by 296. Carson's scheme for the dating of the coinage can be maintained as a general framework for any discussion of the internal chronology of the episode with suitable slight downward adjustment of the date of the very last issue of the reign of Allectus.

• 4 •

THE LITERARY NARRATIVE

THE LITERARY SOURCES GIVE A reasonably coherent story of events at the start of the reign of Carausius though they are partial in every sense. They are also very informative about events relating to the siege and fall of Boulogne and, to a lesser extent, those surrounding the fall of Allectus. They give only a superficial account of the revolt itself and the reasons for that revolt. There is no account of the manner in which Britain fell to the usurper, of why a part of the army on the Continent joined his cause. We are told nothing of his administration of Britain, of the reasons for his overthrow or the reign of his successor except that it was claimed to be oppressive by the panegyricist. But, as the lady said on another occasion, 'He would, wouldn't he?'

Let us examine these accounts in detail in order to extract from them their narrative of events. After this we can look to see whether it is possible to supplement or change that narrative from the archaeological and numismatic evidence, testing the authority of the historical sources by recourse to non-literary studies.

We notice at once that only the later historians actually name either Carausius or Allectus; the contemporary and near-contemporary panegyrics offer no biographical details of the usurpers and refer to them only through periphrases and in demeaning epithets. This is entirely consonant with the contemporary practice which deliberately avoided dignifying criminals or enemies of the state by the use of their names. In a society which held that the remembrance of the dead mitigated the condition of their afterlife existence there was a metaphysical, or at least superstitious, intention to abolish reality through denying it concrete existence. In the most extreme case, that of the *damnatio memoriae* of fallen rulers, measures extended to erasing names from monuments, destroying statues and images and even abolishing their laws and enactments. Carausius and Allectus are normally apostrophized as 'pirate', 'robber', 'desperate creature' or 'the standard bearer of the criminal rebellion'. This, in Roman terms, is mild stuff; a recent study has shown that political enemies were often addressed in terms of very explicit sexual abuse in a ritualized exchange of insults. Even a statesman of the calibre of Augustus ritually insulted his enemy Mark Antony (Adams, 1982).

For details of the life of Carausius, and such few comments we have about Allectus, we must turn to Aurelius Victor and Eutropius. Both texts are assumed to derive from a lost imperial history dating to the first quarter of the fourth century and, since they offer slightly differing accounts, we may be sure that they have used their mutual source selectively. Because the two accounts derive from a single progenitor we may be justified in using them as a single source in reconstructing a composite narrative.

Both Victor and Eutropius name Carausius and Allectus but do not give their full names, and to this day that of Allectus is unknown. In the case of Carausius some of his coins give an abbreviated full name in the form IMP C M AVR M CARAVSIVS ('The Emperor Caesar Marcus Aurelius M(...) Carausius'). A milestone, the single epigraphic record of the British emperors, found at Gallows Hill near Carlisle (RIB 2291), gives a fuller version of the name by expanding the M. CARAVSIVS of the coins to MAVS CARAVSIVS (Pl. c). The abbreviation MAVS does not readily give a common Latin name and scholars have proposed an expansion to MAVSEVS or MAVSAEVS, with the latter being the more acceptable version (Birley, 1981). Thus the full titulature of the emperor would read IMPERATOR CAESAR MARCVS AVRELIVS MAVSAEVS CARAVSIVVS PIVS FELIX AVGVSTVS. The names Marcus Aurelius are very common in the third century being adopted by a large proportion of the population when enfranchised by Caracalla (Marcus Aurelius Antoninus Pius). Carausius may already have had these names or they may have been adopted on accession to the throne. The names Marcus Aurelius were borne by Diocletian himself as well as by Probus, Carus, Carinus and Numerian among emperors in the years leading up to the reign of Diocletian.

Discussions of the etymological origins of the names Carausius and Mausaeus have been inconclusive. Mauseus, or Musaeus, has genuine Roman antecedents and Carausius has been ascribed to a Celtic or Germanic origin without much conviction (Shiel, 1977). It may be significant, however, that the only epigraphic record of the name other than in the context of the revolt, and on an enigmatic coinage issued in Britain in the middle of the fourth century (discussed below), is on an early Christian tombstone (Fig.2) from Penmachno in the Celtic west of Britain which reads CARAVSIVS HIC IACIT IN HOC CONGERIES LAPIDVM ('Carausius lies here in this cairn') (Nash-Williams, 1950). The tombstone probably dates from the late fifth century and has no connection with the usurper (Fig.2).

Aurelius Victor states that Carausius was a 'cives Menapiae' (a 'citizen of Menapia'), this being the coast of Gallia Belgica, incorporating the coast of modern northern France, Belgium and Holland. This region saw very dramatic changes in fortune in the third century. During the reign of Marcus Aurelius, in c.172–4, it was devastated by the raids of two German tribes, the Chauci and the Chatti, the former attacking the area by sea and the latter from across the Rhine. An imperial policy of restoration of settlements and the construction of forts did not enjoy success for very long. Frankish and Alamannic raiding in the 260s, again from across the Rhine, was so

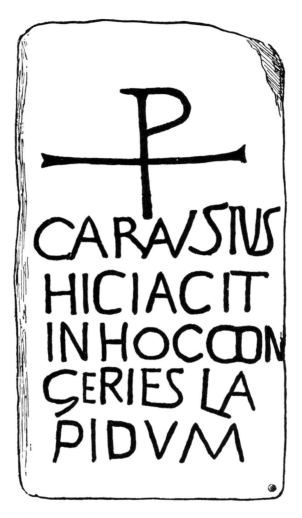

2 Sixth-century Christian tombstone from Penmachno.

intensive that it appears to have led to the start of a depopulation of coastal areas. This trend was brought to a climax by a marine transgression which flooded the coastal plain in c.270, leaving it uninhabited and uninhabitable (Thoen, 1981).

This, then, was the background of Carausius' early life: on the edges of the empire in a province which was threatened with, and periodically subjected to, barbarian attack and natural calamity. As a frontier area it was a zone of ethnic inter-activity where Germanic, Celtic and Romano-Gallic populations intermingled freely and where social and business mores might not conform to the niceties of metropolitan Roman society. It was also an area where the mercantile classes had intimate commercial contacts with Britain. At the mouth of the Rhine stood a temple of the goddess Nehalennia, whose worshippers included merchants carrying on trade with Britain. It was in this environment, we are told by Aurelius Victor, that as a young man Carausius earned his living as a sailor. The text uses the phrase '*gubernandi gnarus*' which means literally 'helmsman' and has been glossed by some writers to mean 'pilot'. There can be little doubt that the profession of pilot existed in the shipping trade of Menapia and that the shifting sands of this coast might well necessitate the service of knowledgeable coastal guides but there is no certainty that this extension of Carausius's status is justified. Dr Roger Tomlin, in discussion of this complex text, notes that the educated Aurelius Victor would know that in the *Aeneid* Palinurus, who steered Aeneas' ship, is described as '*gubernator*'. He further notes that in military contexts *gubernator* was a non-commissioned rank though acting as second-in-command of a ship in the fleet (Tomlin, pers. comm.). In a broader context the phrase might be interpreted as a periphrasis indicating a general naval expertise, especially as the text contrasts his naval talents with those he displayed in the land war against the Bagaudae, citing them as the qualification for promotion to the command of a fleet. Eutropius adds that Carausius was 'a man of very humble origin', perhaps more a comment on his social status than any reference to his economic background. In the context of imperial antecedents in the period, humility of background was no bar to high office: Diocletian was probably the son of a freedman, and Galerius, his Caesar and later ruler of the Eastern Empire, is alleged to have started life as a mere herdsman.

There is no further information vouchsafed about Carausius' life before the events leading up to his revolt; we do not know when he was born nor the names of his parents. On the former point a guess can be hazarded from the age structure of military and imperial commands held during his lifetime. There seems, on the slight evidence available, to have been a rough age correlation between office and rank.

Table 3   *Age and rank of emperors 268–93. (Source: Kienast, 1990)*

Ruler	Birth date	Age at elevation	Last pre-imperial rank
Claudius II	c.214	c.54	Dux Illyrici
Probus	223	44	Dux Orientis
Aurelian	c.214	56	Dux equitum
Carus	224	58	Praetorian prefect
Diocletian	245	39	Imperial guard commander
Maximian	250	35	Unknown
Constantius I	250	43	Praetorian prefect

The highest offices appear to have been achieved by men in their mid-40s and 50s; both Diocletian and Maximian were relatively young and neither had achieved very high rank when they were promoted. We have no indication that Carausius held any high office before his promotion to command a fleet and it might be expected that his age approximated to that of Diocletian and Maximian. His coin portraits, which show an elderly man, are not good evidence for his age because, as was normal, they are designed to increase his *gravitas* by mature representation.

We do not know what sort of career was pursued by Carausius after his early days of seamanship. If he followed a military career we may conjecture that it followed the sort of progress experienced by officers who rose to prominence after the administrative and military reforms of the emperor Gallienus (253–68). These reforms opened a professional military career to non-senatorial officers by depriving senators of their monopoly of high military command, making these posts available to members of the equestrian social order. Being based directly on property qualification, rather than birth or imperial donation, equestrian status, and with it the ultimate prospect of the command of provincial armies, was open to officers above the rank of centurion. At the same time the army was freed from the straitjacket of traditional legionary tactics, large cavalry commands were created and increasingly mobile battle groups formed from a more lightly armed infantry force. These new formations demanded innovative general-ship skills, skills evolved from extended field service in a wide variety of tactical situations. The day of the short-service aristocratic politician in uniform gave way to the professional, long-service officer from the lower social classes, often from a very humble provincial background. It was from this background that the majority of the emperors in the second half of the third century came. It is likely that Carausius's career followed this sort of pattern.

All sources agree on the reason for Carausius's promotion. Aurelius Victor says that he had acquired a military reputation during Maximian's campaign against the Bagaudae in Gaul and that the emperor 'commissioned him to put together a fleet and fight off the Germans who were infesting the seas'. Eutropius adds some further detail in that 'he had been commissioned at Bononia [Boulogne] to bring peace to the sea infested by Franks and Saxons, along the Belgica–Armorica sector'. This sector comprised the coast from the Rhine to Britanny. There is no mention of Britain in any of this and the centre of activity is clearly the coast of the Continent, though any success against raiders in this area would benefit the security of Britain also. Significantly the Panegyric of 297 describes Casausius as stealing 'the fleet that used to protect Gaul'.

The promotion seems to have been granted because Carausius came to the notice of Maximian; this appears to dispel any notion that a cause of the revolt was resentment of his commander's elevation to imperial rank. Maximian's campaign in Gaul is dated in the Panegyric of 297 as taking place after his elevation to co-emperor with Diocletian, after 1 April 286. Maximian held the lower rank of Caesar between the summer of 285 and the date of his promotion to Augustus. If Carausius was promoted because of his activities in that war, then raised a fleet, conducted a successful naval campaign, was condemned and revolted before the middle of 286 – a date derived from the numismatic evidence (below p. 91) – then the compression of events is very extreme. But there is reason to think that the elliptical wording of the Panegyric is misleading. A more reasonable sequence of events is that Maximian was sent to Gaul to take over the administration of the defeated Carinus and to deal with the Bagaudic revolt. Elevation to full imperial rank was surely dependent on the successful achievement of these tasks, otherwise Diocletian would have promoted his colleague to full rank in 285, rather than progressing him by stages from *Filius Augusti* and Caesar to co-emperor. In these circumstances it is perfectly possible for Carausius to have participated in the campaign at an early stage and then to have moved on to hold an independent command. That this was of some duration is made clear by Eutropius's statement that he had 'often captured many barbarians'.

The enemy that was vanquished by Maximian, and against whom Carausius won his military reputation, has excited wide academic interest. *Bagaudae* (they are also called *Bacaudae*) occur in a number of Roman historical contexts, especially in the fifth century in Gaul and Spain (Drinkwater, 1992). The name, of unknown origin and meaning, has been interpreted as encompassing every range of rural resistance to authority from the classic Marxist peasant class struggle to a demand, led by a waning tribal aristocracy, for a reversion to a traditional Celtic stratified social order (Thompson 1974). Modern opinion suggests that *Bagaudae* comprised various elements of society who, having been relieved of the burden of Roman authority by barbarian invasion, resisted its reimposition by a government which had been unable, or unwilling, to protect them in the first place. Whatever later Bagaudae may have been, and the term may have been used as a blanket condemnation of any sort of rural discontent, the text of Aurelius Victor says that:

> ... on the death of Carinus, Aelianus and Amandus, having raised in
> Gaul a troop of peasants and brigands (called locally *bagaudae*) and
> having ravaged a wide area of the countryside, were attacking most of
> the towns.... (Eutr.ix.13)

It is not very clear from this whether the peasants are to be included in the term '*bagaudae*' or whether the local word only refers to the brigand element of the insurrection. In any event the two leaders, who issued their own coinage, took the opportunity given by the temporary collapse of the imperial administration to set up their own government in northern Gaul. The suppression of the revolt does not seem to have taken long since Maximian launched an attack on the Germans in 286, an unthinkable strategic move unless the hinterland of northern Gaul had been secured.

Returning to the career of Carausius, the sources agree that he was a success as a naval commander. According to Aurelius Victor, he 'killed many of the barbarians' (v.39.20) and Eutropius claims that he 'often captured many barbarians' (Eutr.ix.13). These enemy sailors, given the later evidence of the employment of barbarian forces in the navy and army, may have been recruited into his ranks.

Eutropius gives the fullest account of the official reason for Carausius's fall from grace. The accusation was that he kept recovered booty for himself rather than trying to return it to its owners or, failing their survival at the hands of the barbarian raiders, surrendering it to the imperial authorities. He is also accused of developing an innovative strategy for catching pirates. This involved allowing them to penetrate the Roman defensive screen and attack their targets in order to catch them when returning to base exhausted and burdened with loot. The result of these tactics was to accumulate in his hands large resources with which, contrary to all Roman administrative practices, he could pay or reward his own forces. The consequence of this was condemnation to death by an enraged Maximian. Faced by this fate, according to both Aurelius Victor and Eutropius, 'he usurped the imperial power and seized Britain' (Aurelius Victor, v.39.20). None of the accounts says that the condemnation was immediately followed by flight to Britain; this is a modern gloss of the texts. On the contrary, the texts imply that he seized power first and only then took over Britain; the one action was not dependent upon the other.

For literary evidence of developments on the Continent we are confined to the narrative provided by the three panegyrics, there being no mention whatsoever of events outside Britain in any of the historians. From the Panegyric of 289 we learn that a year has been spent in an all-out preparation of an invasion force to root out the rebel. Forests are felled, shipwrights are engaged in a huge shipbuilding programme, the weather is co-operative and the army is eager for the campaign. Success is assured, the inexorable process of imperial retribution is in motion, the gods are willing and 'certainly the day will dawn, when Rome will see you [Maximian] victorious . . .' (*Pan. Lat.* x(ii).13).

On 21 July the next year, another panegyric was delivered before Maximian. Significantly there is absolutely no reference to Carausius, to Britain or to the campaign promised in the speech of the previous year; clearly the enterprise had failed disastrously. The next information that we have comes from the Panegyric of 297, and that of 310, showing that Carausius was in occupation of parts of northern Gaul and had established a naval and military base at Boulogne. In the absence of direct literary evidence we can only conjecture about the chain of events which lead to this situation. At the very least the loss of the invasion fleet by enemy action or, as is hinted, by natural causes, left the coast of Gaul open to Carausian attack. In the event the opportunity was snatched to effect a landing and to occupy imperial territory.

At this juncture the newly appointed Caesar, Constantius, makes his appearance on the stage. Constantius had served as praetorian prefect to Maximian from 288; in this position we must assume that he served in a leading role in the unsuccessful campaigns against the rebel. It seems unlikely that he was himself responsible for any of the setbacks hitherto experienced by the imperial cause, for this would have disqualified him from the position to which he was now promoted. Ever since man started to wage systematic warfare it has been acknowledged that good generals are lucky generals and a lack of *felicitas* would certainly have counted against a candidate for the highest office. Constantius was elevated to the imperial college in 293 as heir apparent to Maximian. He immediately set about the task of bringing Carausius to heel.

The Panegyric of 297 contains eloquent detail of both the campaign in Gaul and of the invasion of Britain; it also gives otherwise unrecorded detail of the support enjoyed by Carausius and of the recruitment of forces to his cause. It is from this source that we learn of the defection of a Roman legion and unspecified auxiliary units, of the support given by Gallic merchants, the recruitment of allies from among barbarian peoples, the building of a further fleet and the training of sailors (*Pan. Lat.* viii(v). 6,12).

There is a detailed account of the siege of Boulogne, which was reduced by cutting the town off from relief by the Carausian fleet by the construction of a timber-based mole. How long this operation took is not stated but it cannot have been less than several weeks and may well have taken several months. The Panegyric of 310 adds the further detail that the garrison was treated with clemency after the surrender of the town (*Pan. Lat.* vi(vii). 6). At this stage, or earlier, Carausius was assassinated by Allectus.

The Panegyric of 297 records this event without mentioning the principals by name. The orator seems to have mixed feelings about the event; although Carausius is described as a 'pirate chief' and Allectus as his 'henchman', the murder is described as a 'crime' (*Pan. Lat.* viii(v). 12). A motive is also offered in that Allectus 'thought that his crime would be rewarded by imperial power'. This seems to imply a belief that he would be recognized as legitimate by Diocletian and Maximian as a reward for the deed. If so he was badly misled.

Both Aurelius Victor and Eutropius record the death of Carausius, though not the siege of Boulogne. The former describes Allectus as having been made Carausius's minister of finance – '*summae rei praeesset*' (v.39.39) – but the latter as 'his only ally' (Eutr.ix.14).

The Panegyric of 297 next deals with the expedition to recover Britain, explaining that the three years' delay between the death of Carausius and the defeat of Allectus was occupied both in the construction and preparation of an invasion fleet and with a campaign in the area between the Rhine and the Scheldt against the Chamavi and the Frisii (*Pan. Lat.* viii(v). 8). These peoples were defeated and transported to the interior of the empire where they were settled as agriculturalists on land which had gone out of cultivation.

The account of the invasion itself is handled with tact. Despite bad weather Constantius prevails, Allectus is defeated, and London is saved from the depredations of the usurper's fleeing and broken forces, specifically Frankish mercenaries. Allectus's body is found on the battlefield together with his entourage. Additionally 'hardly a single Roman died in the victory of the Roman empire'. Constantius is then hailed by a jubilant population of Britain as a liberator (*Pan. Lat.* viii(vi). 5).

The Panegyric of 310 adds nothing to this account except to claim, in contrast to the earlier account, that the expedition was blessed with absolutely calm seas (*Pan. Lat.* vi(viii). 5).

The later historians unite in undermining this account by ascribing the victory in Britain not to Constantius but to his subordinate. 'He [Allectus] was crushed by the agency of Asclepiodotus, the praetorian prefect', says Eutropius (Eutr. ix.14). Aurelius Victor is more specific: '... Constantius sent Asclepiodotus, whom he had made praetorian prefect, ahead with part of his fleet and legions, and destroyed him [i.e. Allectus]' (v.39.39).

This, then, is the outline of events as recorded in the literary sources. Needless to say they are hardly impartial accounts, being, in the main, political documents, laudatory speeches with a framework of their own rules and traditions. And, of course, addressed to the victors. The historical narratives, though written at a period when the political restraints imposed on the panegyricists no longer prevailed, are derivative from a lost work and we do not know what information has been omitted by the authors, nor do we know the political stance of the original work or even its own accuracy. Even in this brief summary it is clear that there are discrepancies between accounts and problems which arise from the silences of the sources. Instances in which specific problems are raised by the texts include the meteorological details, the part played by the praetorian prefect, the fate of Maximian's expedition and the manner in which Carausius came into possession of Boulogne. Nor are we told why a legion, and which one, defected to Carausius or, finally, who Allectus was or how he rose to power. These, and other problems, must be considered in relation to such other evidence, archaeological and numismatic, as is independent of the literary tradition.

• 5 •

THE IDEOLOGY OF
CARAUSIAN AND ALLECTAN
COIN TYPES

THE STUDY OF ROMAN COIN types is the study of the devices, images and mottoes which appear on the reverse, or tail side, of the coins. It is a study with a long history, but the results achieved have tended to bring this aspect of numismatic research into contempt with critical historians. The search for meaning in coin types, in the absence of other documentary reference, has led scholars to claim an almost clairvoyant ability to read the political subtleties of the past through the medium of its coinage. The tirade which this brought forth from A.H.M. Jones is worth quoting in full, since it is the declared aim of this book to refute his dogmatic stance:

> If a modern analogy is to be sought for the varying types and legends
> of Roman imperial coins it is perhaps to be found in the similar
> variations in the postage stamps of many modern countries.... No
> serious modern historian would use them as a clue which revealed
> changes of government policy, even if other evidence were totally
> lacking. It would be better if numismatists took the coin types and
> legends less seriously, and if historians of the empire, instead of
> building fantastic history upon them, frankly admitted that the
> political history of periods when the coins are the sole evidence are
> irrecoverable, apart from the bare bones of the chronology of the
> reigns, the areas which the emperors effectively controlled, and any
> other salient events which the coins directly celebrate.   (Jones, 1956).

Despite this extreme contrary view it seems reasonable to assume that the choice of coin types does reflect something of the concerns of society. This is especially so as, until recently, coins were the only way of circularizing the whole population with images of their rulers. It can even be argued that the symbols on modern coins have a function in mediating between political reality and the population in general. The chosen imagery expresses embedded social norms, concepts or expectations. On ancient coins overt symbols record contemporary events such as the erection of temples or other public buildings, the celebration of victories and the remembrance of anniversaries connected with the ruler or his family. These, of course, can be easily understood not least because an explanatory motto often accompanies the image. But the implications of less specific imagery such as generalized personifications of Peace (*Pax*), Plenty (*Abundantia*) or Security (*Securitas*) can be interpreted in any number of ways. At the lowest level of significance they are simply things which fill an otherwise empty space on the coin. On the other hand, since the chosen themes vary with time it may be claimed that they represent a changing ideological portfolio from which symbolic representations, apposite to the times, were chosen.

If we look at the designs on the current coin of Britain we see a suite of symbols which make a clear statement about inter-regional parity – a leek for Wales, the thistle for Scotland, the arms of England and an obscure local plant for Ireland because the use of the traditional symbol, the Irish harp, would constitute an unacceptable partisan statement in the context of the current political situation. Coins of lesser value display symbols evocative of a historic past – Britannia ruling the waves, a portcullis symbolic of a free parliament, the Prince of Wales feathers implying continuity of the monarchy. These symbols comprise a series of statements which, cumulatively, evoke a static ideology established by reference to a long historic past. They evoke images of unity, stability and continuity. But they may deceive the future interpreter because they are really designed to mitigate the impact of change in a period of dynamic constitutional transition, one in which the institutions evoked by the coinage, and even the coinage itself, is in imminent prospect of being restructured within the European Union.

On a broader scale in the Roman period we can see distinctive trends in the use of coin symbols over several centuries. The grandees of the late Republic used control of the magistracies attached to the production of the coinage to select types which enhanced their political status through references to the achievements of ancestors. Later, changes in the state religion are reflected. In the first and second centuries the dominant types referred to the Roman gods and victories over foreign enemies. In the fourth century such victories were rare to the point of vanishing, but the adoption of Christianity as the state religion opened the prospect of spiritual success, an eternal metaphysical victory over material enemies. Christian imagery was adopted as an imperial theme, accurately reflecting the contemporary imperial social and political ideology. This ideology was not necessarily shared by the bulk of the population, or even by some of the most prominent ministers of the regime. On a narrower scale we can see that the types used in the first half of the reign of Marcus Aurelius (161– 81) are almost all of a pacific nature; those used in the second half of the reign which was entirely occupied by the Marcommanic War, fought on the Danube, are mostly of a military or warlike content.

If coins convey a message from or about the ruler, who made the actual choice of types? We do not know, but the choice must represent what those who served the administration conceived to be representative symbols of its political, social or religious ideology. Though individual types may not permit specific interpretation the overall aggregation of symbols comprises a statement which may be capable of elucidation. It should, of course, be borne in mind that coin types can constitute an aspiration rather than a reality; the selected symbols may proclaim success and disguise failure, enjoin loyalty but represent sedition, celebrate victory but disguise defeat. Even so a case can be made for interpreting coin types as political statements on the broad level.

Can anything be achieved by a study of the coin types of Carausius and Allectus? A useful strategy is to look at them in the light of the coinage issued on behalf of Diocletian, Maximian and, later, Constantius. Here we may be able to ascertain whether the production of the rival camps was representative of a campaign of numismatic propaganda and whether the coinage gives an indication of policy or political intent.

Perhaps before taking this step we should ask to whom all this numismatic fine art was directed. It is unlikely that the bulk of the population, labouring in the fields, elbow deep in clay in the potteries, or sweating in the forests to fell timber for the construction of fleets, gave much thought to the nuances of imperial numismatic ideology; their concerns were with coins as money. To this extent, if the coins had the right head on the obverse and were accepted by the taxman, the rent collector and the baker, all was well. We are in all probability dealing with a phenomenon addressed to an elite to reconcile them to the status quo rather than to influence their minds about things which, in the last analysis, would be decided by the loyalty of the forces or external military events. The exception to this statement is the army itself, which received coin as pay and for whom specific coin types were produced.

To check the validity of arguments advanced for the function of coin types as ideological indices we can contrast the coinage of the British regime with that of its legitimate rival through the widely circulating billon issues of the important mint of Lyons (Lugdunum). While some types are shared with the British regime, the overall 'message' of the Gallic mint is focused on the unity of the twin emperors, Diocletian and Maximian, and their relative ranking within the imperial hierarchy. This ranking was symbolized by the identification of Diocletian with the supreme deity Jove/Jupiter and his junior colleague, Maximian, with Hercules, the adjutant of Jove. The bulk of Diocletian's coins invoke Jove as protector of the emperor (*IOVI CONSERVAT AVGG*; Pl.1, no.9) while a very high proportion of Maximian's refer to Hercules, who is invoked as *HERCVLI PACIFERO* ('The Bringer of Peace after Conflict'; Pl.1, no.10). Maximian himself acquires the attributes of Hercules, adopting the tree trunk club of the heavenly giant as a piece of symbolic regalia (Pl.1, no.11). The bravery of the Caesar, Constantius, and his successes against Carausius on the Continent are celebrated by the appearance of victory trophies and captives (Pl.1, nos 13, 14). In terms of volume of coinage, as represented in hoards, the religious–dynastic and militaristic types predominated in the circulating medium.

By contrast the bulk of the coinage of Carausius is restricted to the single type with the legend *PAX AVG(vsti)* which proclaims and celebrates the blessings of peace. This type was issued throughout the reign by the Unmarked, London and Colchester mints. That the type is a pious hope, rather than a statement of reality, needs no emphasis. Nevertheless, it is an important ideological statement in its own right and must represent the ostensible policy of the regime in the same way that the central empire's choice of types reflects its concern with dynastic stability and military success. The fact that a single type dominates the coinage suggests that the regime was content to direct overtly propagandistic types to a minority and that coinage was not a medium of persuasion of the majority.

Around the basic *Pax* type cluster a number of issues which contribute specific information about the reign. These will be dealt with, in their chronological setting, elsewhere; for the moment it will suffice to give an overview of what might have been the changing concerns of the regime as reflected in its choice of coin types. This aspect of the coinage is perhaps best represented by the products of the RSR mint.

The mint, opened to strike coin to pay an accession donative to the army and provincial bureaucracy, seems to have been active in the early months of the new administration and so presents a conspectus of types representing the ideological outlook at this formative period. The types of the high-value silver coins are very allusive and demand a high level of Roman literary education for their full impact to be appreciated, suggesting they had served a ceremonial function before entering the currency pool. The mint was also responsible for issuing the consular medallions which commemorate the acquisition of Britain in terms of an imperial victory (Pl.2, nos 1, 2). Emphasis is placed on the legitimacy of the regime by claiming that Carausius is responding to a public demand for his presence; the claim is validated by recourse to Vergilian imagery. Adapting a line from the *Aeneid* the coinage proclaims *EXPECTATE VENI* ('Come, O expected one'). Carausius, as saviour, is welcomed by a personification of Britain (Pl.2, no.3). The arrival itself is celebrated with a formal *Adventus* ceremony, which may have involved a series of rituals associated with state visits to London and Colchester (Pl.1, no.4; Pl.4, no.4). The imagery of this issue shows the emperor trampling a captive under his horse's hoofs in the ritual of *calcatio colli*. This representation did not, at this time, represent an actual trampling. Not until the fourth century was the vanquished victimized in this manner. That peace and plenty will flow from the beneficial presence of the new ruler is proclaimed in another Vergilian reference, this on the coin inscribed *VBERTAS* (Plenty). This personification is normally depicted as a woman who stands holding a bunch of grapes, but in the second *Georgic* there is a description of rural bliss and rustic simplicity which harks back to the agrarian roots of Roman society in its uncorrupted state. Among the wonders of nature in this bucolic idyll is the fact that udders (*vbera*) of the cows are always full of milk. The verbal play on *vbera*/udder and *VBERITAS* (Plenty) is united in the image of a Romano-British milkmaid at her work, seated on a milking stool, her head laid against the flank of a contented cow (Pl.2, nos 5, 10).

The province itself is seen in a wider context of the empire as whole, the object of the revolt is to renew Rome, Carausius is depicted as the *RENOVATOR ROMANO(R VM)* ('Restorer of the Romans') (Pl.2, no.6). To achieve these ends he needs two things, the backing of the army (*CONCORDIA MILITVM*) and Good Fortune (*FELICITAS*); the latter he already enjoys and it is embodied in the naval forces depicted on the coin (Pl.2, nos 7,11). The welfare of the state is endorsed by the taking of binding public vows for its safety (*VOTO PVBLICO*), an event normally associated with the giving of a donative (Pl.2, no.9).

If we tabulate the recorded specimens of the silver coinage a clear picture emerges of which issues were the largest in the series, assuming that survival represents relative volume of issue. From this tabulation we may see in which direction the trend of the propaganda effort lay and so ascertain something of the proclaimed policy of the regime.

Table 4   *Type conspectus of Carausian silver coinage*

Type	*Number*	*Percentage*
ADVENTVS AVG	7	6.7
CONCORDIA AVG	2	2.2
CONCORD(IA) MILIT(VM)	18	17.3
CONSERVAT AVG (Neptune)	2	2.0
EXPECTATE VENI	12	11.5
FELICITAS AVG (Galley)	16	15.0
FIDES MILIT(VM)	2	2.0
FORTVNA AVG	1	1.0
LEG IIII FL(AVIA)	1	1.0*
ORIENS AVG (Sol)	2	2.0
RENOVAT(OR) ROMANO	20	19.0
ROMAE AETERN	1	1.0
TEMP FELIC	1	1.0
VBERITAS	6	5.7
VIRTVS AVG	3	3.0
VOTVM PVBLIC(VM)	10	9.6

*probably a modern counterfeit   (after Shiel, 1977, with additions)

A number of peaks are visible in this table, while other issues, though of individual iconographic interest, are scarce and of nugatory political significance. In a very direct sense these coins make up a programmic self-declaration of the antecedents and intentions of the new regime. The situation to be confronted is already in existence, not created by the revolt; a saviour is expected, who has arrived in the person of Carausius. The task

Table 5 *The main types of insular billon issues by mint and mintmark*

	CARAUSIUS	RSR	UM	ML	L/ML	F/O ML	B/E MLXXI	B/E MLXXI C	S/P MLXXI	SP/ML	C
ABVNDANTIA AVG											
ADVENTVS AVG		X	X	X							X
AEQVITAS			X								
APPOLINI CONS AV			X								X
COHR PRAET			X	X							
COMES AVG-Minerva			X	X					X (AVGGG)		
COMES AVG-Victory			X	X					X (AVGGG)		X
CONCORDIA AVG		X		X							
CONCORD EXERCI				X							
CONCORD MILIT		X		X							X
CONSTANT AVG											
EXPECTATE VENI		X									
FELICITAS AVG		X									X
FELICITAS SAEC											
FELICIT PVB											X
FELICIT TEMP					X						X
FIDES MILIT		X				X					X
FIDES EXERCIT											
FORTVNA AVG		X			X						X
FORTVNA REDVX											
GENIVS AVG					X						
GENIVS BRITANNI											X
GENIVS EXERCIT											
GERMANICVS MAX V					X						
HILARITAS AVG				X	X				X (AVGGG)		
IOVE AVG						X					
IOVE VICTORI										X	
LAETITIA AVG						X				X	X
LAETITIA AVGGG											
LEG I MIN				X							
LEG II AVG				X							
LEG II PARTH				X							X
LEG IV FLAVIA			X	X							X
LEG VII CLAVDIA				X							
LEG VIII AVG				X							
LEG XX VV				X							

MC	MSC-SMC	CXXI	MCXXI	S/C C	SC	SP	S/P C	ALLECTUS	ML	S/P ML	S/A ML	S/A MSL	QL	S/P C	S/P CL	QC
							X							X		
										X					X	
											X			X		
X	X															
									X			X		X		
	X								X		X					
X																
							X									
	X															
		X												X		
		X					X							X	X	
							X							X		
									X							
				X			X									
				X												
										X	X	X		X		
X				X			X			X	X	X		X	X	X
							X									
	X															
		X				X										

Table 5 *Continued*

	CARAUSIUS	RSR	UM	ML	L/ML	F/O ML	B/E MLXXI	B/E MLXXI C	S/P MLXXI	SP/ML	C
LEG XXX VLPIA				X							
LIBERALITAS AVG											X
MARTI PACIFIC							X				
MARTI VICTO											
MARS VLTOR							X				
MONETA AVG			X	X							X
NEPTUNE		X		X							X
ORIENS AVG		X							X		X
PAX AVG		X	X	X	X	X	X	X	X	X	X
PAX AVGGG					X			X			
PIETAS AVGGG											
PIETAS AVG											
PROVIDENTIA AVG			X					X			X
PROVIDENTIA AVGGG											
PROVID DEOR											
RENOVAT ROMA		X									X
RESTIT SAEC											X
ROMAE AETERNAE		X									X
SAECVLARES AVG											X
SAECVLI FELICIT											
SALVS AVG			X	X		X			X		
SALVS AVGG									X		
SALVS PVBLICA							X				
SECVRIT PERP					X						
SOLI INVICTO				X			X				
SPES AVG			X								
SPES PVBLICA			X								
TEMP FELIC			X								
VBERITAS		X									
VICTORIA AVG			X	X			X		X	X	
VICTORIA GERMA			X								
VIRTVS AVG		X	X	X		X					
VIRTVS AVGGG									X		
VOTA PVBLICO			X								

MC	MSC-SMC	CXXI	MCXXI	S/C C	SC	SP	S/P C	ALLECTUS	ML	S/P ML	S/A ML	S/A MSL	QL	S/P C	S/P CL	QC
X							X									
X				X		X	X				X	X		X		
							X									
									X	X	X					
X		X	X	X		X			X	X	X		X			
				X												
							X									
									X	X						
				X			X		X	X	X		X	X		
							X									
									X							
		X														
		X					X			X			X			
X																
									X							
X		X		X					X	X	X					
				X												
							X			X			X			
X								X		X	X	X		X	X	
X	X		X					X		X	X			X		X
X					X											
X			X		X			X		X		X		X		
							X									

to be undertaken is not that of dividing Britain from the bulk of the empire but of restoring it to *romanitas* and by this example to restore the Roman state itself to its pristine and uncorrupted condition. These achievements depend for their accomplishment on two loyal agents of the regime – the army, which enjoys concord between its various elements and collectively with their emperor, and the naval forces who are the embodiment of the imperial good fortune, or *Felicitas*.

To summarize the message. The new rule is constitutionally established and the proper forms are observed. The ceremony of *Adventus* is celebrated and vows for the safety of the state are recorded in proper form, though with a perilously misinformed understanding of imperial protocol. The army is happy, peace has been established and the silver coins themselves speak of a new level of monetary prosperity.

Table 5 lists the main types of the insular billon issues by mint and mintmark. This tabulation allows a number of observations to be made about the emission of what constituted the substantive issues of the reigns of both Carausius and Allectus. Other than the *PAX* type, *SALVS AVG(VSTI)* and *VICTORIA AVG(VSTI)* are issued by all mints in most years, types celebrating the welfare and victorious enterprise of the emperor. They are paralleled by issues of the legitimate emperors and, indeed, constitute the normal suite of types employed by imperial regimes from the middle of the third century. As such they are non-specific though the *VICTORIA* issues cluster at the end of the reign at London but are early at Colchester, pointing to a degree of independence in the operation of these establishments and emphasizing the difficulty of drawing political conclusions from too narrow a view of such numismatic research data.

In terms of religious content the Carausian coinage is reticent when compared to that of Diocletian and Maximian. This more accurately reflects the religious basis of Diocletian's constitutional arrangements than a secular policy pursued by Carausius or Allectus. The output of types identifying the emperor with specific deities, or soliciting their direct intervention, is relatively rare. The C mint issued coins, derived from those of Gallienus, with the legend *APOLLINI CONS AVG*, which invoke the sun god as protector of the emperor. This mint also produced a number of special issues on which the bust of Carausius is conjoined with that of Sol. The cult of Sol, with whom Apollo was identified, had been confirmed as a major state religion when Aurelian dedicated a great new temple to the god on the forum in Rome itself. This dedication was the culmination of the spread of the cult of sun worship, which had been gaining popularity through military circles in the third century. The identification of Sol/Apollo with Mithras, already a strongly established cult among the upper ranks of the army, further enhanced the status of the new rite.

The thematic concerns of the silver coinage is reflected in the earliest bronze. Here the dominance of military types hardly survives the first year of the reign. Minerva, in her manifestation as a military deity, is identified as companion of the emperor; so too is Victory. CONCORD(IA) EXERCI(TI) and CONCORD(IA) MILIT(VM) make the usual statement of military support. This appeal for military support is directly solicited by a series of billon coins from the London mint commemorating the individual legions who supported Carausius in his occupation of Britain. These coins are discussed in detail elsewhere (p.92). Two rare issues deserve notice: the first proclaim Carausius to be RESTITVTOR BRIT(ANNIAE) ('Restorer of Britain'), the second appears to depict a mystic marriage between Carausius and his newly won island, CONIVGE A(VG), with the emperor hand in hand with his 'bride'. Both are early issues.

The tone of the C mint tends to be even less militaristic. The earliest issues are devoted to such topics as the happiness of the people (FELICITAS PVBLICA) and the generosity of the ruler (LIBERALITAS AVGVSTI); the acceptability of the new coinage is also a concern of this mint with the issue of MONETA AVGVSTI under four consecutive sequence marks, possibly indicating some otherwise unrecorded, temporary, economic crisis.

A notable feature of Carausius's reign is the issue of both gold and billon coins which recognize the legitimacy of Diocletian and Maximian. This recognition takes the form of coins bearing the portraits and legends of the legitimate rulers or of coins in the name of Carausius which associate the usurper with the legitimate imperial college through the use of the formula AVGGG, as in PROVID AVGGG, to denote the rule of three co-equal emperors (Pl.5, no.8). The most notable case of such association takes the form of the use of a triple-portrait issue, displaying the conjoined busts of the three emperors (Pl.5, no.6). These issues are of primary political significance, offering, as they do, an insight into Carausius's political aspirations or into otherwise unattested diplomatic activity. Such numismatic gestures were not reciprocated.

There is a certain degree of contrast observable in the coinage of Allectus. Numerically the PAX AVG type (Pl.5, nos 10, 11) still constitutes a large element of the coinage, though the mints seem to have issued this only in the first year of the reign. Of equal weight in the Allectan coinage are the PROVIDENTIA AVG issues of both mints, a type only infrequently employed by his predecessor. *Providentia* represents the quality of watchful foresight which anticipates and smooths out problems for the benefit of the commonwealth. Two further types are prominent: LAETITIA AVG(VSTI) and HILARITAS AVG(VSTI). In the first the personification is equipped with an anchor and rudder, or the legend is associated with a war galley (Pl.8, no.3). *Hilaritas* represents not unrestrained mirth but religious joy associated with the festival of the *Hilaria*. The Romans defined various degrees of rejoicing; *Laetitia* was joy occasioned by something giving pleasure, in the case of Allectus his fleet, *Hilaritas* represented religious joy and *Gaudium* an official rejoicing in which the citizen body shared the good fortune of the ruler. Neither Carausius nor Allectus appear to have felt the need to declare a state of *Gaudium*.

Table 6 *Special billon issues*

CARAVSIVS

Mint/Date	Type	Mint	Type	Mint	Type
LONDON	I	'COLCHESTER'	I	'UNMARKED'	I
286/9 ⊥/ML	ADVENTVS AVG	286/9 ⊥/C	CONSERVATOR (Iovi)		ADVENTVS CARAVSI
	PAX AVG		LAETITIA		CONSERVATOR (Iovi)
	COMES AVG		LIBERALITAS		LAETITIA
	II		PAX AVG		PAX AVG
	PAX AVG		PROVID AVG		PROVID AVG
	I		II		COMES AVG
LL/ML	GERMANICVS MAX		RESTIT SAECVLI		II
	I		III		PAX AVG
	PAX AVG	⊥/MC	FORTVNA (Emp/Sol)		FORTVNA (Emp/Sol)
	VICTORIA AVG		SOLI INVICTO (Torso)		INVIC (Torso)
289	II		I		LAETITIA AVG (Torso)
FLO/ML	PAX AVG	289	EXPECTATE VENI		FORTVNA REDVX (Consular)
	III		II		PAX AVG (Consular)
	PAX AVG (Consular)		EXPECTATE VENI		

PROVIDENTIA AVG
SALVS PVBLICA

Date	Mint mark	Legend	Type
		PAX AVG	II
292/3	S|P / MLXXI	PAX AVG	II
293	S|P / ML		
ALLECTVS			
293/4	S|P / ML	LAETITIA	II
		PAX AVG	
		PROVIDENTIA	
295	S|A / ML	PAX AVG	I
			II
296	S|A / MSL	LAETITIA	
		PAX AVG	
		PROVIDENTIA	II
296	— / QL	VIRTVS AVG	II

Date	Mint mark	Legend	Type
292/3	S|C / C	PAX AVG (Emp./Sol)	II
		SPES PVBLICA	I
		TEMP FELICIT	II
		PAX AVG	
293	S|P / C	VIRTVS AVG (Emp./Sol)	III
		PAX AVGGG (Maximian)	II
		CARAVSIVS ET FRATRES SVI	III

Type I: Radiate, helmeted, cuirassed bust left, holding spear and shield.

Type II: Radiate, cuirassed bust left, holding spear and shield.

Type III: Jugate, busts, half length portraits, facing portraits, etc.

Allectus's coinage lacks the programmatic qualities of that of Carausius. Of the state deities only Sol, represented in three issues from the London mint, offers any insight into the religious preoccupations of the regime. There is no appeal to the gods at the end of the reign nor increase in military types. This contradicts any suggestion of an administration under pressure or feeling in imminent danger of collapse. Nor is there much evidence of the Carausian appeal to the unity of the empire: only two rare issues commemorate ROMAE AETERNAE. The coinage exemplifies a stable regime, an impression reinforced by the introduction of a new denomination at the end of the reign.

The normal bust type employed on the Roman coinage depicts the ruler in armour or civilian dress facing right to the spectator looking at the coin; variation from this norm seems to be reserved for ceremonial issues. Both Carausius and Allectus issued coins with left-facing busts. These variations are significant and we may be correct in thinking that such coins fulfilled some non-monetary as well as a normal monetary function; an analogue may be drawn with modern commemorative coins such as the £2 piece issued for the Commonwealth Games, held in 1986 in Scotland, or the special 50p piece which heralded Britain's entry to European Common Market in 1971. The coins which best demonstrates this secondary function are those showing the emperor wearing the robes of a consul, since a consulship was accompanied by a donative. Carausius issued consular coins in every year between 287 and 291, Allectus in 294/5. Because the mintmarks extend across more than one calendar year we cannot say that Carausius held consular office four times, but it can hardly be less than three. Needless to say, these were self-conferred honours unrecognized by the legitimate emperors who designated their own pairs of consuls.

Schematizing these special issues (Table 6) suggests that it was intended to produce a basic suite of three left-facing bust types each year, as a component of the substantive issues. As the Roman army was normally paid three times a year we may have evidence here of coins being produced for the imperial donative which formed an important element of military pay in the third century (Casey, 1977).

A very high proportion of the iconographically most elaborate and innovative coins was produced by the C mint. All of these coins are very rare, suggesting a restricted production rate and a correspondingly small impact in the currency pool as a whole. Since it is likely that the Provincial Council met at Camulodunum, the first capital of the province, it may be that these coins constitute a distribution to this elite section of the civilian community, a distribution which constituted a direct use of coinage to introduce, or at least to reinforce, a political message. The re-issue by the C-mint of the EXPECTATE VENI type (originally a silver accession coin produced by the RSR mint) in billon may be part of the quinquennial celebrations of 289/90, possibly centred on the provincial religious capital.

Overall, there is a strong impression that the coinage was used in a skilful propagandist manner directed at selected elements of the population. Some constitutional arrangements are recorded, as are the conduct of important state ceremonies. Both the Carausian and Allectan administrations express a conciliatory and peaceful image, though in reality events contrived to make them territorially aggressive and bellicose. There is manifest evidence of the management of the coinage and ingenuity was expended on the production of coins which transcended their function as mere monetary units. A sophisticated use of literary allusion adds an unexpected dimension to the coinage of a regime which has, hitherto, been thought to have existed in a state of continuous crisis.

It is clear from the coinage that an obligation was felt to appear to conform to traditional forms of social and political expression, and this ideology was a central element of the usurpers' regimes. The thought devoted to this aspect of administration is, surprisingly, evident from the earliest stage and, though the technical execution of individual coins is not of the highest standard, the use of literary allusion and the employment of traditional motifs in pertinent circumstances points to the production of coinage enjoying a priority above the mere need to have something with which to buy the loyalty of the soldiery.

· 6 ·

THE EVIDENCE OF
THE COINAGE

A DETAILED EXAMINATION OF THE reigns of Carausius and Allectus can only be undertaken within the framework of the abundant coinage which is, after the contemporary or near-contemporary literary material, the principal source of evidence for the period. The coinage can be studied in a number of ways. In the first instance the individual coins and their inscriptions can be studied for direct or oblique allusion to events or, as in the previous chapter, they may be examined in a programmatic manner by their choice of types. Secondly, by studying the spatial distribution of types and issues and their occurrence on sites and in hoards, we may determine sources of production, their circulation pattern and, perhaps, their date of issue.

The need for a date sequence of issues and a firm identification of mints has been the paramount concern of numismatists in the present century and a general agreement has been reached in both of these areas of research. A general agreement only, for there are still, as we shall see, unresolved problems. Minor amendments to the overall scheme are offered from time to time by workers in the field, though Carson's fundamental organization of the series appears to have stood the test of both time and new discoveries. The coinage of Allectus presents fewer problems than that of his predecessor, being of shorter duration and smaller volume, but here too there are problems especially as to how the later issues relate to the contemporary Continental currency system.

Denominations and nomenclature

Coin was struck by Carausius in gold, silver, billon (bronze/silver alloy), bronze and copper. Allectus's coins were produced in gold and billon only. There is a problem of definition in discussing the coins of this period because, for the most part, we do not know the names given to the coins by their issuers and users. Numismatists have adopted a loose and confusing nomenclature of their own. Traditionally Carausius's silver coin is called a *denarius* and his, and Allectus's, large billon coin is called an *antoninianus*. In this discussion a new nomenclature will be used which follows modern Continental practice as regards the name of the billon coins which have been dubbed *aureliani*. This is because after Aurelian reformed the currency in 273 a new coin, probably worth four *denarii*, replaced the so-called *antoninianus* of two-*denarius* value. The identification of the Aurelianic coin with a value of four *denarii* seems to have been confirmed by a new section of the Aezani Inscription. This document is the text of a letter circulated around the empire in 301 to order the revaluation of the currency (Ekrim *et al.*, 1971).

The new coin was not the same as its predecessor, being twice its face value, and confusion can only arise from the misuse of the old conventional name. Carausius's coins were, of course, issued after the Aurelianic reform and are of the new denomination. The Carausian silver coin cannot have been a *denarius* since its intrinsic value is far above the accompanying four-*denarius* billon issue. It is better to avoid the word *denarius* in relation to this coin altogether. Allectus also introduced a new billon coin which seems, by virtue of its weight and composition, to have been valued as a half of the *aurelianus* piece. This coin always bears the letter Q in the exurgue, possibly indicating that it was identified as a *quinarius*; this name will be retained.

Mints

The coinage of the separatist regime was produced at a number of mints, five have been identified for Carausius and two for Allectus. In the reign of Carausius not all of the mints operated at the same time and staff may have transferred between establishments, making attribution on stylistic criteria difficult.

One of Carausius's mints was on the Continent, another was formerly located there but has been reattributed to Britain, while yet another produced coin largely as donatives for the army. Thus the bulk of the circulating medium was issued from three mints, one of which either quickly went out of production or should be identified with one of the remaining operational establishments.

The Continental mint

Coins of the Continental mint are very distinctive (Pl.3, nos 1–5), the portrait of Carausius being closely based on those of Diocletian and Maximian on the coinage produced by the Lyons (Lugdunum) mint (Pl.3, no.6). The features are thinly modelled, with distinctively high cheek bones and a sharp nose, and the hair and beard treated as a series of incised lines. This is in contrast to the productions of British mints which always represent the beard and hair as curls (Pl.3, nos 7–11). Only rarely is a mintmark employed, because the reverse legend often extends into the exergual area where the mintmark would normally appear. When a mintmark is employed it takes the form of the letters PR or R. Issues appear both with and without the inclusion of C(*aesar*) in the imperial title. The base metal coins are not skilfully produced, the legends frequently blundered and poorly laid out on the flan. The weight is not very well controlled, varying between 2.75 and nearly 5g. The style of the coinage strongly suggests that it was produced by workers unskilled in the techniques of the professional moneyer. The general angularity of the portraiture and the reverse figures may indicate that the dies were made by artists normally employed as cutters of sealstones and intaglios.

The mint struck in two metals, one of which was gold; the second metal is more problematic. Ostensibly the bulk of the Continental mint's coins are *aureliani* because they are base metal and the effigy of Carausius wears a radiate crown; however, a non-destructive metallurgical analysis of one of these coins, undertaken for the author, shows that far from having the expected percentage of silver, it had none at all. Despite the absence of silver the fact that these coins are found in hoards with regular *aureliani* suggests that this was the intended value. Other issues of Carausius which lacked a silver content, discussed below, are also hoarded with silver rich coins; it must be supposed that either the state could enforce a notional value for its coinage, irrespective of metallic content, or that it suited the convenience of the public to accept the two versions of the currency on a single basis.

The bulk of the surviving production of this mint derives from the finding of a single hoard. Outside this source less than 50 coins are recorded. Despite the use of a wide variety of individual coin types employed by this mint the volume of surviving coins suggests that the total production was very small (Beaujard & Huvelin, 1980).

The gold coins of the Continental mint, of which there are nine closely die-linked specimens recorded, weigh an average 4.6g, indicating a standard aimed at a striking rate of 70 coins to the Roman pound. This is the same standard as the gold issued by Diocletian and Maximian in the period up to 290, when they raised their gold standard to 60 to the pound (5.46g). One issue of the Continental gold depicts Carausius in the robes of a consul. The appearance of this coin suggests that the life of the mint extended to a date later than 1 January 296, the earliest date for which the emperor could have held the consulship. The view that this coin refers to a regular or an hypothesized suffect consulship held at an earlier stage of Carausius's career can be discounted (Burnett & Casey, 1984). The presence of an RSR silver issue in the Rouen hoard (p.91) confirms that Rouen had an extended existence.

The types employed in the gold coins reflect an emphatic appeal to the military – CONCORDIA MILITVM ('Unity with, and of, the Army'), and FIDES MILITVM ('The Loyalty of the Army'). Also celebrated is the Foresight of the emperor (PROVIDENTIA), his Courage (VIRTVS), and his Well-being (SALVS). The largest issue in the bronze celebrates the Protection the emperor extended to his subjects (TVTELLA). All this is the normal content of the contemporary coinage and can, with the exception of the TVTELLA type, be paralleled in the products of his opponents and their predecessors.

The location of the Continental mint in Rouen (Rotomagus in the Roman period) has been established both by the discovery of a very large hoard of coins in the city and by the distribution of these distinctive pieces

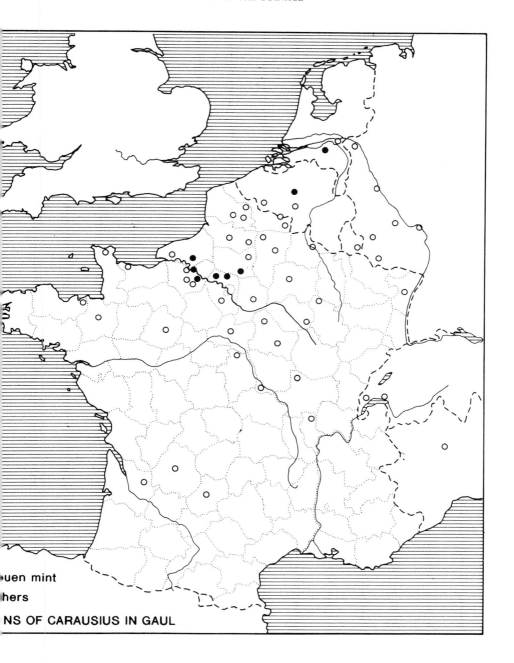

uen mint
hers
NS OF CARAUSIUS IN GAUL

3   Finds of Carausian coinage in Gaul. (After Loriot.)

in Gaul within a circumscribed radius of Rouen itself (Fig.3). In the past these distinctive coins have been attributed to Boulogne (Gesoriacum or Bononia in the Roman period) because of the inclusion of a number of specimens in the collection of Boulogne Museum (Casey, 1977). It is now clear that these coins were part of the hoard from Rouen which had been purchased by the museum and subsequently mistakenly provenanced to Boulogne (Webb, 1933). There is, as yet, no record of the Rouen-type coinage being found in excavation at Boulogne itself. The republication of the original hoard has sorted this problem out so that the coinage can now be studied in its original context. The distribution of Rouen coins in Britain offers no contradiction to their attribution to a Continental mint (Fig.4) and the view that they were produced in Britain and exported to Gaul does not overcome the objection that stylistically they are completely unlike any unequivocally insular products. The portraiture and treatment of the hair and beard, emulating as it does from the Lyons coinage of Diocletian and Maximian, differs so much from the bulk of the usurper's coinage as to suggest a completely different artistic milieu and centre of production.

Dating the coins of Rouen has presented a number of problems and several hypotheses have been advanced:

1   The coins are an emergency issue produced after the loss of Boulogne in 293 to pay the few troops left after the defeat of Carausius's forces by Constantius.

This view was based on a supposed 'emergency' look to these rather ill-produced coins.

2   They were produced as a donative paid to the forces who captured Boulogne after the defeat of Maximian's expeditionary force in 289/90.

This view was based on the mistaken assumption that numbers had been found in Boulogne.

3   They were produced, as outlined above, at the end of 290, not as a once-and-for-all donative but as a regular currency and the emission continued to the end of 291, when it ceased (Beaujard & Huvelin, 1980).

The objections rehearsed under the second hypothesis prevail with equal force against this argument.

4   The coins are the initial issue of the reign, produced in 286 before Carausius extended his regime to Britain. The gold coins are the accession donative paid at the start of the reign (Burnett & Casey, 1984).

Of these hypotheses the present author favours the last. The first can be dismissed on the grounds that Rouen coins appear in hoards in which the terminal dating is provided by issues pre-dating 290. Thus there is a Rouen coin in the Croydon Hoard (Burnett & Casey, 1984), which closes in 286/7, another in the Little Orme Hoard dating it no later than 289 (Seaby, 1956). This early dating is supported by the metrology of the gold coinage, which corresponds to the pre-290 Continental standard. Though Carausius himself maintained this standard in Britain it seems unlikely that coinage designed

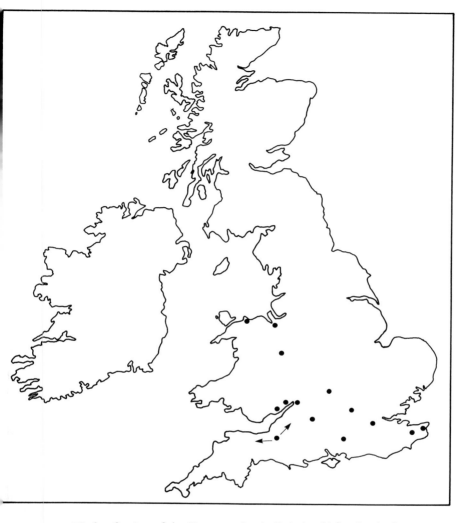

4 Finds of coins of the Rouen mint in Britain. (After Loriot.)

for Continental use would be struck at the old standard after the introduction of the new, especially since insular base metal coin standards were raised to those of the mainland in 290.

The fact that the coins appear in such early contexts undermines the second and third hypotheses, as crucially as does the erroneous provenance. A further argument for a later date for the Rouen coins stems from the fact that some specimens give Carausius the title Caesar, in the abbreviated form *IMP C CARAVSIVS PF AVG.* It has been claimed that the title Caesar was only assumed in 290/1 following the successful repulse of an invasion attempt by Maximian and the establishment of an enclave in north-west Gaul (Carson,

1959). In general this is true of products of the British mints but the evidence of the hoards makes it clear that the Rouen mint included the title Caesar at an earlier date than its general adoption by the insular mints. Even these have pre-290 issues with the title Caesar, though these are of such infrequency as to not invalidate Carson's acute general observation. The implication of the re-dating of this coinage is discussed below.

The RSR mint

The third of the Carausian mints of short lifespan signed its products with the enigmatic letters RSR. The mint produced gold and silver coins (Pl.2, nos 3–11) and bronze medallions (Pl.2, nos 1,2). The rare base metal coins bearing the RSR mark are perhaps unofficial (Pl.2, no.10).

Attempts to offer a geographical interpretation of the enigmatic mint letters resolved itself into two possibilities; that they incorporated in some manner either the name of RUTUPIAE (Richborough) or ROTOMAGUS (Rouen). Both of these attributions have been effectively rejected, the latter on distribution and stylistic grounds and no theory involving a place-name interpretation of these letters can be validated by normal Roman epigraphic practices. Abandoning the place-name approach completely, Webb offered a solution which is accepted by all workers today (Webb, 1906). Noting that in the financial reforms of the Severan period a new administrative post was created, that of *Rationalis Summarum Rationum* or *Rationalis Summae Rei*, and that this official dealt with imperial benefactions and donatives, Webb suggested that the coinage was issued from the *officium* of this administrator of imperial gifts and that the mintmark is simply the initials of his office. This elegant solution to the problem is confirmed by the nature of the coinage issued by the RSR mint. The gold coins and bronze medals are clearly presentation pieces associated with the sort of duties carried out in the fourth century by the better-documented *Comes Sacrarum Largitionum* (The Count of the Sacred Largesses). This official administered taxes raised to provide for imperial donatives to the army and the product of this benevolence took the form of monetary medallions and precious metal coins which were distributed on imperial accessions and at fixed interval celebrations during a reign (Kent, 1961).

Looking at the coins produced by the *Rationalis* we can see that they are overwhelmingly of a donative nature, both in type content and metal. The outstanding component is the silver, which restored a coin of a purity and weight unknown since the reign of Nero to the currency system; a non-destructive analysis of a specimen of this coinage indicates that the refiners achieved better than 96 per cent in the standard of purity. Struck at rather variable weights, the standard aimed at appears to have been a unit of c.3.75g, indicating a probable intended striking rate of 90 coins to the Roman pound.

The range of types employed in this coinage is discussed in detail elsewhere (p.59); for the present, it is sufficient to emphasize aspects of the ceremonial content. One issue commemorates a consulship, presumably that taken on 1 January 287, another an imperial state visit presumably to London or Colchester (Camulodunum), a further the taking of vows for the safety of the state. Each of these activities would constitute an occasion on which donatives would have been distributed. But the bulk of the issue may be regarded as the accession donative paid to the army on the successful establishment of the regime in Britain. Obverses showing the bust of the emperor facing to the left, instead of the normal right, which are characteristic of donative coins, are found in the products of the RSR mint (Pl.2, no.7). The production of presentation medals by this mint, and by none of the other mints, is the best evidence for the special status of this establishment (Carson, 1973). The duration of time that this mint operated will not have extended long into the reign if its function was to pay the accession donative. On the other hand the payment of such donatives could have taken some time and, in any event, would not be payable until the next regular triannual payment of soldiers' salaries. Well-established regimes sometimes took several years to pay the donative, but the tenuous nature of Carausius's situation does not make this very likely. By contrast, Diocletian's donative did not reach the soldiers in Egypt until some five years after his accession (Skeat, 1964).

The location of the mint has been attributed to London which, as the administrative capital, was the obvious place to operate the main precious metal mint of the new regime. It may also be noted that an RSR *aureus* shares a die with an Unmarked mint *aurelianus*, a mint which appears to provide die-cutters for the later marked London issues (Shiel, 1974).

While, as has been noted, there is no direct evidence for the length of operation of the mint, the small surviving numbers of coins and the close stylistic similarity between individual coins, points to a short issue, the bulk of which constituted an accession donative for Carausius's loyal forces. The need to strike an unprecedently fine silver coinage for this purpose may be explained by a scarcity of gold created by the recent accession of Diocletian and the elevation of Maximian. These constitutional developments would have had the effect of draining gold stocks out of Britain to pay the obligatory 'crown gold' levied from the cities of the empire on the elevation of a new ruler. It may be remembered, also, that one of the accusations against Carausius was that he misappropriated recaptured pirate booty. Much of this, to judge by contemporary hoards found in Gaul, would have consisted of silver plate.

The type content of the silver coin contributes to its attribution to a very early date in the reign. Like the Rouen coins the emphasis is on military stability and support with the CONCORDIA MILITUM type forming the largest surviving component. Almost as well represented is the theme of FELICITAS (AVG) illustrated with the war galley (Pl.2, nos 7,11). The association of the fleet with the Good Fortune of the Emperor is, in the case of Carausius, an obvious use of pertinent symbolism. The famous type with the motto

77

EXPECTATA VENI ('Come, O Expected One'), depicting Carausius greeted by a personification of Britannia, once again demonstrates the care and thought which went into the design of the coinage at the earliest stage of the administration (Pl.2, no.3).

A type which appears to be of a later date than the bulk of the silver coinage is the issue proclaiming *VOTO PUBLICO MULTIS XX IMP* ('Vows for the Public Safety Renewed for Twenty Years'). The taking of *Vota Publica* should be at five-yearly intervals and Carausius's first *vota* coins should read *VOT V*, as indeed does a gold issue. At the end of five years a coin issue reading *VOT V MVLT X* ('Five Year Vows Completed, Renewal to the Tenth Year') would be expected. Again a gold coin reading *MVLT X* was issued. *MVLTIS XX* should, therefore, be a reference to vows taken after either ten- or fifteen-year intervals, an impossibility in the case of Carausius. Given the close die links between the RSR coins and their obvious stylistic affinities, we may be justified in ascribing this anomalous type to the lack of experience in imperial protocol in the usurper's court. In short, a mistake was made.

The Unmarked mint

Large numbers of Carausian coins have no mintmark; the location of the mint has been sought by a number of strategies, especially by plotting the coin distribution and by observing stylistic relationships to marked issues. For many years it was thought that the mint was at Boulogne, and began operation after Carausius defeated Maximian's attempted invasion of Britain. This was based on the belief that Unmarked coins were found more frequently in the south-east of England than further inland; suggesting they were produced on the other side of the Channel (Carson, 1959, 1971). A wider survey (Table 7) of excavated material and hoards dispelled this notion, showing there was no southern dominance in the occurrence of Unmarked coins, nor were there many in Gaul itself. This research once again opened up the question of the location of the mint.

Table 7   *Distribution of mint products in Britain*

Sites	Mints:London	RSR	Colchester	Unmarked	Rouen	Coin total
NORTH						
Catterick	23.5	5.8	5.8	64.7	–	17
Corbridge	43.7	1.2	23.5	29	–	87
Malton	28.6	–	21.4	50	–	14
MIDLANDS						
Alcester	20	–	10	70	–	10
Hoveringham	94	–	–	6	–	34
Kenchester	31.6	–	11.4	57	–	44
Leicester	37.5	–	25	37.5	–	16
Wroxeter	38	14.2	14.2	33.3	–	21

WALES						
Great Orme	61.5	–	15.5	23	–	13
Little Orme	18.7	0.2	4	76.8	0.35	566
Lydney	21.4	2.3	28.5	45.2	2.3	42
Neath	44.4	–	55.5	–	–	24
Segontium	26.3	–	10.5	63	–	19
SOUTH						
Canterbury	44	2	14	40	–	50
Colchester	15	–	30	55	–	136
Colchester Hoard	51.5	–	44.5	4	–	99
Croydon	9	–	–	91	–	45
Linchmere	87	–	6.8	6.2	–	530
Richborough	35	1	14.8	49	0.3	559
Verulamium	36.2	0.8	17.7	45.1	–	124
Winchester	73.7	–	10.5	15.8	–	19

(Source: Casey, 1977, with references)

PLATE 1

1   Aurelian. 'aurelianus'.
    Obv. *IMP C AVRELIANVS AVG* Rev. *ORIENS AVG-XXIP* RIC 378 var

2   Tetricus I. Radiate copy Rev. *HILARITAS AVGG*

3   Tetricus I. Radiate copy Rev. *INVICTVS* Copy of RIC 82

4   Tetricus I. Radiate copy Rev. *PAX AVG* Copy of RIC 100

5   Carinus. 'aurelianus'.
    Obv. *IMP CARINVS PF AVG* Rev. *IOVI VICTORI - KA.B* RIC 258

6   Constantius I. Alexandrian *tetradrachm*. Obv. The Caesar with spear, shield and helmet decorated with figure of victory. Dattari 6030

7   Constantius I. Alexandrian *tetradrachm*. Rev. The Caesar spearing a fallen enemy. Weder 5.32

8   Constantius I. Alexandrian *tetradrachm*. Rev. The Caesar in military dress with captives.

9   Diocletian. 'aurelianus' Lyons mint.
    Obv. *IMP C C VAL DIOCLETIANVS PF AVG* Rev. *IOVI CONSERVAT AVGG* RIC 43

10 Maximian. 'aurelianus' Lyons mint.
    Obv. *IMP C VAL MAXIMIANVS PF AVG* Rev. *HERCVLI PACIFERO* RIC 371

11 Maximian. 'aurelianus' Lyons mint.
    Obv. *IMP C MAXIMIANVS P AVG* Rev. *HERCVLI PACIFERO* RIC 375var

12 Maxmian. 'aurelianus' Lyons mint.
    Obv. *IMP C MAXIMIANVS AVG* Rev. *HERCVLI INVICTO AVGG* RIC 367 var

13 Constantius I. 'aurelianus' Lyons mint.
Obv. *CONSTANTIVS NOB C* Rev. *VIRTVS AVGG* RIC 648 (A)

14 Constantius I. 'aurelianus' Lyons mint.
Obv. *CONSTANTIVS NOB CAES* Rev. *VIRTVS AVGG* RIC 648(H)

PLATE 2

1 Carausius. Bronze medallion.
Obv. *IMP C MAVR M CARAVSIVS PF AVG GER* Rev. *VICTOR CARAVSIVS AVG GERM MAX –* RSR
Emperor in consular regalia/Emperor crowned by victory

2 Carausius. Bronze medallion.
Obv. *IMP C M AV CARAVSIVS PF AVG* Rev. *VICTORIA CARAVSI AVG –* INPCDA
Emperor in consular regalia/Victory driving a two horse chariot – the meaning of the letters INPCDA is not known.

3 Carausius. Silver.
Obv. *IMP CARAVSVIS PF AV* Rev. *EXPECTATE VENI –* RSR
The emperor greeted by Britannia. RIC 555

4 Carausius. Silver.
Obv. *IMP CARAVSIVS PF AVG* Rev. *ADVENTVS AVG.*
The emperor on horse, treading down captive. RIC 536var

5 Carausius. Silver.
Obv. *IMP CARAVSIVS PF AVG* Rev. *VBERITAS AV –* RSR
Woman milking a cow. RIC 581

6 Carausius. Silver.
Obv. *IMP CARAVSIVS PF AVG* Rev. *RENOVAT ROMANO –* RSR
She-wolf suckling Romulus and Remus. RIC 571

7 Carausius. Silver.
Obv. *IMP CARAVISVS PF AVG* Rev. *FELICITAS AVG –* RSR
Emperor in consular regalia/Warship sailing left. RIC 560var

8 Carausius. Silver.
Obv. *IMP CARAVSIVS PF AVG* Rev. *VICTORIA AVG –* XXX
Emperor crowned by Victory. RIC–

9 Carausius. Silver
Obv. *IMP CARAVISVS PF AVG* Rev. *VOTO PVBLICO –* RSR
Altar inscribed *VOTIS XX IMP* RIC 595

10 Carausius. Copper.
Obv. *IMP CARAVISVS PF AVG* Rev. *VBERITAS AVG –* RSR
Woman milking a cow. RIC 725var

11 Carausius. Silver.
Obv. *IMP CARAIVSVS PF AVG* Rev. *FELICITA AVG –* RSR
Warship sailing right. RIC 560

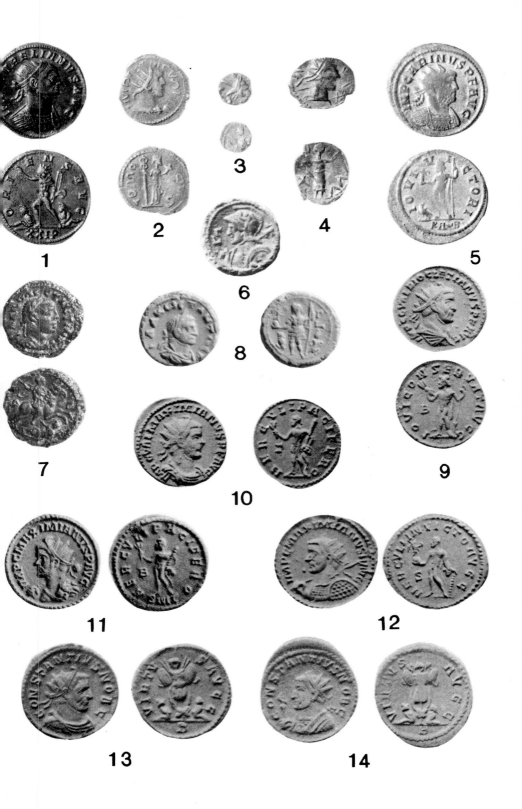

1

2

3

4

5

6

7

8

9

10

11

12

13

14

1

2

3

4

5

6

8

7

9

10

11

1
2
3
4
5

6
7
8
9

10

11
12
13

PLATE 3

1 Carausius. 'aurelianus' Rouen mint.
Obv. *IMP C CARAVASIVS IVG* Rev. *SALVS AVG – R* RIC 665var

2 Carausius. 'aurelianus' Rouen mint.
Obv. *IMP C CARAVSIVS AVG* Rev. *FORTVNA A VG* RIC 638

3 Carausius. 'aurelianus' Rouen mint.
Obv. *IMP C CARAVSIVS AVG* Rev. *LAETITIA – OPR* RIC 649

4 Carausius. 'aurelianus' Rouen mint.
Obv. *IMP C CARAVISVS AVG* Rev. *TVTELA P* RIC 692

5 Carausius. *aureus* Rouen mint.
Obv. *IMP CARAVSIVS AVG* Rev. *CONCORDIA MILITVM* RIC 624

6 Maximian. 'aurelianus' Lyons mint.
Obv. *IMP MAXIMIANVS P AVG* Rev. *VIRTVTI AVGG* RIC 455

7 Carausius. 'aurelianus' London mint.
Obv. *IMP CARAVSIVS PF AVG* Rev. *PACAT ORBIS – OXIVL* RIC–

8 Carausius. 'aurelianus' Unmarked mint.
Obv. *VIRTVS CARAVSI* Rev. *PAX AVG* RIC–

9 Carausius. 'aurelianus' Unmarked mint.
Obv. *IMP CARAVSIVS PF AVG* Rev. *SALVS AVG* RIC 984

10 Carausius. 'aurelianus' Unmarked mint.
Obv. *IMP CARAVSIVS AVG* Rev. *PAX AVG* RIC 883var

11 Carausius. 'aurelianus' Unmarked mint.
Obv. *IMP CARAVSIVS PF AVG* Rev. *PAX AVG* RIC 880

PLATE 4

1 Carausius. 'aurelianus' London mint.
Obv. *IMP CARAVSIVS PF AVG* Rev. *PAX AVG – ML* RIC 101

2 Carausius. 'aurelianus' London mint.
Obv. *IMP C CARAVSIVS PF AVG* Rev. *PAX AVG – S/P ML* RIC 98

3 Carausius. 'aurelianus' London mint.
Obv. *IMP C CARAVSIVS PF AVG* Rev. *PAX AVGGG – S/P MLXXI* RIC 143

4 Carausius. 'aurelianus' London mint.
Obv. *IMP CARAVSIVS PF AVG* Rev. *ADVENTVS AVG – ML* RIC 10

5 Carausius. 'aurelianus' London mint.
Obv. *IMP C CARAVISVS PF AVG* Rev. *PAX AVG – F/O ML* RIC 472

6 Carausius. *aureus* London mint.
Obv. *CARAVISVS PF AVG* Rev. *CONSERVAT AVG – ML* RIC 1

7 Maximian. 'aurelianus' London mint.
Obv. *IMP C MAXIMIANVS PF AVG* Rev. *VIRTVS AVGGG – S/P MLXXI* RIC 39

8 Diocletian. 'aurelianus' London mint.
Obv. *IMP C DIOCELTIANVS PF AVG* Rev. *SALVS AVGGG* – S/P MLXXI RIC 14var

9 Maximian. *aureus* London mint.
Obv. *MAXIMIANVS PF AVG* Rev. *SALVS AVGGG* – ML RIC 32

10 Allectus. *aureus* London mint.
Obv. *IMP C ALLECTVS PF AVG* Rev. *PAX AVG* – ML RIC 6

11 Allectus. 'aurelianus' London mint.
Obv. *IMP C ALLECTVS PF AVG* Rev. *PROVIDENTIA AVG* – S/A MSL RIC 38

12 Allectus. 'aurelianus' London mint.
Obv. *IMP C ALLECTVS PF AVG* Rev. *LAETITIA AVG* – S/A ML RIC 22

13 Allectus. 'aurelianus' London mint.
Obv. *IMP C ALLECTVS PF AVG* Rev. *PROVID AVG* – S/P ML RIC 35

A number of facts emerge. The evidence of hoards, such as that from Croydon, confirms that the mint was operating at a very early date in the reign. Chemical analysis of its products reveals the startling fact that the base metal coins are not billon at all but bronze with such silver as is present being the irreducible fraction found in cupellated lead (Cope, 1974). A slight complication arises from the fact that some Unmarked coins were struck over issues of earlier reigns which, by their nature, would have been silver bearing. But Unmarked mint coin struck on newly produced flans appear deliberately to exclude the precious metal. In this respect they are similar to the Rouen coins discussed above.

Table 8 *Analyses of aureliani of the Unmarked mint*

Reverse Type	RIC No.	Copper	Tin	Silver	Lead
PAX AVG	879	86.42	4.29	0.08	8.78
PAX AVG	880	94.88	1.23	0.17	3.24
PAX AVG	880	97.70	0.48	0.16	1.58
PAX AVG	895	–	–	0.21	–

(Source: Cope, 1974)

The insular location of the mint is problematical, as is its relative date of operation. The use of an obverse die to strike both an *aurelianus* of the Unmarked mint and an *aureus* of the RSR mint, which was itself most probably located in London, suggests that the Unmarked mint was also operating in London. Attention has also been drawn to stylistic links between Unmarked *aureliani* and coins produced by the C mint but arguments of style are not as strong as those of actual die duplication (King, 1985). An explanation for the connection between products of the Unmarked and the C mints could most readily be explained by the transfer of die-cutters, or apprentices trained in their style, from the Unmarked mint to staff the C mint when it was opened. It is also possible that the dies for all of the Carausian mints, with the exception of Rouen, were produced centrally.

Establishing the operational dates of the Unmarked mint is difficult. The absence of silver in the *aureliani* gives an outside date for the series since the issues of the various marked mints do contain silver. The date of this innovation appears to be 287, at the latest, since Cope quotes analyses of coins dated to this year with a meaningful silver component, though the possibility that this is overstruck on an earlier flan must be kept in mind. It is very unlikely that a silver-free and a silver-bearing coinage would be issued at the same time and the latter must have superseded the former. Unmarked *aureliani* stayed in circulation, but not in production, when the London and Colchester mints opened. It is extremely likely that the Unmarked mint, rather than closing, became the signed London mint.

In the light of the foregoing discussion it might be suggested that the Unmarked mint operated in Britain from the start of the reign and continued production until the introduction of the new standard in 287. If Carausius only reached Britain after his eviction from Gaul, the date for which is given a *terminus ad quem* by the issue of consular coins dating to after 1 January 287, there seems very little time for the production of the considerable numbers of Unmarked coins found in the currency pool of the period. It could, on the other hand, be argued that much of the issue was actually produced before the arrival of Carausius in person in Britain. The case for this hypothesis would rest on the belief that Carausius controlled Britain while still engaged in military activity on the Continent and that the island formed part of the *imperium* of Carausius from inception of the revolt in Rouen. This explanation would extend the production life of the mint from mid-286 to mid-287. The large number of irregular coins copying the Unmarked series suggests that there was a widespread illicit production while the population as a whole was unfamiliar with the appearance of the new coinage. This is a contributory argument to ascribing an early date to the issue of the series as a whole.

London (Pl.4)

The attribution of a mint to London presents no problems since the mintmarks employed are self-evident and production was unbroken into the Constantinian period. We have already discussed the probability that the Unmarked mint was located in London; if that is the case, and the Unmarked and London mints are the same, the introduction of a mintmark would become necessary only with the opening of a further operation, the

C mint, which would create the need to differentiate the work of the two establishments. The London mint, in its 'signing' phase, produced *aurei* and *aureliani*. The bulk of the coinage in the reigns of both Carausius and Allectus was produced by the combination of the London and Unmarked mints.

The C mint (Pl.5)

The mint signing its work with C, or variants, has been variously attributed to Clausentum (Bitterne, Hants), Calleva Atrebatum (Silchester, Hants) and Camulodunum Colonia Victricensis (Colchester, Essex). Less likely claims have been made for Glevum (Gloucester) on the grounds that the C on the coins was intended for a G, this despite the fact that Gs are abundantly used in the obverse and reverse legends of the coins and are well defined. The only reason for not accepting Colchester as the location of this mint, apart from localized historical interests which bedevil Carausian studies with their special pleading, is the observation that it would be so close to London as to be an unnecessary duplication of effort and personnel. A further objection is that a very few coins display the letters CL instead of the plain C mintmark. None of these observations outweighs the distributional evidence. Since Camulodunum was the first colony of Roman citizens founded in Britain, in AD 49 and within six years of the Claudian landing, it was pre-eminently 'the colony'; the variant lettering may simply be a contraction of the word *colonia*.

In any event, study of the coins found at Clausentum, both as published archaeological finds and in local museum collections by the author, does not support the location at this site, although the discovery of an *aureus* of Carausius near Southampton emphasizes the importance of the area in this period (Shiel, 1976). Silchester (Calleva Atrebatum) has produced a hoard of Carausian coins of which 65 per cent are London issues and the remainder products of the C mint. But this high proportion is matched by the hoard from Colchester which has 45 per cent of its content of C mint origin. Moreover, there is a high proportion of C mint products on sites local to Colchester. There is no dominance of C coins in the Gloucester region or among Carausian coins found on the Continent.

But why should there be a second mint so close to London? The answer to this may be in the status of Colchester. As the site of the first colony to be founded in the new province, Colchester was also the capital of the newly acquired territory. Colchester lost this status quite quickly when its marginal position in relation to the natural transport network of the country was appreciated and London began to flourish as a port in the second half of the first century. Both the imperial governor and the provincial procurator took up residence in London and it thus became the centre of both the legal and economic administration of the province. Soon London was to become the *de jure* as well as the *de facto* capital of Britain, but Colchester retained its prestige through important religious functions centring around the

Temple of Claudius and the imperial cult which went with it; it was also probably the meeting place of the Provincial Council. Thus, while London became the administrative capital, Colchester retained its function as the ceremonial centre of the province. A dedicatory plaque, possibly from a statue, to Victory and the welfare of the emperor Severus Alexander (222–35) by Lossio Veda, grandson of Vepogenus, a Caledonian, may be interpreted as showing the reception of an embassy, or the housing of diplomatic hostages, in the city in the third century (RIB 191). It is notable that Colchester was the seat of one of the four British bishoprics attested in the early fourth century, but certainly established earlier. Many of the C mint's coins are suggestive of something other than a mere monetary function since they display a high proportion of innovative types associated with religious or public ceremony. The C mint struck billon *aureliani*; there is a single specimen of the silver coinage with a C mintmark but no gold is known.

The BRI mint

A very small number of *aureliani* carry the mark BRI. The first of these coins to be reported was found at Wroxeter (Viroconium) and this led to the suggestion that a mint was located in that city, the argument being that in later Latin the letters B and V have the same phonetic value and are interchangeable. Further finds have upset a distribution pattern optimistically based on a single coin (Shiel, 1979). Stylistically the coins relate to the Unmarked and the London series; possibly the mark was a short-lived experiment intermediate between the Unmarked and marked stages of the development of the London mint. The letters may be interpreted as a contraction for BRI(TANNIA).

The monetary system

As we have seen, the variety of coinage issued by Carausius was extensive, encompassing several denominations, some of which, though issued for only a short period, seem to have remained in circulation as a component of the overall system. How did these coins relate to each other? The only way to establish a relative scale of values is to use the metal content as a guide and to relate them to traditional gold/silver/copper ratios.

Unfortunately, the only figures available for the value of monetary metal post-date the Carausian episode, being found in Diocletian's Edict of Maximum Prices issued a few years after the fall of the British regime. Nevertheless, though prices may have been inflated since the middle of the preceding decade the relative value of commodities is likely to have remained constant.

In using absolute metallic values it should be remembered that it is normal practice to value coins beyond their intrinsic value so as to recover the cost of production and distribution and so give the state a profit. There is no way of knowing the scale of overvaluation in the absence of documentary evidence. That the overvaluation of base metal coinage was probably great is implicit in the circulation of no-silver *aureliani* of the Unmarked mint beside those with silver content of the London and Colchester issues.

The main series of Carausian gold coins was struck at an average weight of 4.33g (N = 10) which compares with the issues of Carus and his family with a gold average of 4.39g (N = 8). In contrast, the bulk of the gold of Diocletian and Maximian was struck, after reform, at a 5g standard. It seems that Carausius either deliberately struck at the weight of the gold coinage already circulating in Britain or used available gold coins to overstrike his own, though examples with undertypes showing have not been recorded. Allectus's gold, which is common compared to his predecessor and apparently issued throughout the reign, was of similar standard to that of Carausius, averaging 4.4g (N = 20).

In Diocletian's edict the price of gold is set at 72,000 *denarii* per pound; silver is valued at 6,000 *denarii* per pound and, what is thought to be monetary standard, copper at 50 *denarii* per pound (Cope, 1977, 109). Thus the relationship between the metals is: gold/silver 12:1; silver/copper 120:1; gold/copper 1440:1. Taking into account the average weight relationships between the main denominations we arrive at the following minimum rounded up values:

> *Aureus* = 1000 *denarii*
> Silver = 70 *denarii* = 14 to the *aureus*
> *Aurelianus* = 2.5 *denarii* = 48 to silver = 670 to the *aureus*

The obvious discrepancy here is in the intrinsic value of the billon coin which we have good reason to believe circulated with a value of four *denarii*. Reconstructions of the Diocletianic monetary system, following the changes implemented by the edict preserved in the fragmentary Aezanic Inscription, suggest that after 301 the 5g *aureus* was valued at a minimum of 375 of the surviving pre-reform *aureliani*. If we adjust this figure to a notional 4.3g coin we would have a relationship of 322.5 *aureliani* to the *aureus*. Since the Aezani Inscription deals with the doubling of value of already circulating coins, without changing their physical composition, it looks as though the *aurelianus* was one of these denominations, the post-301 value being about twice the figure calculated for the Carausian issues.

As would be expected, the tariffed value of the billon coins in circulation is considerably higher than the intrinsic value, the difference being between production value of 2.5 and a circulating value of 4 *denarii*. The overvaluation of the gold and silver is less easy to determine but, if the traditional relationship between the *aureus* and *denarius* was employed, the silver coin might have been circulated at a rate of 25 to the gold coin.

The coinage of Allectus

Compared to that of Carausius, which is still an inchoate mass in the standard reference work, the coinage of Allectus is relatively simple (Burnett,

1984). It was produced in three denominations in two metals, gold and billon, by two mints – London and Colchester. The absence of a silver coinage and the relative abundance of gold further underlines the expedient nature of the Carausian silver issues as well as the recovery of gold stocks in the province during his reign. The innovation of the reign is the introduction of new denomination, the so-called *quinarius* (Pl.8, nos 2–6). Despite the fact that coin was issued with a radiate portrait there is little doubt that this was intended as a half of the *aurelianus*. The mintmark always contains the element 'Q', as in QL and QC for the issues of the London and Colchester mints respectively. It is considered that the letter 'Q' is a denominational sign indicating *quinarius*, used in the by now traditional sense of 'half' when referring to coinage. The weight of 2.7g and silver content of *c.*2 per cent fits this interpretation. The possible reasons for the introduction of this coin, and the date of its issue, are discussed elsewhere (below p.130). All issues of the coin feature a warship as the reverse type with the legend *VIRTVS AVG*, at London, and this legend and *LAETITIA AVG* at Colchester. There are many varieties of the galley but these have no monetary significance, whatever they tell of marine technology of the period.

The coins of the London and Colchester mints all bear sequential mintmarks, increasing in complexity with time. By correlating mintmarks with changes in imperial titulature, and by relative occurrences in hoards, the marked coinage has been put into a sequence with established dates. The scheme, the work of R.A.G. Carson, has enjoyed widespread acceptance and is largely the basis of the chronology discussed in subsequent chapters (Carson, 1959, 1971). It must, however, be borne in mind that the scheme is conjectural and depends on the belief that mintmarks were applied to coins from the start of the reign. We have already noted that the Unmarked mint's products constitute such a large element of the surviving coinage that to compress its operations into a few months, at the very start of the reign, demands a belief that the commission and execution of a vast coinage was within the capabilities of the new regime at a time when its hold on Britain might still have been tenuous. We have also noted that an extension of operations into 287 would be tenable. If this is so, perhaps the inception of mintmarking itself should be deferred. Carson's scheme is an open one as regards the assignment of marks in the three-year period 286–9 and a recent discovery suggests that some revision of this section is in order. A coin, apparently dated by the tribunician power of Carausius, has come to light which suggests that the C mintmark was in use as late as 288/9 (Bland, 1988). Indeed it is suggested that this evidence marks the initiation of all mintmarking (Huvelin, 1992), but this is, perhaps, too extreme a view of the sometimes aberrant use of marks found in this extensive series and the all too frequently attested cavalier attitude of die-cutters to correctness of detail. In any event the extension of mintmarking to 288/9 does not invalidate the arguments which can be derived from the use of marks in a chronological framework.

Table 9   *Mintmark sequences of the coinage of Carausius and Allectus*

CARAUSIUS   IMP CARAVSIVS PF AVG

Mints	London	Colchester	RSR	Rouen
286	ML	C	RSR	R, OPR
	L|	MC		
	ML			
289	F|O	SMC		
	ML			
290	B|E	CXXI, MCXXI		
	MLXXI			
291	B|E	S|C, SC, SP		
	MLXXI	C		

IMP C CARAVSIVS PF AVG

291	B|E	S|C, SC, SP		
	MLXXI	C		
292	S|P	S|P		
	MLXXI	C		
293	S|P	S|P		
	ML	C		

IMP C ALLECTVS PF AVG

293	S|P	S|P		
	ML	C		
	S|A			
	ML			
295	S|A	S|P		
	MSL	CL		
295/6	QL	QC		

It should be observed that the employment of mintmarks and control symbols in a rational and systematic manner is an innovation of the coinage of Carausius which was subsequently adopted throughout the Roman coinage. Why it was felt necessary to introduce such a radical system of record is not known: if, as will be argued, Allectus was the finance minister of the Carausian administration, it is to him that this innovation should be credited. Studies of the coinage of this period have not yet reached a stage where it can be determined whether or not specific mintmarked issues have specific areas of distribution, nor has the relative production volume of individual coin issues yet been determined.

• 7 •

NARRATIVE AND ARCHAEOLOGY I:

THE REVOLT

THE LITERARY SOURCES QUOTED IN Chapter 4 give an account of events in Britain and Gaul which, in the case of Aurelius Victor and Eutropius, is very laconic or in the case of the Panegyrics extremely partial. We are now attempting the reconstruction of events using all other available resources in relation to these accounts. These resources are limited to the numismatic material, some of which has been reviewed in Chapters 5 and 6, and to some pertinent archaeological data. In the latter sphere the problems of close dating loom large since archaeological evidence does not normally lend itself to better than aggregate estimates; without precise inscriptional evidence specific dates can rarely be achieved. Negative evidence is also an important component of archaeological method.

Let us start by examining the account of the escape from Gaul to Britain. The sources state that on receiving news of his condemnation, Carausius fled to Britain with his fleet. The implication is one of unpremeditated flight, a spur of the moment action, and it is in the light of this interpretation that events at the start of the revolt are normally considered. R.A.G. Carson considered things in a different way when he interpreted the output of the Unmarked mint as constituting evidence that Carausius held territory in northern Gaul from the beginning of his reign until the fall of Boulogne to Constantius in 293. Carson stated:

> unmarked coins of Carausius are probably the most common class of his coins: such hoards as have been adequately reported are notable either for the scarcity of these coins or their complete absence. This, and the fact that the hoards and excavated sites in this country [i.e. Britain] in which the unmarked coins appear are all in the south-east, suggest that the mint may not have been in Britain at all
>
> (Carson, 1959).

We have discussed the numismatic evidence for this conclusion and seen that it is based on an inadequate analysis of the widespread distribution of Unmarked coins throughout Britain. Despite the collapse of this theory it can be shown, on other numismatic grounds, that Carausius did indeed hold territory in Gaul at the beginning of the reign. Further, it can be shown that this territory was recovered by the forces of Diocletian and Maximian and that the separatist regime was then confined to Britain until the failure of Maximian's invasion attempt in 289/90; at which point Carausius once again controlled an area of northern Gaul.

The basis of this contention is the evidence of the output and activity of the mint which has been identified as being located at Rouen. In 1846 a black earthenware jar containing some four hundred bronze coins and three of silver was recovered during the excavation of a Roman building in the rue du Petit-Loup in Rouen. After the loss of 80 coins in conservation the residue was identified as comprising 12 examples of issues of Gallienus and emperors of the Gallic Empire, a bronze of Constantine issued in 330–7 which appears to have been added to the original hoard during excavation or during the conservation, and 207 of the distinctive coins of Carausius now recognized as being of Continental origin. Part of the hoard was retained in the Rouen Museum and the rest sold into private collections through the prominent dealer Messrs Rollin et Feuardent. It was from this source that Boulogne Museum acquired the specimens which were mistakenly, and confusingly, provenanced to that town (Webb, 1933; Casey, 1977). The coins being of such distinctive style, a great deal of discussion took place as to where and when they were struck. It was soon recognized that they were a Continental product since specimens from British contexts are very scarce. Attention focused on two sites as the location of the mint, Rouen (Rotomagus) itself, both because of the location of the find and the fact that some coins bear the letter R in the exergue, and Boulogne. Since a vivid description of the siege of Boulogne occupies so much of the surviving literary record it was natural to see this as the site where the coins were produced. The siege also, apparently, gave a context and date for their production in the dying days of the regime on the Continent (Carson, 1959, 1971).

Since the original find other specimens of the coins have been discovered in Rouen during controlled archaeological excavation and none in Boulogne; there is now little doubt that Rouen was the place of their production (Beaujard, 1980). Mapping recorded finds shows clearly the epicentral position of Rouen in the distribution pattern.

As we have discussed the date of the activity of the Rouen mint can be determined by the occurrence of its coins in hoards found in Britain; this date is not at the end of the Carausian episode in Gaul but at the beginning, there being two associations which give an early date, the Little Orme's Head (Seaby, 1956) and the Croydon hoards (Burnett & Casey, 1984). The former contained no insular coins dated later than 289 while the Croydon hoard contained only coins with the mintmark ML, which is normally dated to the first year of the reign. This hoard also contained coins which were obverse and reverse die duplicates, indicating that they had not moved far from the mint or been in circulation for any significant time before being hoarded.

A further indication of an early date is the absence of silver in the *aureliani*, a feature of the insular coinage before the emissions of 287. We have already discussed the unique stylistic features of this group of coins, which so sharply differntiate it from the products of attested British mints.

The implication of all of this is that there was a Carausian presence on the Continent before 289/90 and that this was centred, at least administratively, on Rouen rather than Boulogne. Now it could be argued that some local group of dissidents threw in their lot with Carausius, expecting him to support them militarily but that this expectation was unfulfilled because he was cooped up in Britain, having precipitously fled from Boulogne. This might be an explanation of the uncharacteristic portrait style of the Rouen coins; these hypothetical local supporters, being isolated, had no official image to work from and so copied the portraits of the legitimate emperors. If there is not a precedent for this there is at least an instance of something similar from the next century when Trier revolted against the usurper Magnentius (350–3). The city produced a billon coinage in the name of the legitimate emperor Constantius II, with an unofficial portrait and two reverse types, one based on the emperor's last circulating coinage, the second an invention of the Trier moneyers (Carson *et al.*, 1960). But in contrast to events at Trier, Rouen produced a gold coinage and a subordinate series of base metal coins comprising some dozen substantive types. Nor were the Rouen coins necessarily a hasty production, quickly issued and quickly superseded. One at least of the three precious metal coins in the rue du Petit-Loup hoard was an RSR silver issue. As we have seen, there is reason to think that these coins were produced in London so that the Rouen hoard can hardly have been accumulated at a period when there was no access to insular coinage. It very much looks as though Rouen was still producing when Britain was under Carausian control and coin could still be taken to Gaul. On the other hand, Unmarked coins are virtually absent from Gaul, suggesting a very short period, at the start of the reign, when both sides of the Channel were under rebel control.

The hypothesis that Carausius maintained a Continental base at this time is supported by the text of the Panegyric of 289 which predicts Maximian's forthcoming reconquest of Britain and gives details of the year-long preparations that have been made for the campaign.

> It is proof your good fortune, your success, Your Majesty, that your soldiers have already reached the Ocean in victory, that the tides have swallowed the blood of enemies slaughtered on the shore. That pirate must now lose heart, when he sees that your armies have almost entered those straits which alone have postponed his death until the present, that his men have abandoned their ships and have followed the retreating sea. (*Pan. Lat.*x(ii). 11.7,12)

There does not seem to be much doubt that this passage states that there had been campaigning on the Continent against Carausian forces and that only now, on the eve of the imminent invasion of Britain, has this conflict been resolved in victory. Ocean, in Roman terms, is the sea which girdles the known landmass; it was a conceit of Roman geography to enhance the mysteriousness of Britain by regarding it as beyond Ocean, and thus outside the civilized world. Caesar's attacks on Britain gathered particular glory because they were conducted beyond the bounds of the world and Claudius's conquest was regarded in the same light. Apparently, then, Maximian's forces at this stage have reached the Ocean – the Channel; they have not yet crossed it to Britain. It is on this shore, of Gaul, that waves have sucked up the blood of slain enemies.

If the Carausian revolt was much more than a swift flight with a fleet and actually involved the maintenance of an administrative centre at Rouen as well as land battles with Maximian's army, we must ask what forces were involved in the rebel army? We can get some insight into this from the literary sources but it is the coinage commemorating a number of legions which seems to offer striking evidence of the military strength of the Carausian forces (Pl.6, nos 1–7).

Table 9   *Legions commemorated on the coinage of Carausius*

Legion	Base	Home province
I MINERVIA	Bonn	Germany, Lower Rhine
II AUGUSTA	Caerleon	Britain
II PARTHICA	Rome, Alba	Italy
IIII FLAVIA	Belgrade	Upper Moesia
VII CLAVDIA	Viminacium	Upper Moesia
VIII AVGVSTA	Strasburg	Germany, Upper Rhine
XX VALERIA VICTRIX	Chester	Britain
XXII PRIMIGENIA	Mainz	Germany, Upper Rhine
XXX VLPIA VICTRIX	Xanten	Germany, Lower Rhine

The only unit not comprising a legion commemorated in the coin series is the Praetorian Cohort, the imperial bodyguard which would have been made up of soldiers from the legions.

Coins in the commemorative series are issued by the RSR, London and Colchester mints; the Unmarked mint does not seem to have participated. Specimens of legionary coins ascribed in the literature to the Unmarked mint are, when examined, shown to be poorly struck London products. The early date of the series is given by the employment of the marks ML and C. Commemorative coins of legions IV and VII of Colchester issued under the mark CXXI may indicate that these legions were honoured again in 290, possibly in connection with Maximian's abortive invasion in 289/90.

Since the legions are honoured before the re-establishment of a Carausian presence on the Continent in 290, they must constitute part of the force used to take over the island and thus have been devoted to the cause from ts beginnings in Gaul. There no possibility that Carausius actually disposed of the legionary force enumerated by the coins. On the other hand, the view that the series is merely an attempt to suborn these units was a naive misunderstanding of the composition and deployment of the later Roman army. Taken at face value a force of nine legions would have comprised a bit less than a third of the entire legionary army of the empire and, at full strength, would have numbered 49,500 men. Such a force could have conquered the Roman West, not fled pell-mell to Britain. By the later third century legions were usually deployed in detached fragments, *vexillationes*, either as individual units or in amalgamation with other detachments. The legions of Carausius are in reality vexillations of legions operating in Gaul, possibly drafted there for Maximian's campaign against the Bagaudae or allocated to Carausius as part of his anti-pirate command. It is notable that the legions commemorated, with the exception of *II Parthica*, are grouped in pairs from the provinces from which they derive – two units from Germania Inferior, two from Superior, two from Upper Moesia and, finally, two from Britain itself. It is a characteristic of Roman military strategy to pair legions when creating detached units and the pattern of the Carausian units confirms their vexillation status.

Even as vexillations we should be suspicious of equating them with the 1000-strong detachments attested in the earlier Roman army. By the later third century the legion itself may have been reduced to a 1000-strong unit and vexillations reduced proportionately, perhaps to the equivalent of a couple of centuries of 80 men each. We can get a glimpse of the way in which the legions of this period were split up from documents surviving from Roman Egypt where we find *Lego II Traiana* divided into contingents located in no less than three separate locations in towns on the Nile; by the later fourth century *Legio XIII Gemina* had five contingents at various places on the Danubian frontier, one in Egypt and yet another serving in the mobile field army (Casey, 1990).

The omission of *Legio VI Victrix* from the commemorated legions has drawn comment, especially since medieval fictions about Carausius record a tale of him experiencing difficulties at York, the base of this legion. The reason for the legion not being in the list is that it did not serve in Gaul and was, therefore, not a body which proclaimed Carausius before his descent on Britain. As the legion nearest Hadrian's Wall it was normally excused from detaching troops for vexillation duty. On the other hand the pairing of units drawn from *II Augusta* and *XX Valeria Victrix* is attested in a number of inscriptions in the second and third centuries. Their presence as joint vexillations in Gaul is illustrated by an engraved metal roundel, found in France, which shows the units parading together, each contingent fronted by a standard bearer with a *vexillum*, the flag from which the vexillation as a unit got its name (Fig.5).

While the bulk of legionary forces will have comprised elements from

5   The British legions in Gaul. Third-century officer's badge depicting a
      parade of *Legio II Augusta* and *Legio XX Valeria Victrix*.

vexillations one legion is credited with having gone over to the rebel
in its entirety. The Panegyric of 297 includes a recapitulation of those
who defected:

In that criminal usurpation first the fleet that used to protect Gaul was
stolen by the pirate on the run, then many ships were built in our
style, a Roman legion was seized, several units of non-Roman soldiers
were secured, Gallic merchants were recruited, considerable forces of
barbarians were seduced by the loot of the very provinces

(*Pan. Lat*.viii(v). 12).

Taken at face value this passage says that a legion stationed on the Continent
declared for Carausius. Of the Continental legions for whom coins were
issued, the most likely candidate for identification with that mentioned in

94

the Panegyric is *Legio XXX Ulpia Traiana*. This legion was stationed at Xanten on the Rhine in the nearest legionary base to the scene of the revolt. Even so it is unlikely that the legion was at full strength and the passage may be interpreted as indicating that this was the only legionary force whose commander, or *praeses*, declared for Carausius, vexillations being lead by officers of lesser rank.

The same panegyric passage mentions two other elements of the rebel force, 'units of non-Roman soldiers' and 'considerable forces of barbarians'. The Latin text translated as 'units of non-Roman soldiers' reads '*peregrinorum militum cuneis*'; the literal meaning of *cuneus* is 'wedge' but it also had a technical military sense when applied to cavalry. In the third century units of non-Roman cavalry, usually of German origin, are found among garrisons on the frontiers. One of the best known of these units is the *Cuneus Frisiorum* stationed at Housesteads on Hadrian's Wall. Here, in the reign of Severus Alexander (222–35), they dedicated an elaborate altar to the welfare of the emperor, the war god Mars and their homeland goddesses, the Alaisiagae (RIB 1594). In the inscription the Frisians record that they are Germans. Other *cunei* of Frisians are known from Papcastle, on the Wall, and at Binchester in the hinterland of the Wall zone (RIB 882-3, 1036). Inscriptions mentioning *cunei*, but missing the name of the unit, are known from two other forts of the northern frontier, Brougham and Corbridge (RIB 772, 1136).

The description of the units in the army of Carausius as *peregrini*, non-citizens, is consonant with third-century social developments. In 212 Caracalla gave the Roman citizenship to all free people in the empire, at a

PLATE 5

1   Carausius. 'aurelianus' C-mint.
    Obv. *IMP C CARAVSIVS PF AVG* Rev. *LAETITIA AVG – C* RIC 255

2   Carausius. 'aurelianus' C-mint.
    Obv. *IMP C CARAVSIVS PF AVG* Rev. *PAX AVG – CMXXI*
    Emperor in consular regalia RIC–

3   Carausius. 'aurelianus' C-mint.
    Obv. *IMP C CARAVSIVS PF AVG* Rev. *PACA TOR ORBIS – C*
    Bust of Sol RIC–

4   Carausius. 'aurelianus' C-mint.
    Obv. *IMP C CARAVSIVS PF AVG* Rev. *PROVIDEN AVG – S/C C*
    Conjoined busts of emperor and Sol RIC–

5   Maximian. 'aurelianus' C-mint.
    Obv. *IMP C MAXIMIANVS PF AVG* Rev. *SPES PVBL – S/P C* RIC–

6   Carausius. 'aurelianus' C-mint.
    Obv. *CARAVSIVS ET FRATRES SVI* Rev. *PAX AVGGG – S/P C*
    Busts of Carausius, far left, Diocletian, centre, and Maximian RIC 1

7 Diocletian. 'aurelianus' C-mint.
   Obv. *IMP C DIOCLETIANVS AVG* Rev. *VICTORIA AVGGG* – S/P C RIC 28

8 Carausius. 'aurelianus' C-mint.
   Obv. *IMP C CARAVSIVS P AVG* Rev. *PROVID AVGGG* – S/P C RIC 371

9 Allectus. 'aurelianus' C-mint.
   Obv. *IMP C ALLECTVS PF AVG* Rev. *SALVS AVG* – S/P C RIC 114var

10 Allectus. 'aurelianus' C-mint.
   Obv. *IMP C ALLECTVS PF AVG* Rev. *PAX AVG* – S/P C RIC 86

11 Allectus. 'aurelianus' C-mint.
   Obv. *IMP C ALLECTVS PIVS FEL AVG* Rev. *PAX AVG* S/P C RIC 88

PLATE 6

1 Carausius. 'aurelianus' London mint.
   Obv. *IMP CARAVSIVS PF AVG* Rev. *LEG I MIN* – ML
   Legion I Minervia RIC 56

2 Carausius. 'aurelianus' London mint.
   Obv. *IMP CARAVSIVS PF AVG* Rev. *LEG II AVG* – ML
   Legion II Augusta RIC 58

3 Carausius. 'aurelianus' C-mint.
   Obv. *IMP CARAVSIVS PF AVG* Rev. *LEG XX AVG*
   Legion XX Augusta RIC 275

4 Carausius. 'aurelianus' London mint.
   Obv. *IMP CARAVSIVS PF AVG* Rev. *LEG II PARTHICA* – ML RIC 62

5 Carausius. RSR mint.
   Obv. *IMP CARAVSIVS PF AVG* Rev. *LEG IIII FL* RSR
   Legion IIII Flavia RIC 568

6 Carausius. 'aurelianus' C-mint.
   Obv. *IMP CARAVSIVS PF AVG* Rev. *LEG IIII FLA* – C
   Legion IIII Flavia RIC 273

7 Carausius. 'aurelianus' London mint.
   Obv. *IMP CARAVSIVS PF AVG* Rev. *LEG VII CL* – ML
   Legion VII Claudia RIC 75

8 Maximian. *aureus* Iantinum mint.
   Obv. *MAXIMIANVS P AVG* Rev. *IOVI FVLGENTORI* – IAN RIC—

9 Diocletian. Aureus Iantinum mint.
   Obv. *DIOCLETIANVS P AVG* Rev. *VIRTVS AVGG* – IAN RIC—

10 Diocletian. *aureus* Iantinum mint.
   Obv. *DIOCLETIANVS P AVG* Rev. *HERCVLI VICTORI* – IAN RIC—

PLATE 7

1 Constantius I. Trier mint. Gold medallion of 5 *aurei* (Wt. 27.0g).
Obv. FL VAL CONSTANTIVS NOBIL C Rev. VIRTVS AVGG – PTR
The Caesar in consular robes/Hercules struggling with a stag. RIC 3

The medallion was issued in early 294 to celebrate the elevation of
Constantius to the rank of Caesar; he is shown wearing the ceremonial
robes of the consulship bestowed upon him on his promotion.

2 Constantius I. Trier mint. Gold medallion of 5 *aurei* (Wt. 26.84g).
Obv. FL VAL CONSTANTIVS NOBILISSIMVS C Rev. PIETAS AVGG – PTR
The Caesar wearing the lionskin head-dress of Hercules/The Caesar,
crowned by Victory, raises a kneeling figure of Britannia. RIC 32

3 Constantius I. Trier mint. Gold medallion of 5 *aurei* (Wt. 26.79g).
Obv. FL VAL CONSTANTIVS NOB CAES Rev. PIETAS AVGG– PTR
The Caesar in the robes of a consul, holding a eagle-tipped sceptre/as
No.2 above. RIC 33

4 Constantius I. Trier mint. Gold medallion of 10 *aurei* (Wt. 52.88g).
Obv. FL VAL CONSTANTIVS NOBIL CAES Rev. REDDITOR LVCIS AETERNAE/LON – PTR
RIC 34

This, with the two smaller denominations above, form part of the suite of
commemorative gold medallions struck to reward the participants in the
recovery of Britain.

5 Constantine I. Trier mint. Gold medallion of 8 *aurei*, or 9 *solidi* (Wt.
40.70g).
Obv. IMP CONSTANTINVS PIVS FELIX AVG Rev. PRINCIPI IVVENTVTIS – PTR
The emperor in military dress/Constantine with spear and globe.
RIC 801

This medallion commemorates the fifth anniversary of Constantine's
accession to power on the death of his father, Constantius I, at York. The
reverse bears the inscribed name of the owner, Vitalianus.

PLATE 8

1 Allectus. 'aurelianus' London mint.
Obv. IMP C ALLECTVS PF AVG Rev. PAX AVG – S/P ML RIC 33var

2 Allectus. 'quinarius' London mint.
Obv. IMP C ALLECTVS PF AVG Rev. VIRTVS AVG – QL RIC 55

3 Allectus. 'quinarius' C-mint.
Obv. IMP C ALLECTVS PF AVG Rev. LAETITIA AVG – QC RIC 128

4 Allectus. 'quinarius' C-mint.
Obv. IMP C ALLECTVS PF AVG Rev. VIRTVS AVG – QC RIC 128

5 Allectus. 'quinarius' London mint.
Obv. IMP AC ALLECTVS PF AVG Rev. VIRTVS AVG – QL RIC 55var

6 Allectus. 'quinarius' C-mint.
   Obv. *IMP C ALLECTVS PF AVG* Rev. *VIRTVS AVG– QC*
   A figure of victory stands on the prow of the galley. RIC 128var

7 Postumus. double *sestertius*.
   Obv. *IMP C CASS LAT POSTVMVS PF AVG* Rev. *LAETITIA AVG* RIC 143

8 Postumus. *dupondius*.
   Obv. *IMP C CASS LAT POSTVMVS PF AVG* Rev. *LAETITIA AVG* RIC 143

9 Constantius I. *aureus* Trier mint.
   Obv. *CONSTANTIVS NC* Rev. *VIRTVS ILLYRICI – TR* RIC 88

stroke abolishing the distinction between soldiers serving in the legions, who were citizens, and those in the auxiliary regiments, who were non-citizens. In future the only military formations who could be described as peregrine were tribal units like the Frisians. Whether such units were mercenaries or captives shipped to remote parts of the empire to serve in the army is uncertain. The number of *cunei* found on Hadrian's Wall tends to imply the latter origin (Casey & Noel, 1993).

In these circumstances it seems probable that Carausius had Germanic cavalry at his disposal, possibly units originally intended to conduct land operations in pursuit of the pirates the fleet was dealing with at sea. We also read of 'considerable forces of barbarians'. These are not given any sort of technical military title and are thus to be distinguished from forces already serving in the Roman army. From references elsewhere in the panegyric we can conjecture that these barbarians were Franks from the northern borders of Gallia Belgica.

Of forces stationed in northern Gaul itself there is very little evidence. By the end of the fourth century the Channel coast was furnished with a number of forts which protected harbour installations and inland areas against sea-borne attack. The *Notitia Dignitatum* gives details of 11 forts stretching down the coast from the Rhine to the mouth of the Loire (ND.Occ.XXVII). Excavation of these sites has, as yet, made little progress and even the identification of some named forts is still uncertain. Of the sites which have been explored the general tenor of the evidence suggests that they were constructed after the period under review, but not very long afterwards (Maxfield, 1989). In general these forts seem to have been built to counter the sort of attack Carausius was employed to prevent, thus abandoning a maritime strategy to avoid putting another fleet in the hands of another potential rebel.

The last group to be considered in the list of the traitorous are the Gallic merchants. Who are these merchants and why should they be singled out in a list which is otherwise concerned with military matters? It might be supposed that, if most of the coast and inland ports, such as Rouen, were in rebel hands, anyone earning a livelihood from overseas or coastal trade would, perforce, have to recognize or treat with the separatist regime, especially if that trade was with Britain. There is little archaeological evidence of trade in commodities such as pottery, which leave material traces behind them, but epigraphic evidence from a slightly earlier period bears witness to the existence of cross-Channel trade conducted by wealthy entrepreneurs. From an inscription on an altar from Bordeaux set up by M. Aurelius Lunaris in 237 which tells us that he was a priest of the imperial cult at both York and Lincoln, we may assume that he was also a trader (AE, 1922). From the Rhineland comes a series of dedications by merchants whose trade was with Britain; unspecified dealers at Cologne (CIL,XIII, 8164a) and Castell, near Mainz, the base of *Legio XXII Primigenia* from which one of Carausius's vexillations was drawn (CIL,XIII, 8793). From Domburg, where the temple of the goddess Nehalennia stood at the mouth of one of the many channels which connected the main waterway with the North Sea, comes an altar dedicated by a pottery merchant whose market was Britain (Hodius-Crone, 1955). An inscription from York makes the wealth and wide social connections between the mercantile classes of the northern sea routes even clearer. The stone records the erection, in 221, of an arch and a shrine, dedicated to 'Iuppiter Best and Greatest of Doliche and the Welfare of the Emperors', by L. Viducius Placidus. Placidus records that, besides being a priest of the imperial cult, he is a citizen of Rouen (Hassal & Tomlin, 1977). A further inscription of Placidus from the temple of Nehalennia shows that his trading empire stretched from Britain to the Rhineland and into the very heart of what was later to be Carausian territory (Stuart, 1971).

Conceivably it was the support of the descendants of merchants such as these which is alluded to in the texts; merchants who may well have been the source of the gold used in the Rouen coinage. Little is known in detail about the mercantile class in Gaul, but the magnificent marble monuments raised by individual merchants in Lugdunum to commemorate the holding of office in the provincial council and priesthoods in the imperial cult suggest that this class was a very powerful element in the politics of the province. We may even conjecture that there was a tension between the landowning and the mercantile classes, with the latter throwing their weight behind Carausius for political advantage. Certainly it is the landowning classes who will have suffered most in the tumult of the barbarian attacks on Gaul in the third century – with their property destroyed and their slaves in revolt their traditional status might well have been threatened.

To suggest that Carausius may have been the front man for a more extensive conspiracy is only to place him in a familiar context. In the fourth century two such insurrections were raised which came within a very narrow margin of success, significantly both started in Gaul. In 350 the revolt of Magnentius was engineered by Marcellinus, the *Comes Sacrarum Largitionum* of Constans, and at the end of the century the elevation of Eugenius was engineered by Arbogastes, the *Magister Militum*, following the suicide of Valentinian II, an event in which Arbogastes played a provocative role. As to the part played by Allectus in the revolt of Carausius, we unfortunately lack any specific ancient information but his later role fits him into the sort of position held by other manipulative ministers lurking behind an imperial candidate of their own manufacture.

We must ask the pertinent question: Why did anyone support Carausius? No question but he had the very best personal reasons for revolt if his life was in danger, and in all probability a number of his officers were condemned with him, but what of the rank and file? This question is posed in a broader context by the historian E.H. Carr (1987, 52):

> Here I should say something about the role of the rebel or dissident in history. To set up the popular picture of the individual in revolt against society is to reintroduce the false antithesis between society and the individual. No society is fully homogeneous. Every society is an arena of conflicts, and those individuals who range themselves against existing authority are no less products and reflections of the society than those that uphold it. Richard II and Catherine the Great represent powerful social forces in ... England ... and ... Russia ... : but so did Wat Tyler and Pugachev, the leader of the great serf rebellion. Monarchs and rebels alike were the product of the specific conditions of their age and country. To describe Wat Tyler and Pugachev as individuals in revolt against society is a misleading simplification. If they had been merely that, the historian would never have heard of them. They owe their role in history to the mass of their followers, and are significant as social phenomena, or not at all.

By the same token Carausius and Allectus owe their role in history to the great mass of their followers. Unfortunately we have no information about the motives of the individuals who comprised the mass. But we should bear in mind, as their leaders must have done, that action without the consent of these followers would be no action at all. Policies engendering loyalty and enthusiasm for the cause must have transcended Septimius Severus's simple aphorism, 'Pay the soldiers ... damn the rest.'

So far we have suggested that a successful campaign was conducted by Maximian against Carausian forces on the Continent which resulted in the expulsion of the rebel forces to Britain. It has also been suggested, on the basis of the presence of RSR coin in the Rouen hoard, that Britain had fallen to Carausius before Diocletian and Maximian had expelled his forces from Gaul. All of which raises the acute problem of why and how did Britain succumb to Carausius?

There have been a number of conjectures advanced, of which the most popular are that he must have enjoyed a reputation in Britain gained during unrecorded military service in the province, or that the situation was such as to make a new administration, prepared to devote itself to the affairs of the island instead of maintaining a distant control from Trier, a welcome alternative to that already in place.

NARRATIVE AND ARCHAEOLOGY I: THE REVOLT

The notion of a pre-revolt military career which earned the respect and affection of the provincials, though without any independent evidence, has been elaborated in a number of ways (White, 1961). An example of this is the claim that Carausius served as commander of the *Classis Britannica*, the fleet based at Dover and Boulogne that served as the imperial transport link between the mainland of Europe and the empire's offshore possession. Another of the fleet's activities would have been the protection both of shipping and vulnerable coastal areas from seaborne attack. Attention has been drawn to the numbers of coin hoards found in the south-east of Britain which date from the second half of the third century and to compare these with hoards of similar coins from Gaul as evidence for a widespread threat to the region, or even attacks (Frere, 1987). These hoards consist of the basest issues of the Gallic empire's coinage and, while it is possible to point to allegedly historically attested destruction in Gaul by barbarian activity in the third century, and especially between 268 and 278, it does not follow that the hoards are witness to these events. Indeed, there is evidence of attempts to suppress the hoarded coinage by Probus (276–82) in order to implement further the monetary reform of Aurelian and it can be argued strongly that these hoards are no more than coins which were abandoned because they had lost most of their monetary value. Further, the distribution of these hoards is not confined to the south-east; in reality they are as widespread as any other class of hoard encountered in Britain (Casey, 1986). On the other hand, the creation of coastal forts on the Wash, the coast of Suffolk and the Thames estuary cannot be overlooked. Nor can the conversion to a watchtower of the monument at Richborough be taken as anything less than a sign of difficulties.

That problems which called for military solutions had arisen by the last quarter of the third century is clear from the involvement of the emperor Carinus (283–5) in Britain. By mid-284 the emperor bore the title *Britannicus Maximus*, a title which he shared with his brother Numerian, indicating a victory in Britain (ILS 608). The inscription, from near Ostia, lists the British title after that awarded for his German victory, showing that any campaign was fought after April 283, the earliest date recorded for the German acclamation.

The situation, or specific event, which necessitated the campaign and the location of the military activity is not known, but the personal intervention of Carinus in Britain is probably alluded to in the *Cynegetica* of the contemporary Carthaginian poet Marcus Aurelius Nemesianus.

Hereafter I will gird myself with fitter lyre to record your triumphs, you gallant sons of the deified Carus [i.e. Carinus and Numerian], and will sing of our sea-board beneath the twin boundaries of the world, and of the subjugation, by the brothers' divine power, of nations that drink the Rhine or Tigris or from the distant source of the Arar or look upon the wells of the Nile at their birth: nor let me fail to tell

> what campaigns you first ended, Carinus, beneath the Northern Bear
> [*sub Arcto*] with victorious hand, well nigh outstripping your divine
> father . . . . (Nemesianus, *Cynegetica*, 65–75)

The phrase '*sub arcto*' is a poetic reference to the Pole Star and is a frequently employed equivalent for 'the far north'. As such, it may well be a reference to campaigning in Britain. Mann has suggested that the poetic nature of the phrase suggests naval warfare. Though not stated, the inference is that the Pole Star, as the mariner's guide, serves to convey a seaborn context to the reader (Mann, 1989). On the other hand, a number of pieces of evidence, none in itself conclusive, suggest that Carinus was himself in Britain. At a period when imperial gold coinage is otherwise unknown in Britain, a number of specimens of Carus and his sons are found; an *aureus* of Numerian from Richborough, another, in a private collection, of the deified Carus from Wroxeter. A bronze medallion of Carinus is recorded from an East Anglian location. There is no direct reference, however, to events in Britain among the numerous coin types of Carinus and Numerian celebrating victory. Nor, for that matter, is there any record in the coinage of Carinus and Numerian of a single type featuring ships, the god Neptune or any hint of a naval victory. An inscription of Carinus, as Caesar, from the villa at Clanville, Hants (RIB 98) and a number of milestones recording attention to the roads in the reign of Carus (RIB 2282, 2307, 2250) are no more significant than the similar inscriptions for emperors of the second half of the third century relatively commonly found in Britain.

The title *Britannicus Maximus* was also conferred on Diocletian early in his reign. An inscription, now in Rome but probably originally from Ostia, records the honorific title at the time when Diocletian was sole emperor, before the elevation of Maximian (ILS 615). The event commemorated must, therefore, fall between 20 November 284 and October/December 285. The inscription itself dates to after 9 December 284 as it records Diocletian's second tribunician power (Barnes, 1982). But, it is thought, Diocletian was not in control of the West until after the death of Carinus, which took place in August or September 285, and it hardly seems likely that serious campaigning, with or without the emperor, could be undertaken in the short period between August/September and December 285. A solution to the problem is that Diocletian simply took over the title *Britannicus Maximus* from Carinus as part of his imperial titulature, without having done anything to earn it himself. But Carinus's titles at the end of his reign were *Germanicus Maximus, Persicus Maximus* and *Britannicus Maximus*, the first two titles being conferred in 283 and the latter in 284. Diocletian is recorded as *Britannicus Maximus* and *Germanicus Maximus* on the Rome inscription and since he numbers his five later German victories sequentially from this one it is not likely to have been a mere adoption of another man's title. If this is so, then the integrity of the British honour should be given credence.

We may conjecture that Carinus's forces were once again conducting a campaign in Britain, which was concluded very shortly after his death and that the new ruler, Diocletian, gathered the symbolic fruits of the victory. The title was not used while Britain was outside imperial control during the revolt of Carausius and Allectus. There is no other direct evidence for a Diocletianic intervention in Britain.

It is conceivable that Carausius took part in campaigns fought in Britain by Carinus or Diocletian. What seems less likely is that Carausius commanded the *Classis Britannica* and was thus involved in operations in the Channel which would have endeared him to the garrison of Britain or to influential sections of the civilian population. Excavation of the British naval base at Dover indicates that the fort housing the sailors of the fleet had ceased to function by 270 (Philp, 1981). Excavations at Boulogne, where the fleet maintained its Continental base, suggest a similar pattern of occupation with an abandonment of the installation well before the end of the third century. Even before the final closure, whole blocks of barracks had gone out of use, pointing to a reduction in the size of the fleet earlier in the century (Brulet, 1989). Rather than offering a context for Carausius's early career, this evidence gives one for his later command since not only did he have to gather a fleet, suggesting that none existed, but also conduct operations which would normally be within the operational remit of the *Classis Britannica*. The demise of this fleet was probably instrumental in setting in motion the piratical activities which Carausius was appointed to crush.

Once established in Britain the new regime must have sought to reinforce its integrity both against internal dissent and external attack. It is impossible to disentangle which steps were taken while a hold was maintained on the Continent and which were those taken after the loss of this territory, or indeed which date to a period after the recovery of northern Gaul following Maximian's campaign. The organization of a mint, or mints, and dissemination of money bearing the effigy of the new ruler appear to have been a priority. The distribution pattern of Carausius's early coinage only hints at the need to assuage the army with the payment of a donative, but the presence of an *aureus* found at Neath, in south Wales, the site of an auxiliary fort (Evans, 1886), a silver coin in the fort at Piercebridge, Co. Durham (Casey, forthcoming) and the issue of bronze medallions by the RSR mint, one of which has an unspecified northern provenance, point to this priority. There is also ample evidence, in the form of the surviving products of the Unmarked mint, that a vast quantity of coinage was immediately injected into the insular economy. This move was a very much-needed corrective to the monetary situation inherited by the new administration. Coins of the Aurelianic reform are very scarce in British hoards or site finds and the continued use of unofficial copies of the issues of the long defunct Gallic Empire, despite Probus's efforts to suppress them, is eloquent testimony to the scarcity of coinage in the British economy.

Such care for the economy, through the introduction of an ample medium of exchange, cannot but have engendered a renewal of economic activity. Not least it provided the administration with a medium for the purchase of supplies, the payment of the army and the collection of taxes. The fact that the bulk of the coins masqueraded as *aureliani*, though they had no silver content, probably did not matter in the context of the closed economy of isolated Britain. The exploitation of insular economic resources can be traced in Wales where the hoard from Little Orme's Head points to the exploitation of the copper resources of Anglesey at an early date (Seaby, 1956). The volume of Carausian coinage from the fort at Caernarfon shows that the centre of military and economic administration in north Wales and Anglesey was in full use at this time (Casey & Davies, 1993). An indication that the gold mines at Dolaucothi, in Carmarthenshire, were probably being worked can be traced in the presence of coins of Carausius in hoards from Erw-hen and Cynwyl Gaio in the vicinity of this remote mining complex (Boon, 1967).

The disposition of the forces evacuated from the Continent is problematic. Since we do not know the actual manning levels of individual forts it is impossible to say whether their garrisons were reinforced. A study of the coinage from selected forts on Hadrian's Wall suggests that these were maintained at low garrison strength throughout the Carausian period, ultimate integrity of the northern frontier being dependent on the garrisons of the larger hinterland forts (Curteis, 1988). On the other hand, at Brecon Gaer in Wales a fort which had been abandoned in the late Antonine period appears, judging by the coinage, to have been reactivated about this time, and we have already noticed a gold coin of Carausius in association with Neath, where the fort had been run down in the Hadrianic or Antonine period (Nash-Williams, 1969).

It might be thought that strategic considerations would require a shift of military resources away from the more remote parts of Britain, such as Wales and the extreme north, to a more southerly dispersal in anticipation of a counter-attack by Maximian. The preparations for this took a whole year and it is inconceivable that an espionage network was not employed by the regimes on both sides of the Channel. Further, the Panegyric of 297 specifies that 'many ships were built in our style' and were manned by new recruits to the navy, 'all of these being trained in seamanship'. We would expect the harbours and rivers of the south and east coasts to have been the scene of this activity, though so woefully lacking is knowledge of Roman harbours and shipbuilding in Britain that it is impossible to identify specific Carausian naval bases. Once again recourse to the exiguous evidence of a find of a gold coin points to Clausentum (Bitterne, near Southampton) being a candidate, and this is supported by the reappraisal of the numismatic dating of the site which gives a *terminus post quem* for the construction as being after 268. The aggregate of the phased evidence thereafter suggests a construction date in the third quarter of the third century (King, 1991). The replacement of the *Classis Britannica* fort at Dover with a shore fort, if at this date, indicates that the traditional harbours played a central role. This last point must inevitably lead to a discussion of the problem of the part which may, or may not, have been played by Carausius and Allectus in the construction and use of the so called Saxon Shore Forts.

NARRATIVE AND ARCHAEOLOGY II: THE SECOND CONTINENTAL EPISODE

THE PANEGYRIC OF 289 MAKES IT clear that an invasion of Britain had been planned in considerable detail; there is no reason to doubt that the attempt took place and suffered a complete reversal. The silence of the Panegyric of 291 is deafening, while the oblique reference in the Pangyric of 297 to the 'sea's difficulty which had inevitably postponed your victory' may indicate a natural disaster which engulfed the invasion fleet. Whether or not this covers up a defeat or simply records what really happened it is clear that Maximian suffered a setback of enormous magnitude. Deprived of a fleet, the coastal areas of Gaul were vulnerable to Carausius who, once again, established rule over areas in the northern part of Maximian's domain. The extent of the territory seized, to judge by the distribution of coin finds, included Boulogne, Rouen and Amiens. Significantly, all three cities offered port facilities, the latter sites on the Somme and Seine respectively (see Fig.3).

A number of changes in the coinage took place at this time. The style improved dramatically: the broad-busted, rather uncouth, portrait hitherto employed was replaced by a smoother more practised model, probably a the result of the importation of Gallic die-sinkers recruited from the new territories (Pl.4, no.3). In 290/91, also, the coins were brought into line with the monetary standards of the rest of the empire, the *aureliani* now being issued with a silver content of about 3 per cent to create a billon coinage. The revaluation is marked on the coins themselves by the addition of the numeral XXI to the mintmark, as in the form MLXXI (Pl.4, no.3, Pl.5 no.2). In late 291, the obverse legend changed from *IMP CARAVSIVS PF AVG* to *IMP C CARAVSIVS PF AVG*, thus assuming the title Caesar as a regular component of the imperial titulature.

The date of Maximian's defeat, or setback, is not very certain. The Panegyric of 291 was probably delivered on 21 July, which gives a *terminus ad quem*, or outside date. But there is nothing to fix the invasion itself. An analysis of the non-Rouen coins of Carausius found in Gaul, for which the sequence and mintmarks are available from publications, points to the resumption of a Continental *imperium* taking place in late 290 or early 291 rather than in 289 (Table 10). No Continental mint coins can be ascribed to this later occupation.

Table 10   *Carausius and Allectan coins in Gaul: mints and issues*

		London	Unmarked	Colchester	Rouen
IMP CARAUSIUS PF AUG	286	I		3	240 +
	287				
	288	I			
	289				
	290				
IMP C CARAUSIUS PF AUG	291				
	292	IO			
	293	2	2		
MP C ALLECTUS PF AUG	293	8			
	294	6			
	295	2		2	
	296	I			

Aurelius Victor implies that Carausius achieved a degree of recognition from Diocletian and Maximian:

> Only Carausius was left with imperial power [of the various usurpers fought by the emperors early in their reign] over the island, after being thought amenable to orders to protect the inhabitants from warlike peoples. (v.39).

This may be a genuine echo of events at this period though it must be stressed there is no evidence that any gesture made by Carausius was reciprocated by his adversaries. The assumption of the title Caesar might indicate a temporary rapprochement but is more likely to be an honour bestowed by the usurper upon himself. Similarly, the issue of consular coins by the London mint in 289 represent another self-awarded consulship. The assumption of the highest honour in the Roman state hardly ranks as a persuasive act of reconciliation with the Continental rulers, who had already appointed their own nominees, M. Magrius Bassus and L. Ragonius Quintianus, for the year in question (Degrassi, 1952).

Just as the garrisoning of Britain must have been a priority in the early days of the revolt so the redeployment of forces on the Continent and the establishment of a land frontier with the imperial authorities demanded attention. No forts or fortifications can be certainly associated with these events but there are tantalizing hints of activity at Boulogne which, from the account of the fall of the city, is known to have been fortified with walls and ramparts.

Archaeological investigations in the difficult environment of a busy modern port city have yielded some information (Brulet, 1991). The *Classis Britannica* base has been identified in the middle of the modern city – in antiquity it would have occupied a plateau of a bluff rising above the lower

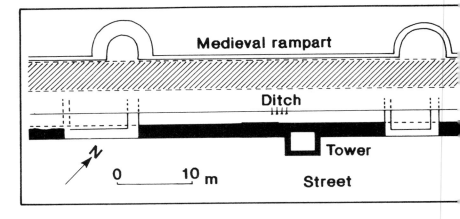

6   The Carausian defences of Boulogne. (After Brulet.)

town and dockyards which crowded the banks of the estuary of the rive
Liane; coin evidence indicates that the fort was dismantled in about 27
Later, a new circuit of walls was built, using the ditches of the *Classis* fo
as a foundation trench, this enclosed an area of *c.*13 ha. The new wall w
furnished with the now obligatory semicircular external towers. Intermedia
between the *Classis* fort and the new circuit of defences is a phase represente
by two square towers (Fig.6). Possibly these represent a scheme of defenc
planned and partly executed during the earlier Carausian occupation. Th
later defence circuit is also claimed as Carausian.

Events before the attack on Boulogne in 293 are obscure but it is possib
that a campaign against Carausius was launched as early as 291. The evidenc
for this depends upon the interpretation of the significance of a small grou
of gold coins struck in the names of Diocletian and Maximian by a mi
identified as Iantinum (Meaux), to the east of Paris (Bastien, 1980). Hither
these coins have been attributed to the period immediately before th
invasion of Britain by Constantius, their function being seen as a donati
to inspire the invading forces. But an examination of the types employe
by these coins offers a different insight (Pl.6, nos 8–10). The imagery of th
coins seems closely to reflect that used in the Panegyric of 291 in which th
emperor Maximian's struggle against Carausius is compared with even
associated with the Labours of Hercules. Specific parallels, with a maritim
emphasis, are drawn with Hercules's successes against pirates and his defe
of Antheus, son of Poseidon. The types for Diocletian depict Jove/Zeus
struggle with the Titans (Loriot, 1981). If this interpretation is correct an
the coins represent a special issue as a pre-campaign donative at the earli
date, it would seem that a thrust was contemplated along the valley of th
Seine perhaps in an attempt to retake Rouen. This interpretation gains som
credibility from the fact that Maximian is known to have been in Rein

in February 291 (Barnes, 1982). The proposed later date for the arrival of Carausius on the Continent, outlined above, would give a good context for Maximian's counterthrust and for the issue of the coins as a direct economic appeal to the loyalty of the imperial forces.

Writing after the collapse of the Tetrarchic system in the reign of Constantine when the new emperor encouraged the denigration of his pagan former enemies, a Christian polemicist gave a character sketch of the emperor Maximian. As a recent convert to Christianity Lactantius was, of course, an extremely prejudiced commentator on those who persecuted his new faith. His view of Maximian was that:

> They [i.e. Diocletian and Maximian] differed only in this, that Diocletian was greedier but more hesitant, whereas Maximian was no less greedy but bolder – though bolder at doing evil, not at doing good. Although he controlled Italy, the actual seat of empire, and although highly wealthy provinces like Africa and Spain were in his power, he was not particularly diligent in guarding the wealth of which he had such an ample supply. When the need arose there was no shortage of extremely rich senators who could be claimed on the basis of suborned evidence to have aspired to imperial power. In consequence, the senate's luminaries were constantly being snatched from it, while Maximian's purse, soaked in blood, bulged with ill-gotten wealth. There was in the man, pestilential as he was, a lust directed not just at the hateful and detestable practice of debauching males, but also at violating the daughters of leading citizens. Wherever he travelled, maidens were at once seized on the spot from the embrace of their parents. The only thing in which his government rested was the denial of nothing to his lust and nothing to his evil desires.
>
> (Lact. 8.2–6)

In contrast to this view it can be shown that in the years of Carausius's ascendancy the western Augustus was fully occupied in warfare, securing the Rhine frontier against the Alamanni, the Heruli and the Chamavi and the lower Rhine against the Franks, who may or may not have acted in concert with Carausius. Apparently the only enemy that he could not suppress was Carausius himself, presumably because when Roman arms met Roman arms the usurper was the better general. In the winter of 290/91 the joint emperors, Diocletian and Maximian, travelled from their respective territories to meet at a summit conference in Milan. The failure to eradicate Carausius must have been a feature of the agenda. If the campaign deduced from the issue of coins at Iantinum took place at this time it will have been as a result of decisions made at Milan. Diocletian is known to have been hard on colleagues who, in his perception, failed in military ventures. Galerius, the eastern Caesar, was defeated by the Persians in 297; he returned in person to Antioch to report the disaster. Gibbon reports the subsequent treatment of the erring Caesar:

Diocletian received him not with the tenderness of a friend and colleague, but with the indignation of an offended sovereign. The haughtiest of men, clothed in his purple, but humbled by the sense of his fault and misfortune, was obliged to follow the emperor's chariot above a mile on foot, and to exhibit before the whole court the spectacle of his disgrace.

In March 292 the campaign against the rebel was taken out of the hands of Maximian and put into those of his newly appointed deputy, Flavius Valerius Constantius, who was promoted from the office of praetorian prefect to Caesar, or emperor designate. Constantius, like Maximian and Diocletian, was from the Balkan provinces of the empire and like them had served in the armies of Aurelian and Probus. He was forty-two years old when promoted and had served with Maximian throughout his reign, no doubt participating in his various campaigns. On his promotion a new praetorian prefect, Julius Asclepiodotus, was appointed.

The elevation of Constantius sent a clear message of intent which was not ignored by Carausius. No doubt the defences of the regime were further reinforced but the only activity of which we have a record is a flurry of diplomatic approaches to Diocletian and Maximian. The creation of a legitimate heir-apparent should have spelled the end of any hopes of a constitutional position being created which accommodated Carausius's own pretensions to the title of Caesar. The diplomatic drive, the evidence for which is enshrined in the coinage, directly associates Carausius with the emperors as a co-equal ruler rather than supplicant junior colleague.

In 292 the mints of London and Colchester were geared up for the production of coins in the names of Diocletian and Maximian (Pl.4, nos 6–9; Pl.5, nos 5–7). Billon *aureliani* were issued in the names of the legitimate emperors while an *aureus* in the name of Maximian, from the London mint, probably represents a much more extensive coinage in the name of both rulers (Pl.4, no.9). All issues use the extended form AVGGG (*Augustorum*) on the reverse, indicating the reign of three emperors (Pl.5, nos 7, 8). This claim to equal constitutional status is made explicit by one of the most famous coins in the entire Roman series on which Carausius, Diocletian and Maximian are presented in a triumviral portrait group with the inscription CARAVSIVS ET FRATRES SVI ('Carausius and his Brothers') (Pl.5, no.6). There are some twenty recorded specimens of this coinage, of which all but one bear the mintmark S/PC, or the variant SPC; one specimen is recorded with the London mark MLXXI. This should date the London coin to 291 but, since the nature of the reverse leaves no space for any letters in the field, we can be confident that it is contemporary with the C mint issues. The marks S/PC and SPC are the last used by Carausius at the C mint and they are the first used on the coinage of Allectus. At London the mark S/P MLXXI was superseded by a short-lived issue of coins marked S/P ML, also the first used by Allectus. No collegiate issues are known for this mark. The last issue of Carausius also dropped the use of the mark of value XXI, its use not being resumed by Allectus. The gold coin bears the mark ML, used unmodified throughout both the reign of Carausius and that of Allectus. On the combined evidence of the C and London mints the triple portrait issue can be placed near the end of the reign but not at the very end (Carson, 1987).

It seems likely that these coins were produced in anticipation of, or as part of, an overture to secure some sort of recognition by Diocletian and Maximian in the period immediately before the promotion of Constantius. The creation of the Caesar cannot have taken place without preliminary speculation, and since Carausius was firmly established on the Continent at the time we may see these coins in the context of diplomacy provoked by the imminent creation of a ruler devoted to his destruction. Their issue ceased when the promotion of Constantius extinguished the hopes of a peaceful solution to the crisis. It is just possible that the diplomacy may not have been one-sided, though the issue of coins was not reciprocated by Diocletian or Maximian, and that some sort of negotiation was conducted while preparations were made for an attack on Carausius' main base, Boulogne. At the same time a further series of negotiations may have been going on with dissidents in the Carausian party, possibly Allectus.

The Panegyric of 297 gives an account of the fall of Boulogne, suggesting that a planned operation was put into effect at a speed which took the enemy completely by surprise. The arrival of Constantius in front of the walls of the city outran the news of his accession, leaving the garrison penned up inside their defences, their fleet unable to offer assistance or break the grip of the encircling forces. Constantius himself conducted a land-based operation, either having no fleet himself or none that could compete at sea with that of Carausius. Certainly he was unable to establish a naval blockade. To exclude any attempt of relief or retreat by sea a mole was constructed across the harbour by driving piles into the entrance and dumping stones over them. Presumably Constantius planned to conduct a formal siege and intended to reduce the garrison by privation to a state of surrender rather than take the site by direct assault. This would minimize the loss of life among the Roman troops in the garrison, an asset which the empire could ill afford to lose. Such tactics would also send a message of clemency to rebel forces in Britain. These tactics would involve denying flight to the besieged by the construction of a circumvallation around the attacked city; should a relief force be expected a contravallation would be needed to encircle and protect the siegeworks. Caesar's circumvallation and contravallation at Alesia, in 52 BC, comprised 18km of ramparts, towers, breastworks, ditches, mantrap pits, entanglements of thickets and swathes of disabling coltrops. The supremacy of the Roman army in siege warfare had not diminished in the period between the Republic and the late third century. Only a few years before the present events, in 278, Terentius Marcianus, the *praeses* of Lycia and Pamphylia, successfully besieged the city of Cremna after it had

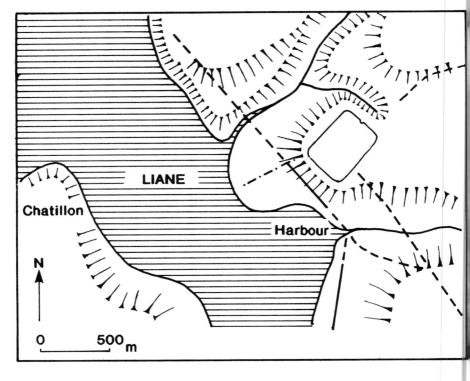

7   The topography of the Roman port of Boulogne. (After Brulet.)

been taken over by Lydius, an Isaurian brigand. Evidence on the site shows
that the Roman army mounted a formal siege, employing a contravallation
to prevent attack by the defenders. For their part the Roman army erected
a huge ramp against the walls, from which to mount an assault, meantime
bombarding the defenders with artillery which hurled stone balls some 0.5m
in diameter (Mitchell, 1987, 1988). In the event, the siege was terminated
by the death of Lydius, shot down by a well-aimed dart from a catapult
(Zos. I. 63–4).

The key to Constantius's siegeworks was the mole which sealed off the
harbour; it was the construction of this that caused the defenders to lose
heart and forced their surrender. The nature of the mole's structure and its
location in relation to the defences of Boulogne presents a puzzle. The
Carausian defences themselves occupy the plateau on the north-east bank
of the estuary of the river Liane with low-lying ground extending for about
400m to the water's edge, an area formerly occupied by a civil settlement
and the dock facilities of the *Classis Britannica*. The plateau is further defined
by streams to the north and south. The modern harbour of Boulogne is
largely a construction of breakwaters, basins and quays on the western

seafront and south-west bank of the river, but in the Roman period ships sailed into the tidal estuary to quays adjacent to the *Classis Britannica* fort. There is no reason why the civil facilities should not have been maintained after the demise of the fleet.

Recently published reconstructions of the topography of pre-modern Boulogne are seriously misleading in showing an estuary with a mouth about a kilometre wide (Brulet, 1991). These reconstructions take the cliffs of the Butte de Chatillon as being co-terminous with the south bank of the estuary (Fig.7). But it is clear from the bird's-eye-view of the port published in c.1760 (Brulet's fig.18), and from naval charts of the eighteenth century (Pl.i), that a tongue of dunes and shingle extended from the Butte de Chatillon, closing the estuary to a width of only c.300m. The anonymous 'Plan of the Town and Harbour of Boulogne' of c.1750 (Pl.j) shows that at low tide a causeway connected the south and north banks of the river at its narrowest point. Naturally, the topography of the estuary will have changed considerably since the Roman period, reflecting silting and rises in mean sea level. But this feature is likely, in some form, to have been present throughout because it is produced by the action of the northern tidal current of the Channel, which is unchanged since antiquity. The strong tidal current carries sand and gravel from further down the coast and deposits it at the mouth of the Liane. This landscape feature was only removed, or rather built over, when the modern port and dry dock were created.

Before modern improvements Boulogne was not an easy harbour for the sailor: 'Boulogne is a Tidal Harbour, and entirely dry at low water, consequently it should not be entered but at high water' (Serres, 1802). The French hydrographic survey of the mid-nineteenth century, before the modern developments, shows that at full tide the narrowest point of the estuary had a depth of 3.84m of water. If we accept a channel width of c.300m instead of 1km and the height of the individual piles needed to close the channel at high tide of being just in excess of 4m, reinforced with a bank of rocks and shingle, we get some idea of the magnitude of the siege works – quite small in comparison to those of Caesar at Alesia, Scipio Africanus at Numantia or Flavius Silva at Masada. Nevertheless, the novelty of an underwater rampart, if only submerged twice daily, demonstrates an impressive strategic grasp.

The completion of the mole seems to have brought about the surrender of the garrison following the negotiation of terms which the defenders could accept; the Panegyric of 297 says that 'dire straits and a trust in your mercy had ended the siege'. The very next tide smashed the mole and would have allowed a relieving fleet to outflank the besiegers.

The fall of Carausius is shrouded in impenetrable mystery – the date is uncertain, the place of his death unknown, the motive for his killing obscure. It is generally assumed that his death was a consequence of the loss of Boulogne and the agent of his death was Allectus, but we do not know who struck the blow. The presence of Carausius himself at Boulogne during the siege can be discounted. Any terms granted the defenders would have involved the surrender of Carausius, an event which he would have probably anticipated by suicide. Nothing in the extant literature actually associates Carausius's death with the fall of Boulogne and it has been suggested that he was already dead before Constantius opened his campaign. The wording of the Panegyric of 297 could be taken to imply that Carausius was killed before the Boulogne siege, at a time when the rebels felt that the emperors had given up the attempt to overthrow them:

> A protracted impunity for their crime had swollen the desperate creatures' audacity, making them claim that the sea's harshness which had inevitably postponed your victory was only a cover for your fear of them and making them believe that war had been abandoned in despair, instead of interrupted on purpose; and so the henchman [i.e. Allectus] killed his pirate chief.... (*Pan. Lat.* viii(v). 12)

The clear indication is that Carausius was killed not because warfare was raging but because it was not. The Panegyric further asserts that by his action Allectus would be rewarded by the emperors since he 'thought his actions would be rewarded with imperial power'. Does this indicate an expectation based on negotiation? On the other hand, Aurelius Victor imputes the motives of fear of punishment by Carausius for unspecified crimes as the motive for Allectus's coup against his leader. There is no reason to discard either piece of evidence in favour of the other since neither is incompatible with the other.

· 9 ·

THE SHORE FORTS

THE SERIES OF FORTS (Fig.8) listed under the command of the *Comes Litoris Saxonici* in the *Notitia Dignitatum* had a century of existence before being noted in the late Roman army list (ND. Occ.XXVIII). At this late date the forts constituted a single, unified defence system, but we do not know that they were intended as such when originally conceived. That something had changed in the intervening decades is clear from the fact that the *Notitia* does not list the fort at Cardiff, which on date and stylistic grounds must be considered to be one of the original structures. The reason for the omission being that at the date of the compilation of the *Notitia* list, Wales had, effectively, been demilitarized (Casey, 1989).

The notion that the series of forts stretching from Cardiff, on the Severn Estuary, to Brancaster, on the Wash, constituted a Carausian defence system has been examined on a number of occasions and the arguments for and against are most cogently put by a number of authors (White, 1961; Cunliffe, 1977; Johnson, 1979). White's view was that 'only Carausius and Allectus could conceivably have built this defensive system. Only they had the type and size of fleet with which the forts of the Saxon Shore were to complement. Only they had the type of enemy for which the forts were manifestly designed.' He supports his claim by reference to the presence of Carausian and Allectan coins in the forts but does not use this evidence in relation to wider numismatic problems of the period. It must be observed, in passing, that sometimes a certain air of xenophobia permeates criticisms of White's work, as if the Shore Forts were a property peculiarly vested in British scholarship which cannot be trespassed upon from Wisconsin in the midst of the prairies of distant America.

Johnson seeks to rebut the argument of a Carausian origin by recourse to a powerful strategic argument:

Carausius not only held the Channel fleet, but with it he had complete control of the approaches to Britain. There was nowhere on the Channel coastline where Maximian could build a fleet in 288–9, and so he had to build it on the Rhine and the Moselle. This fixed the line of approach along the Rhine, and although the system of defences in Britain was concentrated on the eastern coast, we need not suppose

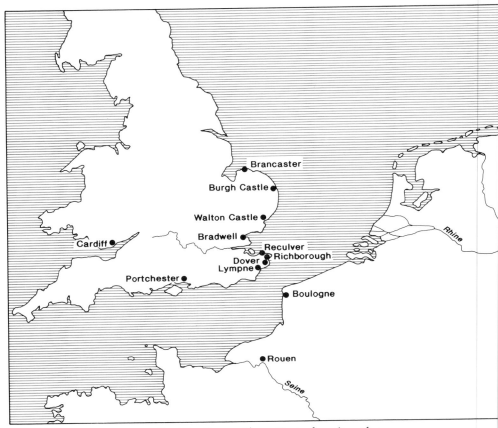

8 The Saxon Shore Forts, location plan.

that Carausius' eastern-facing forts were designed to intercept
Maximian alone. Only after the emperor had chosen the river on
which to build his fleet could Carausius be certain from what direction
the attack would come; in the short winter of 288–9 there was
insufficient time for building and completing a series of forts facing the
Rhine, from whose mouth Maximian was expected to launch his new
campaign. . . . The explanation, therefore, that the new series of forts
was constructed by Carausius against the forces of Rome is unlikely.
The forts could be of little use against the Roman fleet and are too
widely spaced for effective precaution against Roman landings.

(Johnson 1979, 104)

Cunliffe's views are based less upon strategic arguments than morphological
considerations. Noting that there is a dearth of dating evidence from
stratified contexts, he examines the variety of disparate architectural details
displayed by the forts. On these grounds he places Brancaster and Reculver
in the earlier part of the third century; Burgh Castle is then seen as
intermediate in style between these and later constructions. The divergence

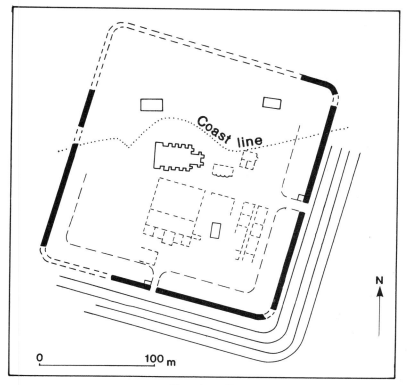

9 Reculver Fort.

of Burgh Castle from strict rectangularity is noted and compared with the same feature displayed by Bradwell, Richborough, Lympne and Dover. He concludes that 'It is tempting to regard them all as broadly contemporary and possibly belonging to the 260s and 270s, but such a contention must be regarded as highly tentative...' (Cunliffe 1977, 3). Portchester, on the grounds of size and regular rectangularity, is seen as later, a conclusion apparently supported by coin evidence of the 280s. Pevensey is placed at a later date on coin evidence and because of the novelty of its construction.

In summary the contemporaneity of most of the Saxon Shore forts with Carausius and Allectus is not disputed in the current literature but the date of their construction is not at all clear. Pevensey is normally seen as a later addition to the series, Cardiff is not discussed. A summary of the sites will serve to give further background to the various views.

Two sites — Brancaster on the Wash, and Reculver on the Thames Estuary — are claimed to date to the earlier part of the third century. Brancaster was built in the tradition of 'classic' auxiliary forts, rectangular with internal corner towers, opposing gates, the normal grid of roads and the headquarters building standing on the *via principalis*, facing down the length of the *via praetoria*. In the *Notitia Dignitatum* the garrison is given as the *Equites Dalmatae*. Tiles of an earlier garrison, the *Cohors I Aquitanorum Equitata*, have been found on the site. This latter unit is attested on Hadrian's Wall, at Carrawburgh, in the second century, the date of its transfer to, or length of its stay at, Brancaster is not known.

Reculver is similar in appearance to Brancaster (Fig.9). An inscription records the construction of the headquarters building during the governorship of a certain Rufinus. Since the governorship of Britannia Superior was a relatively lowly position in the top echelons of the Roman provincial administration, this man will have been a suffect consul and so not recorded in the consular lists, or *fasti* (Mann, 1977). An outside date for his governorship is given by the administrative changes brought about by Gallienus (258–68) who closed governorships to senatorial candidates and opened the rank to equestrian *praeses*: a *praeses* is recorded as governor in 262/66 (RIB 605). We must assume that the fort was constructed at some time between the reign of Septimius Severus (193–211), or Caracalla if he, rather than his father, was responsible for the division of Britain into two provinces, and that of Gallienus.

Two further sites are claimed to be of a relatively early date in the sequence of coastal defences: Burgh Castle on the Suffolk coast, and the earthwork fort at Richborough in Kent. The former is an irregular quadrilateral, distinctively different from the 'classic' fort since it has external drum towers spaced around the walls. The architecture is of a type known to military archaeology elsewhere in the empire from an earlier age but only introduced to the west in the third century. Burgh Castle has been seen as transitional between the 'classic' fort and the fully developed rectangular, high-walled, externally towered structures which comprise the majority of Shore Forts (Fig.10). The new features appear to be an afterthought since the walls are furnished with rounded corners on which the towers sit awkwardly, giving poor inter-tower visibility. It is normally claimed that the fort was furnished with internal towers of the 'classic' fort variety and that these were abandoned in favour of the new-style external defences. This interpretation, based on the presence of a very short section of a single enigmatic wall, has been challenged and the presence of internal towers now appears to be unlikely (Johnson, 1983). The dating of the fort is thus freed from a stylistic comparison with forts like Reculver and Brancaster.

The pre-Shore Fort structure at Richborough provides a context for arriving at a date of the later building. In the first century a great triumphal arch, celebrating the conquest of Britain, was erected in the middle of the civil port area. In the third century this monument was furnished with a series of concentric ditches, it was stripped of its marble cladding and converted into a watchtower. At a later date the ditches were filled, the monument reduced to its foundation platform and the Shore Fort laid out over the site. The refill of the ditches is rich in coins, though, with what is

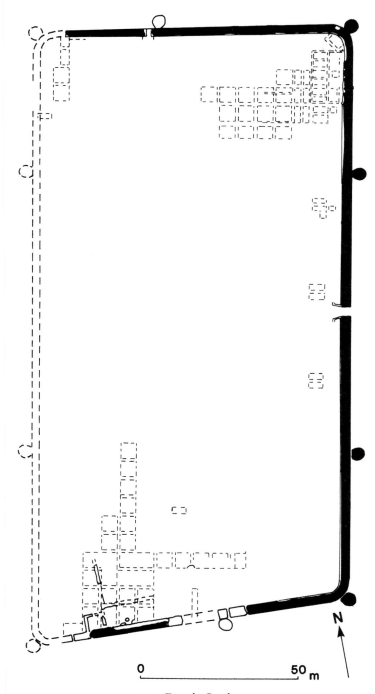

10 Burgh Castle.

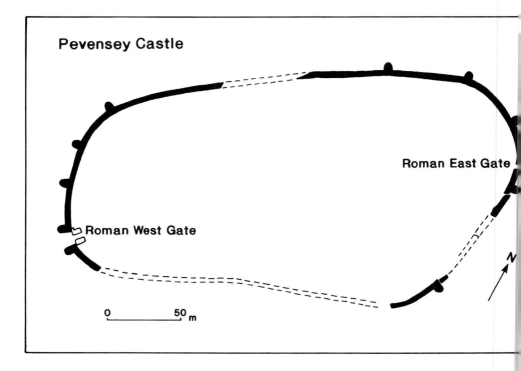

11   Pevensey Castle.

described as a 'doubtful exception', there are no coins of Carausius. Nor are such coins found in the foundations of the Shore Fort itself, though there are many in primary contexts within the fort. Thus, it is argued, the fort predates the reign of Carausius by some short period of time (Johnson, 1970).

Elsewhere, a Carausian date has been advanced for the construction of the fort at Portchester (Pl. d). Here, on a previously unoccupied site, material dug up in making the foundation trench for the walls was heaped up to form a low, sloping bank, or was piled against the walls themselves. Associated with this activity was a coin of Carausius, in clay deposits 'tipped into position at a very early stage of the fort's existence, possibly as the last act of the construction process following the completion of the wall' (Cunliffe, 1976).

For the remainder of the forts there is no direct evidence for the foundation date. A partial exception to this statement must be made for the fort at Pevensey. Morphologically this is exceptional in the series, being a rough oval which hugs the contour of a hill rather than being the usual low-lying, rectangular shape of the other forts (Fig.11). Excavations in 1932 brought to light a coin of Constans as Caesar dating to 330–5. The coin is described as having been recovered from a void left by the decay of a beam forming part of the foundation of one of the external towers (Bushe-Fox, 1932). This find gives every appearance of constituting a *terminus post quem* for the building of the fort. The date appears to gain further significance because of a hurried visit by Constans to face a sudden, grave crisis in Britain in the winter of 342/3 (Thompson, 1990). The building of Pevensey, to close a gap in the coastal defences, has been attributed to this visit (Frere, 1983).

Unfortunately the site at Pevensey has been bedevilled with planted, false evidence, almost certainly the work of the Charles Dawson who is so deeply involved in the Piltdown Man scandal. Tiles stamped with the name of the emperor Honorius (395–423) were found during excavations in the first decade of the century (Salzman, 1907). These tiles appeared to confirm that the resolution of a crisis in Britain by Honorius's *magister militum*, Stilicho, in 399 included the restoration of Pevensey. The tiles were shown to be fakes only after the development of thermoluminescence dating some sixty-five years after their publication and acceptance by the academic world (Peacock, 1973). It is worth noting that the probable perpetrator of this fraud contrived a number of discoveries which enhanced the historic past of Sussex. Notable is the case of the 'Sussex Rareties', birds from the Antipodes apparently blown half way round the globe but in reality imported in the newly developed refrigerated ships carrying frozen produce to Britain. The coin was found years later than the tiles but the possibility of an earlier plant cannot be discounted, nor since the circumstances of discovery are not recorded can the validity of the excavation of the coin be examined. It might well be an intrusion, of a very common coin, by animal activity into the cavity.

The reason for such scepticism about the date of this site is because of the aggregate evidence from the material available from a long series of well-conducted excavations, hitherto unpublished. From this evidence it is clear that Pevensey in no way differs from sites occupied, and built, in the fourth quarter of the third century. A study of the pottery and the coins from previously unpublished excavations points to a much earlier date than that suggested by the hitherto all-important coin (M. Line, pers. comm.). Re-dating Pevensey tends to undermine the typological approach to the dating of the forts as a whole and weakens the argument that the building of the Shore Forts was a cumulative process extending well into the fourth century, with installations being added as problems arose in different areas.

Attempts have been made to establish the date of construction and occupation of the forts through the overall study of the coins found in them (Reece, 1976, 1978). The volume of material available varies dramatically from site to site with several thousands of coins at Richborough to less than a hundred from Burgh Castle. Reculver and Dover, which are still being explored, do not yet have fully published coin lists. Histograms of Shore Fort coins published previously have encompassed the total coinage of the sites. Methodologically this has a shortcoming in that the relative proportions of the third-century coinage are influenced by coin deposits of earlier, in the case of Richborough, and later periods, and not all sites necessarily shared the same history in the fourth century. In the following histograms the coinage from the middle of the third to the beginning of the fourth century is examined, for such sites as there are lists available, in a way which highlights the relationship between Carausian/Allectan coin, that of the Gallic Empire, the period between 273 and 286 when issues of the Aurelianic reform should have circulated, and the issues of the Diocletianic period.

A number of problems need to be confronted in this analysis. Firstly, the coinage of the Gallic Empire embraces unofficial copies which rightly belong in the Aurelianic period but published reports do not always distinguish between regular and irregular coins so that there is no alternative to presenting a conflation. Secondly, the Diocletianic coin includes material dated as late as 318, when the Diocletianic billon 20-*denarius*, revalued from its previous value of 10-*denarii*, was replaced by a new Constantinian denomination. Almost all of the material represented in this period belongs to the end of series, when the 20-*denarius* had fallen from a weight of 10g to about 5g. Besides the pattern of coin finds produced by the occupation of individual sites there is an underlying pattern which is produced by imperial monetary policy. In brief, for the period under review, Gallic Empire coinage is very heavily represented on sites occupied in the third century, the Aurelianic reform's high value pieces are rare, the coinage of Carausius is common, Allectus less so, and the high-value, high-weight issues of the Diocletianic reform are very scarce (Casey, 1984).

The analysis proceeds from the reasonable assumption, confirmed by hoard and stratified site find evidence, that the volume of Gallic Empire coinage, and its copies, falls off as Carausian issues enter widespread circulation. A situation in which the relative strength of Carausian coinage is greater than that of the Gallic Empire suggests a date of inception in that reign, since Gallic Empire coinage still dominated as a circulating component of the economy of the Aurelianic period. The overstriking of early issues of Carausius on Gallic Empire period coins suggests that there was a deliberate attempt to drive them from the currency pool. On the other hand, Carausian and Allectan coins did not circulate in the following, Tetrarchic period (Fig.12).

On the basis of the strategy outlined above, Burgh Castle is confirmed as a pre-Carausian site, so too is Pevensey and Richborough. Bradwell-on-Sea, Lympne and Portchester are placed in a later category but so too is Brancaster. Leaving the last site for further discussion, we may note that both Burgh Castle and Richborough produce independent evidence of an early date. In the light of the discussion above there is nothing in the material from Pevensey that need confound the analysis. Portchester has produced a

12   Late third-century coin deposits in Saxon Shore Forts.

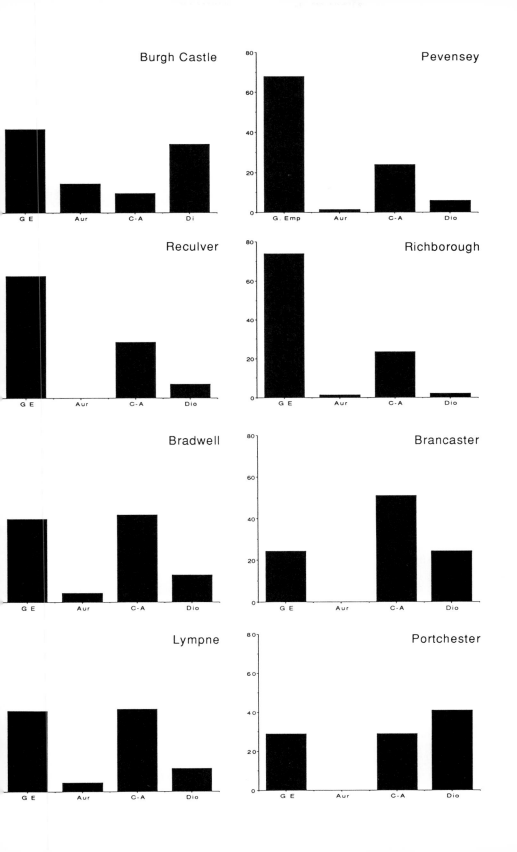

Burgh Castle

Pevensey

Reculver

Richborough

Bradwell

Brancaster

Lympne

Portchester

coin of Carausius from a foundation context and so fits the analysis perfectly Nothing known from Lympne need contradict the conclusion reached here The result for Brancaster is altogether surprising since the fort appears to be a regular early third-century structure.

The Brancaster coin record is not a good one. A list of 64 coins was published by J.K. St Joseph which were assumed to be from the fort (St Joseph, 1936). Since that date an extensive pre-fort settlement has been identified and partly excavated, adding about about hundred coins to the list for the site (Hinchliffe, 1985). The bulk of these coins was found in extramural, non-fort, contexts and are not included in the analytical data Fifteen coins were found in the fort itself but are, unfortunately, not published individually with standard numismatic references, being listed in period tables and histograms which conflate the coins of Carausius and Allectus with those of the Gallic Empire. Of the 67 coins published in 1936 4 predate the Gallic Empire and 13 are ascribed to Carausius. In the new list of 15 coins from the fort there is only a single pre-Gallic Empire specimen (dating to 231–59). Regrettably, the misguided method of non-standard publication does not permit their inclusion in this analysis but clearly, as a group, they do not significantly differ from the earlier published list. It seems odd that a site claimed as a Severan foundation produced only a single Severan coin, especially since this coinage is not scarce in military contexts elsewhere in Britain. Morphology notwithstanding, an open mind should be maintained about this site until a full study of pottery from fort contexts is undertaken, especially since the fort may have been laid out over a previously inhabited landscape, or even, given the presence of epigraphic evidence for the presence of the *Cohors I Aquitanorum Equitata*, an unlocated earlier fort such as is now known to have existed at Dover.

At Cardiff the port protecting the Severn estuary is of the same general type as those of the Saxon Shore system, with a square shape and external towers. Dating evidence from below the internal bank, removed in its entirety in the nineteenth century, gives a construction date of after 268. Despite the removal of most of the late deposits during landscaping operations in the last century a number of coins of Carausius and Allectus survive from the site, though insufficient material is available to undertake any meaningful statistical analyses (Webster, pers. comm.). The omission of this site from the *Notitia Dignitatum*, as a consequence of Arbogastes's withdrawal of forces from Wales in the late fourth century, has resulted in almost complete neglect of the site by scholars discussing shore defences (Casey, 1991).

On the results of the very limited investigation undertaken here, there seems to be a reasonable possibility that Carausius inherited a coastal defence system which was already under construction and that he, or Allectus, augmented it with two or more sites. This independent investigation of the coin evidence offers gratifying confirmation of the general results achieved by Cunliffe's morphological analysis.

A further investigative refinement might be to look at Carausian coins in Shore Forts for evidence of internal chronology. Since many coins have mint and sequence marks, which relate to date of issue, it should be possible to judge whether there is an internal pattern in the assemblages. Unfortunately, the publication of the coins without the sequence marks has been normal until recently and an analysis is impossible on currently available data. It cannot be too firmly stated that the publication of the coinage of this period by Roman Imperial Coinage (RIC) reference numbers only, without sequence marks, should be discouraged. In anticipation of further research Dr Richard Reece has kindly supplied the details of the Richborough coins from his personal records. The percentages are: Unmarked 47.5; RSR 0.7; BRI 0.5; Rouen 0.1; 286/9 15.4; 290/1 15.4; 292 10.5; 293 2.3.

The arguments advanced by Johnson for Carausius not having built the Shore Forts depended very largely on the plea that such structures make no strategic sense in the light of his naval power and the assumed tactical options available to Maximian when planning an invasion of Britain. As we have seen, Johnson is perfectly correct in his assumption as regards most, but not all, of the sites under review. But the argument that the usurpers did not build the forts, and thus by implication that they held no strategic benefit for them, does not really confront the fact that the forts are full of Carausius's coins and no one denies that they are deposits of his, and his successor's reign. The evidence of hoards deposited in the decades immediately after the death of Allectus shows that the usurpers' coinage had no circulation after their fall (Leeds, 1946; Sutherland, 1954; Mossop, 1958). If the forts were used by Carausius and Allectus then they must have fulfilled some perceived strategic function. This may have been a mistaken perception, but that does not invalidate the fact that they were used and that some considerable body of available forces must have been committed to them. And one of them, Portchester, has reasonable stratified evidence to suggest that it was indeed built by Carausius or Allectus. It follows that Carausian strategy not only included the use of the Saxon Shore Forts but extended to increasing their number.

Elsewhere, a building discovered at Shadwell on the north bank of the Thames about 1.2km downstream from the Port of London, has been interpreted as a watchtower built at this time. The structure, 8m square, had 2m wide foundations indicating that something of considerable height could have been erected on them. Adjacent timber buildings may have been barrack blocks for a garrison. The bulk of the coins from the site were of Carausius and Allectus (Perring, 1991). Of itself the Shadwell tower makes very little sense, being so close to the city that its inhabitants would have already been aware of the approach of any enemy coming to the attention of the Shadwell watchers. Rather, it must have been at the end of a chain of towers stretching down to the estuary. No evidence for such a system has yet been forthcoming.

At Cold Knapp at Barry, in south Wales, a complex building, with a colonnaded internal courtyard, some 20 rooms and an external veranda, has been tentatively identified as a Carausian naval store. The evidence is not compelling, the pottery is of later third-century date and of the three coins found one is a pierced *quinarius* of Allectus and a second an issue of Constantius I dated to 298/9. The building was demolished before completion (Evans, 1985).

Fortification of inland sites in this period is not well attested. Many towns in the Midlands, and south and west of Britain had earthwork defences which had been erected in the late second or early third centuries; a few towns boasted stone walls. There seems to have been no burst of defensive activity at the end of the third century with the exception of the walls of Canterbury, which are given a *terminus post quem* by a coin of Postumus sealed under the internal bank (Frere, 1982). The provision of defences for this town may indicate an expectation of trouble in the area, but, on the other hand, the erection of walls may have been a civic gesture made possible by a new prosperity coming with the stationing of Shore Fort garrisons in the region. It is notable that Canterbury has roads leading to the forts at Reculver, Richborough, Lympne and Dover, as well as to London. Possibly Canterbury served as a 'rest and recreation' centre for troops stationed in these forts. Certainly as a centre at the hub of a nexus of forts Canterbury would have profited commercially.

· 10 ·

ALLECTUS

IF THE DETAILS OF THE origins, rise and demise of Carausius are scarce, those for Allectus are nearly non-existent; as a result his career is seen as a mere adjunct to that of his leader. There is also an historiographic problem which has clouded the study of Allectus and so obscured consideration of him as a person in his own right. The implicit attitudes of modern scholars towards the protagonists scarcely vary from those expressed by Stukeley in the eighteenth century. The tendency is to see in Carausius a big, bold and brazen leader – founder of 'the queen's navee', an heroic figure. On the other hand Allectus has been relegated to the position of the villain of the tale, whose function was simply to put an end to the life of the bluff sailor hero and then to wait, supinely, to be extinguished by another heroic figure in British history, Constantius, the father of Constantine the Great.

Nothing is known about the origins of Allectus and even his full name is unknown. Allectus appears to mean something like 'chosen' or 'promoted'; there is nothing to suggest that the name represents a title assumed on taking the throne. A recent discussion of the career of Allectus, before his assumption of the throne, draws attention to a number of epigraphically attested instances of names very similar to Allectus. An inscription from Cologne names a Q. Allectius Marcellus (CIL XIII 12051), this of Antonine date, while two early fourth-century inscriptions from Rome (CIL VI 241, 464) record the name Adlectus (Loriot, 1992). The lack of *praenomina*, or forenames, is a problem which will be resolved when an accession coin of the emperor is found or, as in the case of Carausius, an inscription is discovered. The absence of coins with the full imperial titulature is curious; normally accession issues advertise not only the features of the new ruler to his subjects but also his names, even if in abbreviated form.

The only specific evidence about Allectus's position in Carausius's entourage is given by Aurelius Victor who states that 'Carausius made him his chief minister of finance' (v.39). The wording of the text is '*summae rei praeeset*'. The *summa res* was a financial department of state in the second half of the third and first half of the fourth centuries, though the title of 'chief finance minister' is not attested. In the fourth century the *Comes Sacrarum Largitionum* levied taxes to pay the imperial donatives, or largesses, which his title mentions. The existence of a special mint, the RSR

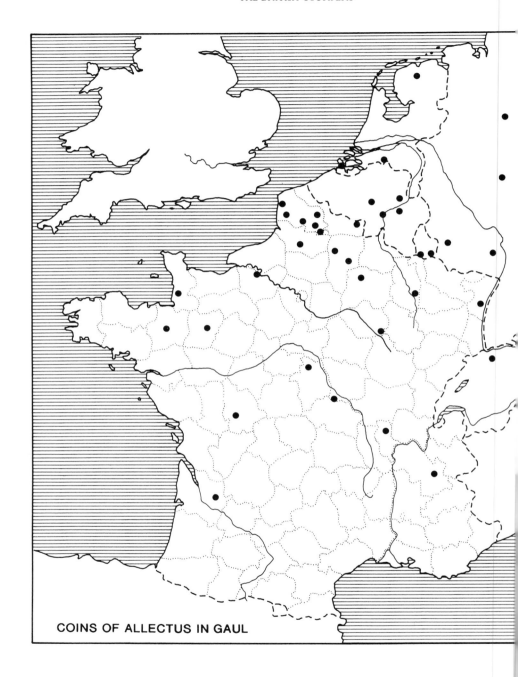

13 Finds of Allectan coins in Gaul. (After Loriot.)

mint identified as that of the *Rationalis Summae Rei*, which operated to pay donatives for Carausius, suggests that Allectus occupied a position similar to the later *Comes Sacrarum Largitionum*. The fact that Victor refers to Asclepiodotus as Constantius's praetorian prefect immediately after discussing Allectus's offices implies that the latter cannot have held this post. As finance minister, Allectus will have controlled the issue of coinage, the collection and levying of taxes, and probably had direct access to the army through the distribution of pay and donatives. Whether his previous career or experience qualified him in some special manner for these tasks is not known but, given the currency innovations which distinguish the reign of Carausius and the coin reform of Allectus himself, it is unlikely that financial affairs were entirely outside his experience. Eutropius is less specific about Allectus's position, dubbing him the 'ally' of Carausius. By this he appears to mean co-conspirator rather than equal. To the author of the Panegyric of 297, Allectus is merely Carausius' 'henchman' (*satelles*). In the circumstances of a revolt the participants probably did not enjoy the luxury of the full range of officials and government posts found in an established court, and too precise a definition of the functions of individuals may be misguided. Allectus might have embodied a number of responsibilities which would in other circumstances be shared by several members of the administration.

Tacit approval for the death of Carausius can be assumed by the fact that Allectus survived for three years and that there is nothing to suggest that his troops were ever less than entirely enthusiastic for his cause in the final struggle. The transition of power appears to have gone smoothly and the sequence marks on the coins continue uninterruptedly through the issue of 293 from Carausius to Allectus. Coin production was limited to the Colchester and London mints.

The general historical dustbin to which Allectus has been consigned – 'his reign...was uninspired and brief' (Frere, 1987) – has contributed to the view that he was confined to Britain throughout his reign and that the fall of Boulogne extinguished the only Continental holding of the separatist regime. That the territory controlled by Carausius was wider than Boulogne and its environs is suggested by the spread of his coinage in northern Gaul (Fig.13). If we separate out the Rouen coinage, which we have ascribed to an earlier period of occupation, the pattern concentrates most densely in the region between Boulogne and the Loire: we have already noted that the bulk of these coins date to the issues of 291 and later. The circulation of this coinage can be explained by his occupation of areas adjacent to the Channel ports but the circulation of British coin does not cease with his death. There are finds of coins of Allectus from Gaul which compare in relative volume and circulation area with those of Carausius. The significance of these finds has received little discussion since the long-accepted explanation for their presence is that they arrived in Gaul with Constantius's soldiers returning from the reconquest of Britain (Evans, 1890). Efforts have been made to examine this view in light of the hypothesis that Allectus did not immediately quit Gaul (Casey, 1977). The arguments are numismatic.

The distribution pattern of Allectus's coins in Gaul is so similar to that of Carausius that the same factors could account for their presence and deposition. If the pattern is not the effect of post-reconquest events in the case of Carausius, why should it be so in the case of Allectus? The similarity of context is only partly explained by coins of the two rulers appearing together in hoards. The explanation of returning soldiers is not strengthened by the pattern of finds: few coins are found on the Rhine frontier, which was the area in which the bulk of forces were concentrated and to which returning troops might be expected to be posted. A coin of Carausius from Autun might indeed be a post-revolt deposit introduced to the site by the British stone-masons sent to the town by Constantius in 297 to repair the ravages of the destruction in the 270s – not, incidentally, destruction wrought by barbarian attack but by the Roman army itself. A panegyric is not the place to mention this embarrassing fact (*Pan. Lat.* viii(v). 21).

It has also been contended that internal evidence argues against Allectus's coins reaching the Continent in significant quantities after 295/6. On currently accepted dating, proposed in the relevant volume of Roman Imperial Coinage, the central empire undertook a comprehensive restructuring of its coinage system in 294, at about the same time as the creation of prefectures and diocesan mints (Hendy, 1985). The reform involved the introduction of new denominations and the revaluation of extant coins, the main new denomination being a billon coin weighing *c.*10g, tariffed as a 10-*denarius* piece. This change in the coinage may have provoked a partial reform in the monetary system of Allectus who, while not issuing the new 10-*denarius*, did issue one new denomination. The new coin seems to have been as a half to the standard 4-*denarius* denomination, weighing 2g as compared to the 4.3g of the larger coin (Pl.7, nos 2–6). Though the new coin has a radiate rather than the laureate bust, which would normally differentiate a half denomination from the double unit, the supposition that it is a fraction is reinforced by the use of a mark of value in conjunction with the mintmark, the letter Q being interpreted as *quinarius*, in the traditional sense of a monetary half unit. The new coin may have been introduced to fit into the new Diocletianic system of 2-, 4- and 10-*denarius* copper and billon coins. The use of a single reverse type featuring a warship is both a comment upon the naval power which maintained Allectus's rule and the fact that the new coinage may have served as a medium for improved military pay.

If all this represents an attempt to bring the insular currency into line with the Continental, the corollary of the move is that the two currencies were expected, in some sphere, to interact economically. Where would this interaction take place where Allectus to be confined to Britain? To pose the question is not to say that the *quinarius* actually circulated on the Continent, for events overtook that development and, as we shall see, there are other interpretations of the significance of the *quinarii*.

Turning to the coinage of Allectus found on the Continent it appears, from a study of the coins for which sufficient detail is published to determine the mint sequence, that the latest coins of the reign are not present (Table 10) and finds of *quinarii* are very rare: up to 1977 only a single specimen from Namur being on record (Casey, 1977). It could be argued that had the coins of Allectus found in Gaul been drawn from the currency pool of Britain in the reconquest period, they would have included the latest issues. In contradiction it can be argued that *quinarii* would be ignored if they did not fit into the prevailing currency system of the Continent at that period, but there is no evidence to elucidate this point. In Britain *aureliani* and *quinarii* tend to be hoarded separately, confirming that it was a new denomination and not a late debasement of the *aurelianus* produced at the end of the reign as a result of a shortage of coining material (Burnett, 1984).

In considering the arguments for an Allectan presence in Gaul after the fall of Boulogne we can turn to the location of coin finds. The Noyelles-Godault hoard, found east of Boulogne, comprised 134 coins ranging in date from Valerian to Allectus. The latest section of the hoard consisted of ten coins of Carausius, five struck in the name of Maximian and one of Diocletian, and seven of Allectus. The mintmarks indicate that these coins date to 293 and 294. Two individual finds from the site are a coin of Carausius and another of Allectus dated to 293 (Gricourt, 1967). The Amiens Hoard closed with six coins of Carausius and ten of Allectus, of these, three date to 293, five can be dated no closer than 293–5 and to 295 (Evans, 1890). Is it possible that Allectus maintained a presence on the Continent as late as 295?

Events in 293, as far as the recovery of Boulogne was concerned, went with dash and efficiency but this brief burst of activity was followed by several years' delay before the imperial forces embarked on the invasion of Britain. The author of the Panegyric of 297 feels the necessity of commenting on this and offers a reason for the lack of action: 'For with the momentum of your courage and success, unconquered Caesar, you could have finished the whole war at once, if circumstances had not insisted that time was needed to build ships' (*Pan. Lat.*viii(v).7).

Two, and possibly three, years is a long time to take in constructing a fleet, especially since only a year or so previously the dockyards had built an invasion fleet for Maximian and experienced shipwrights will not have been in short supply. The account of Maximian's preparations, recounted in the Panegyric of 289, makes it clear that the building of the dockyards themselves, the felling of timber and the construction of the fleet took at most a year. The failure of Maximian's venture may have owed something to under-preparation and might have been on too small a scale to guarantee success, and to this extent Constantius might have been prepared to await the assembly of an overwhelming force. But Julius Caesar built invasion fleets for use against Britain in both 55 and 54 BC in less than ten months, while in 357–8 Julian collected 200 vessels and built another 400 to transport grain from Britain to the armies of the Rhine. This task was, as Julian relates, no mean achievement 'on account of the neighbouring barbarians who kept attacking me' (Julian, *Letter to the Athenians*, 275–83).

The numismatic material is suggestive, though far from conclusive proof, of an Allectan presence in Gaul after 293. That it is not attested by any literary evidence need not be entirely inimical to the suggestion. Only the account of the capture of Boulogne in the Panegyrics of 297 and 310 and two ambiguous words in Aurelius Victor's *de Caesaribus* tell us that Carausius had Continental possessions, neither the main work of Aurelius Victor nor Eutropius, nor any account derived from them, mentions this episode. Were it not for the panegyrics we would have to reconstruct the Carausian presence in Gaul from exactly the same sort of numismatic evidence that we have discussed for Allectus.

If we consider the strategic situation we may note that at this stage the British fleet was still intact and that the Continental emperors were still without any naval forces. At least two fleets are credited to Allectus by the hostile literary sources which recount his fall. In the absence of any means of interdicting communications with Allectan garrisons stationed elsewhere in Gaul where access was by sea routes or by navigable rivers, it may be premature to see the fall of Boulogne as evidence that his domains were confined to Britain.

Whatever the situation in Gaul there is clear evidence that, far from taking a negative view of his situation and awaiting his fate supinely, Allectus was an energetic ruler who was active in more than one area. The introduction of a new denomination in the currency has already been discussed. In the precious metals there are no known genuine issues of silver but a study of the gold coinage indicates that it was issued throughout the reign in considerable quantitites – 24 specimens of this coinage are recorded, all of the London mint. This is a residue, as the large number of recorded dies shows, of a very large original issue. In contrast to Carausius none was issued in the names of Diocletian or Maximian. Provenanced *aurei* have been found at Tingry near Boulogne, Bath, where there are two specimens among the votive offerings to Sulis Minerva (Walker, 1988), Reading, Silchester, Chittenden (Kent), Cynwyl Elvet (Carmarthen), the Isle of Dogs (London) and, finally, Minden in Germany, where, since the coin has been mounted as a jewel, it is probably of post-Roman date of deposit and a well-travelled object (Shiel, 1977). The widespread distribution suggests that the gold acted as a widely accepted medium of exchange and saving and was not confined to a donative function. The gift of two *aurei* at the sacred spring of Sulis Minerva suggests a high level of personal wealth among some individuals at this time, as indeed does the donation of Carausian gold coins to the Thames in the London Bridge votive deposit (Rhodes, 1991). It has already been noted that an accession coinage is yet to be found in this series, nor are any gold consular coins recorded.

Despite the general historical denigration of this reign, lack of confidence does not seem to have spread to Allectus himself. The billon coinage shows that Allectus celebrated a self-conferred consulship commemorated by coins with the mintmarks S/P ML and S/A ML, mintmarks attributed to the period 293–5. The latter mark is later than the former, probably indicating a date of 294, the year in which the legitimate consuls were the Caesars Constantius and Galerius, jointly rewarded for the former's successes in Gaul. It would be normal for a consulship to have been held from the next 1 January after the accession; this is what Allectus appears to have done following his coming to power in 293. The use of the mark S/P ML may indicate that its use extends into 294 or that Allectus already held office when he came to power. It might be that Allectus held the consulship with Carausius in his capacity as 'chief minister' during one of the latter's periods of office, though no consular coins are recorded for his last year. In any event, the celebration of a consulship would entail a range of public ceremonies including a consular procession, the distribution of largesses to the population and the army, and the celebration of public games. Possibly a co-consul was chosen from the imperial entourage to grace the highest state office; in each year of the regime at least one pair of consuls would need to be selected from the military or aristocracy of Britain.

Already a revisionist picture of an active Allectus is building up which contradicts the negative views of a previous generation of historians. This is further enhanced by the discovery of a group of buildings in London, accurately dated to his reign, which may comprise an imperial administrative complex (Williams, 1989, 1993). Here, in the south-west corner of the Roman city adjacent to the riverside wall, which had been built in or shortly after the 270s to complete the circuit of London's defences, a series of massive foundations has been discovered which relate to at least two monumental buildings (Fig.14). The foundations themselves consist of rafts of oak piles driven into the unstable riverside soil with cross timbering on top, over which was laid a platform of massive stone blocks (Pl.a). The timbers of the piling consist of freshly cut trees which were driven into the ground with the bark still intact (Pl.b). Thus the complete radius of each trunk was preserved, giving a full spectrum of the growth rings. Analysis of these rings and comparison with the tree-ring sequence of Roman London shows that the timber was felled in the spring of 294. Although it could be argued that the trees, once felled, were a reserve stock and that the dendrochronological date is merely a *terminus post quem* there is merit in the excavator's argument that the bark of these trees would certainly have been stripped from seasoned timber in the very act of driving piles into compacted London Clay, a tenaciously difficult material to penetrate.

The nature of the structures, one of which was probably colonnaded, invites the conclusion that they were of an imperial nature. A ceremonial and administrative centre in London separate from the palace of the *Praeses* of Britannia Superior, which was on the riverside some half a kilometre to the east, suggests that Allectus's regime was stable and saw its future as

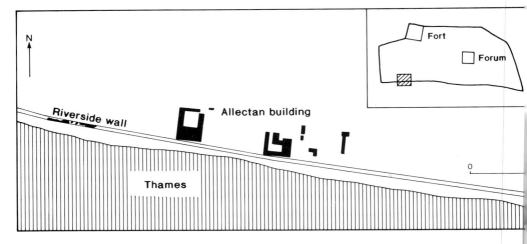

14   Allectan building sites in London.

secure, at least within the confines of Britain itself. Building work in the northern capital of York has not yet been identified; it is not impossible that the rebuilding of the southern defences of the legionary fortress to incorporate external towers, could fall into this period, since the actual dating evidence of this work rests on two stratified coins, dating to the 270s. The similarities of style between the restored defences and the Saxon Shore Forts has received comment (Ottaway, 1993). Given the evidence for a building programme in London, the possibility that Allectus undertook the maintenance, completion or commissioning of new coastal defence sites cannot be discounted.

If the collapse of the Allectan administration was seen as less of an inevitability by its participants than by modern historians armed with perfect hindsight, it can only be because every precaution was taken to protect it. We have very little information about civil or military affairs during this short reign and what is known has all too frequently been fleshed out by unsupported speculation. The Panegyric of 297, which is our only detailed source for the reconquest of the island by Constantius, is at pains to minimize the damage done to the Allectan army by emphasizing that casualties were sustained not by Roman troops but by Frankish mercenaries.

The Franks were the main concern of emperors campaigning in north-western Gallia Belgica and Lower Germany in the last quarter of the third century and represented an ever-present threat to Gaul, a country which they were to make their own in the fifth century. The employment of Franks as mercenaries by the rebels would be seen as a deviation from all that was Roman; the employment of the enemy of the Roman people by the enemies of the Roman state. This does not mean that Franks – 'our'

Franks, as it were – did not find employment in the regular Roman army. Roman policy was essentially pragmatic; as an instance of this we may cite the case of Constantine, brought to power in York by the British army and the assistance of Crocus, a chieftain of the Alamanni, serving with the army in a campaign against the Picts.

The numbers of such mercenaries employed are not known, nor are the formations in which they fought. If the practices of a slightly later period were followed, individual units, or bands, would have served under their own leaders rather than Roman officers. The leader would have been paid a lump sum which he, in turn, would divide among his troops in the Germanic tradition of heroic leadership maintained through gifts to follow-ers. The leader himself might have been rewarded personally by the emperor with prestige gifts, such as gold or silver medallions, armour and weapons. No medallions of Allectus are yet recorded.

Of the location of formal Roman units, the only evidence takes the form of coins of Allectus found in the coastal forts discussed above, confirming that they were garrisoned during his reign. Assessing occupation by reference to the presence or absence of Allectus's coins is difficult. Because his reign was only half the length of Carausius's his coins are relatively less well represented in absolute numbers. Of particular relevance is the problem of Hadrian's Wall and whether the garrisons of the forts were withdrawn to meet the threat of invasion in the south.

The generally peaceful nature of the northern frontier in the third century, evidenced by the growth of undefended civil settlements, has already been discussed. The picture given by excavations at Halton Chesters and Rudchester is of a reduction of garrison strength in the last quarter of the third century, while in the area adjacent to Birdoswald the curtain of the Wall itself seems to have been in disrepair (Breeze & Dobson, 1987). As we shall see, epigraphic evidence from both Birdoswald and Housesteads shows that major buildings were in need of replacement or repair. Cumulatively the evidence suggests a rundown frontier with garrisons in poor military condition; certainly the Wall was not a reservoir of hardened troops at battle readiness.

A further impediment to the hypothesis that frontier units were withdrawn is the listing of Wall regiments in the *Notitia Dignitatum* (ND. Occ.XL). This list, in a document compiled in 395 at the division of the empire between the sons of Theodosius (Jones, 1964), shows that the units attested by dedications and other epigraphic evidence as being in garrison in the third century were still in the same forts at the end of the fourth. Of the 23 forts listed in the *Notitia Dignitatum* independent evidence for the earlier garrison is available for no less than 13. Scholars, in an attempt to maintain the credibility of the 'withdrawal' hypothesis have resorted to a number of arguments. A now discredited view is that the *Notitia* list is a bureaucratic fiction maintained by an idle and indifferent late Roman civil service, who finding a third-century garrison list in some sort of cache of obsolete documents gave it a spurious currency either to maintain a façade of imperial invincibility or to perpetuate some sort of swindle by drawing pay for ghost garrisons. A less incredible view is that the garrisons were withdrawn by Allectus for the campaign against Constantius and restored to their forts by the victor (Frere, 1987). This has the merit of possibility, if not probability, since the families of the frontier soldiers would have been left behind in their homes round the forts during any emergency which called for the rapid deployment of their menfolk and one way to gain the affection and loyalty of the defeated troops would be to restore them safely to their families.

The claim that the Wall was stripped of its troops is based on the assumption that Allectus needed all the forces he could raise to meet the double thrust of the imperial invasion. From this assumption arose the belief that the withdrawal of the frontier garrisons allowed hostile forces, the Picts or the tribes to the north of the Wall, to cross the frontier on a mission of destruction and pillage. The origin of this view is found in the discovery of inscriptions at Birdoswald and Housesteads recording rebuilding work by Constantius in the names of Diocletian and Maximian. Claims of evidence of destruction and burning in this invasion have been made in relation to a number of forts and milecastles, but most, if not all, fall into the category of self-fulfilling prophecies, the strata being dated by reference to the postulated invasion. Selective digging is often the root of the problem, with results from very small excavated areas being extended into wider contexts in an unwarranted manner. At the fort at Greta Bridge (Co. Durham) a stone-built house in the *vicus* was gutted by fire, in the refurbishment the debris of the conflagration was capped by a newly laid flagged floor which sealed a coin of Allectus, this lay on the top of the burned material and must have been deposited during the rebuilding (Casey, forthcoming). Such evidence might well be taken as showing that destruction took place as far south as the Tees valley in the claimed barbarian invasion were it not that the *vicus* comprised at least 20 other buildings which, on examination, showed no signs of burning or destruction. A single domestic disaster seems to have occurred, not an invasion.

The alternative view that Allectus drew reinforcements from the forts of the Pennines has been canvassed. The *Notitia Dignitatum* certainly lists units which are completely new as compared to those known to have been in these forts at an earlier period. This might suggest that they suffered casualties while serving with Allectus, but the later history of military events in the fourth century is itself full of unresolved problems and there are numbers of known imperial interventions, any of which might have resulted in garrison changes.

In summary, the nature, numbers and disposition of the Allectan forces which met the invasion of Constantius are largely unknown factors in the events that follow. For details of the overthrow of Allectus we are entirely dependent on the account given in the Panegyric of 297, the tendentious nature of which is slightly modified by the later historians in regard to the parts played by the principals Constantius and Asclepiodotus. Archaeology has made virtually no impact on this account.

The delay of up to three years from the fall of Boulogne has been accounted for by the panegyricist by the necessity of campaigning in the area of the mouth of the Rhine against the Chamavi and the Frisii; defeated, they were settled inside the empire with their families as *laeti*, cultivators of the soil and providers of offspring who were compelled to join the regular Roman army. By the time that the *Notitia* was compiled at the end of the fourth century, Chamavi and Frisii no longer appear in the lists of *laeti* settled in Gaul and Italy; presumably after a century of uneventful settlement they had been entirely absorbed into the provincial population. During these campaigns the time was also taken up with building a fleet, or rather two fleets.

The undecorated facts about the expedition to Britain that can be derived from the Panegyric are:

1   The fleet sailed in two divisions. One from Boulogne, the other from further south at the mouth of the Seine, having made its way down the river.

2   The Boulogne division, which set sail first, was under the personal command of Constantius.

3   The southern fleet was commanded by the praetorian prefect Julius Asclepiodotus. Significantly, this detail is given by Aurelius Victor and Eutropius, not the Panegyric.

4   The departure of Constantius took place in rough weather. The southern fleet sailed when it learned of his departure, though against the best advice of its officers, the wind being from the wrong quarter. The fleet had to tack to make progress.

5   The southern fleet proceeded towards the Isle of Wight (Vectis) where a sea fog allowed it to slip past a waiting Allectan fleet.

6   Asclepiodotus landed his forces, burned his boats and met Allectus in battle. Allectus was defeated and died on the battlefield, his body was recognized though he had stripped himself, or been stripped of, the imperial regalia.

7   Allectus failed to organize effective resistance and did not marshal all the forces available to him before meeting Asclepiodotus.

The Panegyric, and later sources, say nothing about the activity of Constantius after he sailed from Boulogne. The text may imply that he reached London with forces, who had been lost in a fog, in time to save it from being looted by barbarian deserters, or soldiers fleeing from Allectus's defeated army. On the other hand, it might have been a section of Asclepiodotus's force that did this. We do not know where Allectus was when news of the landing came to him. The Panegyric observes that he was unprepared, and that he abandoned a fleet and a coastal site of some sort: 'Why did the very standard-bearer of the criminal rebellion abandon the shore he was holding, why did he desert fleet and harbour..?' (*Pan. Lat.* viii(v). 15).

The answer to this question may well be that Allectus knew only of a single threat presented by Asclepiodotus in the west, hence he headed off to deal with it with all speed. After all, a fleet would be little use to him in fighting a land battle. The text does not tell us where the shore he left was, nor where the fleet was stationed. Clearly it was a different fleet from the one stationed off the Isle of Wight. The claim that he was on the coast of Kent is an unwarranted guess. The reference to abandoning the shore could mean that he took garrisons from shore forts to supplement his mobile forces. The hyperbole about desertion of the coast being caused by the arrival of Constantius offers no insight into Allectus's decision-making. The text suggests no rational explanation for Allectus's action except: '... unless the sight of your looming sails, unconquered Caesar, made him fear that you were coming yourself at that moment'. This can be discounted since Constantius was not in sight; at best, he was in a fog or a storm somewhere between Britain and Boulogne. The Panegyric of 310 offers the tantalizing suggestion that Constantius had been forced to return to his base in Gaul, the weather conditions on his departure being so different from those described in the earlier panegyric: 'The sea was so calm when he sailed there [i.e. to Britain] that the ocean seemed to have been stunned by its passenger's greatness into losing all motion: his journey was such that victory did not escort him, but was already awaiting him' (*Pan. Lat.* vi(vii).5).

Taking the text and the knowledge and intentions of the panegyricist at face value, this could be seen as constituting proof that Constantius took no part in the actual action in Britain, only arriving in time to receive the benefits of victory. Indeed the whole passage can be seen as a tactful gloss on a less than glorious participation in the actual fighting by the Caesar. Like the orchestra which kept perfect time and tempo when the lights went out, the invasion of Britain was a success without the involvement of its conductor.

This is as much as can reasonably be reconstructed from the texts of the recovery of Britain. The poverty of information about the invasion has not inhibited speculation, however. The numerous unsupported conjectures are best summarized, and added to, by Eicholz (1953). The claim that the Saxon Shore forts played no part in the events of 296 cannot be substantiated since we know absolutely nothing about the actions of individual military units at the time (Frere, 1987).

The location of the final battle is also unknown though, given the known area of the landing of Asclepiodotus, sites between Portchester, Winchester, Silchester and Farnham have all been advocated. It is still sometimes claimed that the Blackmoor Hoard of approximately 30,000 coins represents Allectus's war chest and therefore places the final struggle in the vicinity of Woolmer, Hampshire. This does not bear close examination. The idea drew credibility from the reports which circulated at the time of discovery in 1873 when Lord Selborne, the owner, wrote of finds of broken swords and spearheads being found 'one or two years before' in the vicinity of the hoard. The coins were found in two pots 'pear-shaped, rather more than a foot high with a maximum diameter of about a foot'. The notion that such a hoard of late third-century coins constituted a war chest bears little relationship to the intrinsic value of the coins themselves. The bulk consisted of debased *antoniniani* (28,126) a smaller element comprised *aureliani* (1687), many of the coins of Allectus were *quinarii*. If we reduce this mass to notional *denarii* the whole hoard is valued at approximately 73,000 *denarii*. In the edict of prices promulgated by Diocletian in 301 the government price of gold was sat at 72,000 *denarii* a Roman pound. At this value the Blackmoor Hoard would be the equivalent of about a single pound of gold; since Allectus struck his *aureus* at a weight of *c*.4.4g the value of the hoard converted to gold would amount to no more than 72 coins. Hardly a war chest and in a most inconvenient form.

The defeat and death of Allectus brought the separatist regime down at a blow. With their leader died 'only the old ringleaders of the conspiracy and groups of barbarian mercenaries'. These were pursued so that:

> all those plains and hills . . . were covered by none but the fallen bodies of the foulest enemies. Barbarian, or imitating barbarism in the clothes they wore and their long, reddened hair, they lay filthy in the dust and blood in the various postures dictated by the agony of their wounds; and among them the flag bearer, of the usurpation himself . . . .
>
> (*Pan. Lat.* viii(v). 16)

Thus a clear-cut and satisfactory end was achieved; or fabricated after the event. Only the original conspirators suffered, only barbarians were killed. Allectus was disposed of without embarrassing revelations of any diplomatic accommodations, temporary treaties or other relationships that might have existed between the British separatists and the emperors in the years since 286. Britain was restored, once more to bask in the *lucis aeternae*, the perpetual light, of the empire.

• 11 •

AFTERMATH

THE ISLAND OF BRITAIN BEING brought back under imperial control the celebrations began, or would have done so had other crises not supervened on the Rhine, in North Africa and in the border states with the Persian Empire in the east. It was not until November or December 303 that Diocletian and Maximian celebrated the triumph at Rome which was the cumulation of their years of joint reign. By then the victory in Britain had faded and it was the great defeat of the Persian empire which formed the centrepiece of the ceremonies.

Rewards for the conquerors are found in the form of honours and gifts of precious metal commemorative medals. Intangible rewards will also have been issued, promotions for officers, donatives to the invasion forces. Of this latter category of celebration only the consulships awarded to Constantius, and his eastern co-Caesar Galerius, are recorded. In 296 the consulship was held by Diocletian, the eastern emperor, and Constantius, the western Caesar. In the following year the honour was shared by Maximian, the western emperor and Galerius, the Caesar of the east. After this carefully orchestrated division of imperial honours among the rulers, the system reverted to normal; thereafter the emperors always held the consulship jointly, as did the Caesars. Julius Asclepiodotus, the Praetorian prefect who had actually won the victory in Britain, was not honoured since this would have diminished the status of the Caesar and underlined the subordinate strategic role played by Constantius's forces in the actual reconquest. In any event he had been awarded the consulship in 292, the same year that Constantius had been made Caesar and Asclepiodotus was raised to the Praetorian prefecture vacated by Constantius.

Elsewhere rewards were in monetary terms and items produced for the donatives are preserved in the Beaurains (Arras) Hoard (Bastien, 1977). This hoard, discovered in 1922 in the suburbs of Arras in northern France, consisted a mass of gold and silver coins, silver vessels, jewellery in the form of collars made up of gold coins set in pendants, a silver candlestick and various other items of precious metal. The hoard was quickly dispersed by the finders, though significant parts were recovered and acquired by the museum at Arras. Another portion was distributed in the trade through a number of prominent coin dealers of the period and items ended up in private collections in Europe and America; some of the jewellery, and the silver candlestick, was acquired by the British Museum. Although the whereabouts of all of the items cannot now be traced an estimate of the original composition of the hoard suggests that it consisted of 100 *aureii* and 100 *denarii* of the early empire, and 30 to 35 gold medallions, 400 *aurei* and *solidi*, and 70 silver coins of the late third and early fourth century; a burial date of shortly after 315 is suggested by the evidence of the latest coins. The early coins which date from the first to the second century, were no longer currency at the period when the treasure was concealed.

Since the nature of the other items indicates that much of the treasure was accumulated by someone who received very high-status imperial donatives over a period extending from the recovery of Britain down to the reign of Constantine, we may be justified in identifying the obsolete precious metal as a benefaction paid out by Constantine after he sequestrated the treasures laid up, often for centuries, in the pagan temples in his domains. This might also be the source of the *aureus* of Carausius in the hoard. The date of this sequestration is uncertain but a date around 315 is likely since it is at this time Constantine introduced a new, and very successful, gold coinage. St Jerome dates the sequestration to as late as 331 but he is talking about the situation in the east, which had only come under Constantinian control in 324. The collection of old *denarii* in the similarly dated, but much smaller, hoard from Sully in south Wales is attributable to the same factor (Evans, 1890).

Among the items in the hoard were five gold medallions issued by the mint of Trier to commemorate the reconquest of Britain. Four are issued in the names of Diocletian, Constantius and Galerius and there would also have been one for Maximian which has not survived. These medallions are multiples of the monetary unit struck as 5-*aureus* pieces. The reverse is common to all, depicting Constantius raising a kneeling figure of Britannia who is armed with spear and rectangular shield. Behind the Caesar stands Victory, who crowns him with a laurel wreath (Pl.7, nos 2, 3). There are two obverse types for Constantius, as consul in the *toga picta* of the office and holding the eagle-tipped sceptre of office, and as Hercules in the lionskin head-dress of the god (pl.7, no.2). The latter type, by assimilating the attributes of the deity identified with Maximian, as Maximianus Herculeus, identifies the emperor with the success of his Caesar. The armed figure of Britannia contrasts with the images of the island employed by Carausius. In these she is shown as bereft of weapons, at the mercy of her enemies and grateful for the presence of the saviour emperor. The armed figure has its antecedents in the earliest images devised by the moneyers of Hadrian and employed widely in the Antonine period. The imagery implies a province which has been down but not, to extend a vulgarism, out; a province, furthermore, which has materially assisted in its liberation, which has a vital part to play in the affairs of commonwealth and is ready to contribute to the defence of the empire as a whole.

More explicit than this is the so-called Arras Medallion (Pl.7, no.4). This magnificent product of the moneyer's art is a multiple of 10-*aurei*. The obverse depicts Constantius as commander of the army with the *paludamentum*, the red cloak of a general, worn over his armour. The reverse summarizes the entire campaign in a series of vignettes which can be interpreted at two levels. Firstly, as individual comments on the campaign and, secondly, as an illustration of a single dramatic incident, the relief of London from the marauding bands of Allectus's barbarian allies.

On the first level we have the Caesar as armoured warrior urging his horse forward with the momentum, the eagerness for reconquest, which is commented on by the panegyricist. Below him is the fleet, the chief weapon of the campaign, depicted as a war galley, its ram cutting the waves, its armed crew filling the decks. London, represented by the *tutela* or spiritual embodiment of the city, named to avoid any uncertainty as to the location, kneels before her gates, hands raised in supplication, welcome and thanks for her deliverance.

On the second level the scene is refocused. Constantius makes his triumphal entry into the city welcomed by the population, represented by the *tutela*, after his fleet, or Asclepiodotus's, has sailed up the Thames just in time to save the city from Allectus's defeated army. The inscription which enfolds the Caesar, REDDITOR LVCIS AETERNAE ('Restorer of the Eternal Light') is reflected in the words of the Panegyric of 297:

> And no wonder they [i.e. the Britons] were sated with such
> joy ... when they were at length free, at length Romans, at length
> refreshed by the true light of the empire.   (*Pan. Lat.* viii(v). 19)

The Beaurains Hoard also contains a number of single *aurei* which reflect on the campaign. These, issued in the names of all of the members of the tetrarchy by the Trier mint, show very much the same scene as the Arras Medallion (Pl.8, no.9). Both the naval forces and the Caesar are depicted but the figure of London kneeling before her walls is omitted. No doubt reasons of size dictated what elements of the medallic design should appear on the smaller coin. The reverse inscription, VIRTVS ILLYRICANI, can be interpreted in two ways. By the late Roman period the word *virtus* could be used in the sense of 'army' and if this were so in the present case the coin might commemorate the part played by troops from Illyricum in the conflict. On the other hand the emperors and their Caesars originated in Illyricum so that the motto might simply reflect that it was the *virtus* (bravery and military skill) of the Balkan emperors which brought about the victory. Had troops transferred from the Balkans been employed in the campaign it might be a further factor contributing to the long delay in launching the retributive expedition. Such a transfer of forces from the imperial recruiting grounds controlled by Diocletian would powerfully symbolize the unity of purpose of the joint emperors and the territorial integrity of the empire despite its administrative division into two parts.

Almost the latest object in the Arras Hoard, and the largest single gold object, is a medallion issued by Constantine the Great in 310 (Pl.7, no.5). Scratched on the reverse of the medallion is a graffito which appears to be the name, in the genitive, of the owner of this item and, presumably, of the rest of the hoard – VITALIANI *pp(?O)* . . . ('Belonging to Vitalianus pp'). The letters 'PPO' are normally used in inscriptions as the abbreviation for *Praefectus Praetorio* (praetorian prefect); 'PP' are for *Praepositus*, or regimental commander. There is no record among the *praefecti* of the period of a Vitalianus but the records are not complete. It may be that the owner of the Arras Hoard had achieved this rank in the reign of Constantine. The hoard shows that he had received high-value donatives for a long period and it may be that as commander of a regiment, or some larger formation, he took part in Constantius's invasion of Britain (Casey & Tomlin, forthcoming). Here, for the first time, we have evidence for one of the minor characters in the drama advancing into the limelight of history.

There are no records of show trials or sanctions being imposed on the adherents of Allectus such as those which followed the fall of Magnentius in 353. On that occasion, as Ammianus Marcellinus records, a commission headed by Paul the Notary behaved with such merciless rigour that a governor committed suicide after a futile protest about the severity of the proceedings (Amm. xix, 5.1–3,6–8). The Panegyric of 297 implies that those who constituted the central core of the revolt fell with their leader, but the fact that he advanced to battle without the main body of his forces contradicts this statement and the execution of dissidents, especially if barbarian, can be expected to have taken place. The head of Allectus himself, easily identifiable because of the excellence of his coin portraits, would probably have been paraded around the army of Britain to ensure that pretenders could not rise in his name. Any laws passed by the usurpers, promotions made, contracts issued or treaties entered into would be revoked, rescinded or renegotiated.

The dispersal of forces may also have been a priority. We have already seen that some, or the bulk, of garrisons in the Pennines may have been replaced now or later but that forces on Hadrian's Wall remained as they had been before and during the revolt. The legions, now of very little strategic significance as major tactical units, continued to occupy the legionary fortress of York and, so far as is known, Chester. The accepted view that Constantius embarked on the building of large cavalry forts at Elslack and Newton Kyme (Yorkshire), and at Piercebridge (Co. Durham) needs to be re-examined in the light of the excavations at the last-named site. Here, extensive area excavation has examined, in detail, the south-east quarter, the east gate and the extensive defensive ditches of the fort. The stratified ceramic and numismatic evidence, which includes a silver coin of Carausius, are in agreement that the fort was built in the middle of the third century, not at the end (Scott, forthcoming). A programme of building during the Gallic Empire appears to have taken place which probably encompasses the other sites hitherto ascribed to Constantius. The abandonment of Caerleon may have been partly reversed but the evidence for forces being concentrated in the south Wales fortress is exiguous and may refer to a very much later period (Evans, 1992). In north Wales garrison forts appear to have been maintained.

Possibly the largest single military component of the forces awaiting relocation was the fleet. It is clear from the sources that Allectus deployed more than one fleet, though none of the naval forces contributed to his defence. They were, thus, intact at the end of the campaign. It may be at this stage that the British fleets, with their unrivalled accumulated knowledge of both coastal waters and the strategies of northern pirates, were allocated as tactical units to the individual Shore Forts. That naval forces were stationed at forts is clear from the *Notitia Dignitatum* where the *Classis Anderetianorum*, which derived its name from long service at Anderida/Pevensey, is shown as having been transferred to service on the Seine (ND.Occ.xlii.23). It might also be at this stage that the unified command of the coastal forts was created; whether fleets were deployed on the Continental side of the Channel is uncertain. The Panegyric of 297 claims that Constantius's victory had saved not only Britain but the whole of the Mediterranean region from pirate attack (*Pan. Lat.*viii(v).19). It is difficult to see how events in Britain could possibly influence maritime affairs in the Mediterranean. Contemporary marine technology allowed for coastal attacks in the Channel, but probably not a direct North Sea crossing to East Anglia.

PLATE 9

1 Diocletian. London mint.
Obv. *IMP C DIOCLETIANVS PF AVG* Rev. *GENIO POPVLI ROMANI* RIC 6a

2 Diocletian. London mint.
Obv. *IMP C DIOCLETIANVS PF AVG* Rev. *GENIO POPVLI ROMANI* – LON RIC 1a

3 Constantine I. London mint.
Obv. *FL VAL CONSTANTINVS NOB C* Rev. *ADVENTVS AVGG* – PLN RIC 82

4 'Carausius II'.
Obv. *DOMNO CARAVSIVS CES* Rev. *CONSTANTI* –
Overstruck on a coin of Constantine I similar to No.6

5 Constantius II. Lyons mint.
Obv. *DN CONSTANTIVS PF AVG* Rev. *FEL TEMP REPARATIO* RIC 189

6 Constantine I. Trier mint.
Obv. *CONSTANTINVS MAX AVG* Rev. *GLORIA EXERCITVS* – TRP RIC 525

7 Giovanni Pesaro. Silver ducatone Venice.
Obv. *S.M.VEN. IOAN. PISAVRO.D* Rev. *MEMOR. ER.O.TVI.IVSTINA.VIR*
The doge, Pesaro, kneels before the lion of St Mark/St Justina presiding over the ocean and the Venetian fleet.

1

2

3

4

5

6

7

a St Peter's Hill, London. Monumental foundations of Allectan date.

b St Peter's Hill, London. Monumental foundations with underpinning of tree-ring-dated oak piles.

c Milestone of Carausius from Gallow's Hill, Carlisle.

d Portchester Castle, Hants. The outer defences comprise the walls of the Saxon Shore Fort. The castle in the north-west corner was built in the Medieval period.

e Fourth-century boat from Nydam.

f The flight of Aeneas from Carthage depicted on the fourth-century mosaic from the Low Ham villa. The artists have taken as their model the warships familiar in British waters in the third and fourth centuries.

or the coast of Yorkshire. But it would be a bold or desperate pirate who would accept the challenge of the Bay of Biscay in an open boat. The passage might mean that British crews were dispersed as far afield as the Mediterranean, but it is more likely a piece of groundless hyperbole on the part of the panegyricist.

By the end of the fourth century the coastal defences, augmented by a number of forts on the coast of Gaul, were under the command of the Count of the Saxon Shore (*Comes Litoris Saxonici*). This officer is probably alluded to in an earlier context by the historian Ammianus Marcellinus who describes the death, in 367, of Nectaridus the *Comes Maritimi Tractus* in the barbarian attack on Britain mounted in that year (Amm.xx.1; xx.9,9). A count, as such, could not have been appointed as early as the late third century since the rank was only instituted by Constantine some fifteen years later. But the title, when conferred, presents a problem in itself because the command of frontier defence forces should have been at the subordinate rank of *dux*, especially as the *comes* had at his command many less troops than the *Dux Britanniarum*, disposing, as he did, of all the forces on the Wall, in the Pennines and at York (Mann, 1977). It is possible that the original command was vested in a *dux* and that the command was upgraded when the forts in Gaul were added. The mobility of the fleets may have been seen as a justification for regarding the command as being over all mobile forces such as constituted the tactical field armies of the period.

The suggestion that Portchester was abandoned in the period immediately following the fall of the British regime needs to be examined in the light of more extended numismatic studies. These indicate that coin issues of the period 296 to 305 are very rarely present as site finds in Britain, reflecting monetary events rather than the occupation pattern of individual sites (Cunliffe, 1975).

On Hadrian's Wall the inscriptions from Birdoswald and Housesteads show that work on the frontier was undertaken with immediate effect. The evidence from Birdoswald (RIB 1912) shows that, in the governorship of Aurelius Arpagius, equestrian governor of the northern province, the commanding officer's house, the baths and the headquarters buildings were restored (Fig.15). The commander's house had, indeed, fallen down and was covered in soil (*erat humo copertum*). Excavation has shown that other buildings were constructed, or reconstructed, at the same time, including barracks and new officers' quarters. The inscription from Housesteads (RIB 1316) is too fragmentary to allow interpretation of its contents.

Elsewhere in the north restoration of structures has been claimed at a number of sites based on stratigraphical relationships and on the widely held, and uncritical, belief that decay and destruction is attributable to the activities of hostile forces during the reigns of Carausius and Allectus. The reasoning behind these claims needs re-examination before acceptance. There is no doubt that improvements of accommodation, amenities and restoration of defences would have been included in any programme designed to raise

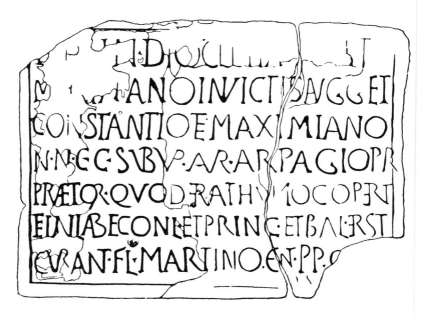

15 Tetrarchic building inscription from Birdoswald.

the effectiveness and morale of the northern garrisons following the fall of
their emperor (Breeze & Dobson, 1987). North of the Wall itself the outpost
forts which protected approach to the frontier are also assumed to have
received attention. At High Rochester (Bremenium) the west gate was
rebuilt in finely dressed masonry blocks and is usually attributed to the
aftermath of the British revolt; the headquarters building may also have
received attention. Inscriptional evidence for this is lacking, as it is for the
claimed restoration of barrack blocks at Risingham (Habitancum). Given
the recent detailed work on the dating of the latest occupation of the outpost
forts the date of unattributable structural changes is best regarded with
reserve (Casey, 1980, 1992). Indeed, given the evidence of a vigorous
building programme elsewhere in the island during the reigns of Carausius
and Allectus, there is no reason why some, or even the majority, of the
changes attributed to Constantius could not have been undertaken by his
enemies themselves. In a completely revisionist situation it could be pointed
out that the inscriptions attesting reconstruction are completion slabs, not
foundation stones, and may only relate to those in power when projects
were finished, not when they were commenced.

It is clear that the northern frontier of Britain, later events notwithstanding,
was not regarded as a high-priority zone. None of the forts were remodelled
in the style then current elsewhere in the empire, and exemplified by the
Shore Forts, with high walls and external towers providing overlapping

146

fields of fire; rather the traditional low-walled fortifications of the age of Hadrian were retained and maintained. Even completely rebuilt forts, such as Vindolanda (Chesterholm), which may have been reconstructed in this period and its entire axis turned through 180 degrees, retained the traditional shape and internal layout of buildings such as the granaries, headquarters and commandant's house. Elsewhere in the empire small fortifications, so-called *quadriburgi*, which were economical of garrisons, were a feature of the period but do not seem to have made their appearance in Britain.

On the other hand, it may be at this time, or earlier, that a new kind of barrack accommodation was introduced. The traditional barrack consisted of a series of pairs of double rooms, usually ten, arranged in line and accessible from a veranda. At the end of the block, and occupying about a third of the available space, was an apartment for the centurion. The new barracks, while retaining the linear scheme, provided individual 'chalets' rather than conjoined rooms: the centurion still retained his quarters at the end of the block (Daniels, 1980). The significance of these changes is as difficult to determine as the date of the introduction of the new style accommodation. Possibly it gave space for soldiers to live with their families within the confines of the fort.

In contrast to the view that the fall of Allectus brought disaster to northern Britain in its train is the fact that a relatively low-grade official was in charge of completing restoration work on the Wall. The policy of Diocletian and Maximian in provincial administration was to separate the civil administration from military command. That this policy had not been implemented in Britain by 305, the outside date for the Birdoswald inscription, indicates that no substantial threat was present on the frontier (Donaldson, 1990). The argument draws on analogies with the frontiers of Africa, which retained praesidial governors with military powers for a long period into the fourth century. Threats to these frontiers were what, in current military jargon, are called 'low intensity' – they normally suffered the depredations of cattle raiders and bandits rather than being the scene of potential or actual invasion by numerous and militarily organized enemies. It was therefore perfectly in order to leave them in the care of equestrian officials whose expertise was in the legal sphere rather than the military. In such circumstances, it is suggested, the employment of a high-grade military officer would have been supererogatory. It should be remembered, however, that it was in 306 that Constantius, by now no longer Caesar but emperor, crossed to Britain to campaign against the Picts.

It is in the areas of economy and the imperial administration that the citizen of post-Allectan Britain would have noticed the most immediate changes, and of all changes it was that in the pocket that would be soonest felt. While it cannot be proved formally that the money of the usurpers was declared unacceptable, it seems very likely since coins of Carausius and Allectus do not appear in hoards of the following period, with the exception of a single gold and two silver coins, no doubt valued for their metal. Vast numbers of coins of Carausius, and a proportionately plentiful number of Allectus, however, are found in excavations, by metal detecting and in unrecovered hoards. Lack of inscriptions precludes proof of *damnatio memoriae* in the form of erasures of the condemned names, though the milestone from near Carlisle survived long enough to be up-ended only in the early years of Constantine to receive an inscription of Constantine as Caesar (306–7). Possibly in a remote area, the stone was overlooked until repairs were carried out on that stretch of road. In any event, the otherwise complete absence of epigraphic material is, in itself, a significant pointer to the extirpation of memorials of the fallen regime.

In 294/6 the Diocletianic administration launched a reform of the billon currency in which all local currencies were brought to an end and, for the first time, a uniform monetary system was in use from one end of the empire to the other. This followed earlier adjustments to the *aureus*, issued at a weight of 5.4g, and the introduction of a *c*.3.4g silver denomination in *c*.293. The main change in the billon was the phasing out of the *aurelianus*, which was no longer issued but still accepted, and the introduction of new denomination of about 10g weight and about 3 per cent silver content (Pl.9, nos 1, 2). Without ancient warrant the coin is called the *follis*; but evidence does exist to show that it was tariffed as a 10-*denarius* piece, later to be retarrifed to 20-*denarii* (Cope, 1977). The new coin was issued, with uniform weight and type (*GENIO POPVLI ROMANI* – 'The Genius of the Roman People'), from mints established in nearly all of the *dioceses* into which, under new administrative arrangements, the empire had been divided. The system of mint and sequence marks introduced by Carausius was adopted in the new coinage. Additional minor denominations were also issued: a copper *denarius* and a larger radiate copper coin, similar in appearance to the old *aurelianus* and intended as a 2-*denarius* piece. Neither of these coins appears in British contexts and they cannot have formed an important component of the local circulating medium.

Hoard evidence shows that the coinage of Britain after the reconquest consisted of diminishing numbers of *aureliani*, never supplied in quantity in the first place, and the new 10-*denarius* coin. The latter is not well represented in site finds but this absence should not be taken as indicating a shortage of coin; rather it reflects the relative value of the coin and its size and ease of recovery when dropped. Nevertheless, the high value of the main denomination in the currency pool was the equivalent of a demonetization of some areas of the economy, which could only have been made good by an extension of credit to individuals in small transactions. In this credit system the 'slate' could be cleared when transaction volume and available coin denomination reached equilibrium. At the same time, a general rise in prices to boundaries set by the new coins may have taken place, if modern experience of changes such as decimalization is pertinent to the ancient world. In compensation the reintegration of Britain into a world currency system allowed British trade to expand into foreign markets.

It may also have encouraged the movement of capital from overseas into an area relatively unaffected by the problems of barbarian population movements and near constant warfare. Some of the prosperity of the agricultural community, with the growth of large villas attested in the fourth century, may owe something to the redistribution of the assets of adherents of the rebels. Certainly, by the date of the publication of the Edict of Maximum Prices in 301 the costs of British textiles were advertised in the eastern provinces of the empire; by the first quarter of the fourth century Britain was experiencing an economic boom.

One branch of industry which did flourish during the usurpation was shipbuilding. It is probably in this period that the tradition of expertise was established which enabled Julian to build his grain fleet half a century later and which produced the warships whose deployment against sea raiders was noted with approval by Vegetius in his work on military tactics (Veg. 37).

The mechanism for the introduction of the new coinage is not known but the production of the mint of Lugdunum (Lyons) was stepped up to supply the island economy. At the same time as the mint established by Carausius at London was maintained and immediately assumed production of the new denomination, the Colchester mint was closed. The skilled mint personnel working at London under Allectus were kept in their jobs; the distinctive work of individual die-cutters can be easily recognized in the last coins of Allectus and the new London issues in the names of Diocletian, Maximian and the Caesars (Pl.9, no.1) (Carson & Kent, 1956).

Administrative changes were also implemented. The empire, already divided between eastern and western emperors, was further divided into compact administrative units, or prefectures. These, in turn, comprised a number of smaller units, *dioceses*, which were themselves made up of groups of individual provinces. The latter proliferated under Diocletian, with traditional provinces being cut up into ever smaller components. The case of Britain well illustrates the process. Divided in two by Severus, on the fall of Allectus Britain consisted of Britannia Inferior and Britannia Superior. The latter comprised the west, Midlands and south-east, with a capital in London; the former, with a capital at York, encompassed the Pennines and the north – the bulk of the military forces were located in this province. On reunification Britain was divided into four provinces – Britannia Prima (Wales and the west), Britannia Secunda (the north), Maxima Caesariensis (the south) and Flavia Caesariensis (the Midlands and East Anglia). The latter two provinces received their recorded names in the reign of Constantine, and bore different, but probably dynastic, names in the period under review (Casey, 1978). Each province was governed by an equestrian *praeses*, and each had its own capital; respectively Cirencester, York, London and Lincoln. The governors were subordinate to a *vicarius* who administered the newly created *diocese* of Britain. The *diocese* was a component of the Prefecture of the Gauls, the *vicarius* being subordinate to the praetorian prefect who, in turn, was responsible for the Caesar – the latter owing responsibility to the emperor.

A gradual division was made between military and civil spheres, the military commanders and provincial governors having separate functions. Virtually the last *praeses* with military responsibilities for whom we have a record is the Aurelius Arpagius who appears on the Birdoswald inscription and whose significance in Britain is discussed above.

Almost coincidental with the recovery of Britain came the introduction of a new system of taxation. Monetary taxation was largely abandoned in favour of levies of goods and services graded to the estimated needs of the imperial army. In 296, a census was undertaken on a scale which makes the Domesday survey look like a minor administrative exercise. The productive value of every economic process and resource in the empire was reviewed and tax levied in relation to productivity. Thus less-productive soil was taxed at a lesser rate than highly productive soil, whether arable land, orchard, vineyard or whatever. The unit of assessment was the *caput* or productivity of a man and his assets, including wife, children, dependants, slaves and livestock relative to the estimated productivity of these assets. The tax liability of individuals would be rated in terms of multiple *capita*, the poorest paying only a fraction of a unit. The individual's liability to tax was subsumed into the estimate for his community, village or city; this in turn was aggregated into the levy for the province, the *diocese* and, ultimately, the Prefecture. Estimates of the requirements of the army were prepared by the praetorian prefect, originally on a five-year and later at a fifteen-year cycle. Special levies, or superindictions, were imposed in case of emergency or shortfall. As a further economy the management of the taxation and its collection was imposed on the magistrates of the individual towns, shortfalls having to be made up from their own resources. All of this brought the individual into a contact with the provincial administration in a way never before experienced. Serving soldiers were not subjected to these tax levies but their sons were compelled to enrol in the army.

If there had been a national consciousness engendered by the Carausian regime or its successor it is likely to have been quickly dissipated by the events outlined above. Britain was now several fragments of a larger polity. This may explain the eagerness with which it embraced later usurpers such as Magnus Maximus who offered it an imperial identity. The Panegyric of 297 offers an official view of the rapture with which Constantius was greeted by the citizens of London:

> ...the moment you reached the shore, a triumphant procession met
> Your Majesty as you deserved; the Britons, jumping for joy, with
> their wives and children presented themselves, not merely falling down
> to worship you yourself, whom they regarded as coming down from
> heaven, but even the sails and oars of that ship, which had brought to
> them your divinity, and they were ready to throw themselves upon
> the ground and thus feel your coming. And no wonder they were

elated with such joy, after the outrages committed upon their wives, after the degrading servitude of their children they were at length free, at length Roman, at length refreshed by the true light of the empire.... They devoted themselves and their children to you both [i.e. Maximian], to your children they devoted all their posterity.

(*Pan. Lat.*viii(v).19)

Though the deliverer of this unctuous speech could not know it, he was right in one particular: Britain developed a strong affection for the House of Constantius as embodied in his son Constantine. When Constantius died at York in 306, while campaigning in the north against the Picts, the army rose in support of Constantine and, despite the prevailing constitutional arrangements which excluded him from imperial office, elected him emperor. Nineteen years later, after civil wars fought in Italy, the Balkans and the East, he became sole ruler of the Roman empire.

But the joy of the citizens may have been less wholeheartedly rapturous than the panegyricist thought, or cared to mention. We have said that, in introducing the new coinage system, Docletian and his colleague adopted the Carausian system of mintmarks. The first issue of the new coins from London, produced by Allectus's staff in the first few weeks of the operation of the mint under the restored administration, bears the mintmark LON; it is an issue of great scarcity, with less than twenty specimens recorded in the standard numismatic corpora (Pl.9, no.2). The following issue bears no mintmark nor does any coinage issued by London until the year 307, when the mark was restored in the form PLN; it was in this year that Constantine visited London, coins being issued with the type and legend, *ADVENTVS AVGG* (Pl.9, no.3), appropriate to a state visit (Casey, 1978). The restoration of the mintmark in conjunction with the presence of Constantine may indicate that London had lost its municipal, or colonial, status within a few weeks of Constantius's arrival in the capital and did not regain it until the visit of his son a decade later. If this is so, it can only be as a result of something connected with events following the overthrow of Allectus. Could it be that the people of London rained tiles down on Constantius rather than flowers and garlands?

There is a strange coda to the revolt of Carausius and Allectus which finds it setting in the lamp-lit depths of the Catacomb of St Mark and St Marcellus, just outside Rome. During the persecution initiated by Diocletian in 303 some Christians appear to have used the catacomb as a refuge. Here, surrounded by two centuries of Christian dead, they took their minds off their present troubles by gambling. With them they had a board for playing *ludus duodecim scriptores* – 'The Game of Twelve Lines' (Huelson, 1904). Evidence for the popularity of this game has been found on sites all over the Roman empire both in the form of portable boards and others scratched on the flagstones in public places. The board is set out with 36 'points' arranged in 12 vertical lines. Often the 'points' are the individual letters of six-letter words, of which a set of six make up a suitable motto. An example, in bad Latin, from North Africa reads:

VENARI — LAVARI
LVDERE — RIDERE
OCCEST — VIVARE
'TO HUNT — TO BATHE/TO PLAY — TO LAUGH/THIS IS — TO LIVE'

The board from the catacomb reads:

PARTHI — OCCISI
BRITTO — VICTVS
LVDITE — ROMANI
'PARTHIANS — KILLED/BRITON — DEFEATED/PLAY — ROMANS'

The combination of a Parthian victory with one over a Briton fixes the events commemorated on the board very precisely to the triumph of Galerius over the Persians and Constantius over Allectus. By a curious irony it was only after the defeat of Allectus in the West and the Persian enemy in the East that Diocletian could afford to divert the resources of the state to the elimination of a perceived internal enemy, Christianity.

• 12 •

SHIPS AND NAVAL WARFARE

THE EVENTS SURROUNDING THE REGIMES of Carausius and Allectus all hinge on the possession and deployment of overwhelming naval forces. A simple listing of the main events makes the point clear. It was the demise of Roman naval power with the running down and eventual abolition of the *Classis Britannica* which led to the growth of piracy in northern waters. As a result Carausius raised a fleet to extirpate these pirates. The loss of Maximian's invasion fleet cost him parts of northern Gaul and gave his opponents full control of the western seaboard of the empire. In turn the interdiction of a relieving fleet cost the British regime Boulogne. The invasion of Britain waited upon the raising of two fleets by the central empire and the success of the invasion depended upon the misuse by Allectus of his fleet. At every turn the control of naval forces is the key to success or failure and the physical and tactical nature of these forces should be considered.

Unfortunately, very little is known about the nature of the opposing forces. Despite the growth of underwater archaeology and the investigation of a number of ancient wrecks, no warships of the third and early fourth centuries have yet been discovered. Any information we have about the appearance and armament of the craft engaged in the events under review has to be garnered from contemporary illustrations and later literary sources.

Of some things we can be sure from the general advance in knowledge which has come with underwater archaeology. For instance, the ancient world had two distinct traditions of naval architecture. In the Mediterranean ships were built on the shell principle, while in the north-western provinces they were frame-constructed in a fashion which has its antecedents in native Celtic practices. The difference between methods is fundamental: in the former the planking of the hull, the strakes, are fitted together edge to edge with tenons, the shape of the boat being achieved by bending and warping the strakes. Only when a hull shape is achieved are ribs inserted to strengthen the total structure. Boats with tenoned planks do not need caulking since the close fit of the edges of the timbers, combined with their expansion when immersed, creates a watertight hull. In the northern Romano-Celtic tradition the shape of the boat is determined by a completely pre-formed framework of keel and ribs to which the strakes are individually attached. The bulk of Roman period vessels known from north-western Europe also have the strakes laid edge to edge, with long nails employed to secure the planking to the frames (Marsden, 1990; Rule, 1990), but because the individual strakes are not joined together to give a waterproof seal it is necessary to caulk the seams of these vessels. An advantage of this method of frame-building is that it allows a broader limit of tolerance to be set in construction and less skilled workmanship can be deployed. This might be counted as a consideration when fleets had to be built in haste.

The main source of illustration for the naval vessels operating in the Channel and the North Sea in the late Roman period is the contemporary coinage. Both the coins of Carausius and Allectus, especially the latter, depict the ships on which their power was based, and two issues of the Continental emperors bear military vessels as parts of their reverse types; they also make an appearance on the coins and medallions of Maximian and Constantius and on a fourth-century mosaic in the villa at Low Ham, in Somerset (Pl. f). The largest aggregation of warships is found in the bronze coinage of the Gallic emperor Postumus (259–68), though the representations are of poor artistic quality, displaying little evidence that the artists were familiar with what they were trying to depict. Military transports which must have made up a large part of the various invasion fleets attested by the literary sources and specialized craft (*hippagines*) would have been needed to transport cavalry horses and draught animals. A vessel of this type is depicted on a mosaic with representations of 30 different named types of Roman ships, of second-century date, from Althibunis in Tunisia (Gauckler, 1905). The *hippago*, complete in this case with a cargo of named racehorses, displays a number of features: there is no mast or sail and no steering oar, propulsion is provided by six sweeps – three on each side. Normally a vessel of this type would be towed by a troop transport and the ropes stowed along the gunwales may represent towlines (Fig. 16).

Before considering the evidence in detail, a number of points pertinent to the interpretation of coin iconography may be noted. Firstly, specific details vary from coin to coin even when the same object is depicted. This is especially so in the case of large coin issues, where many sets of dies would have been needed to keep up with the demands of the mint's output. Where more than one mint is engaged in the work, discrepancies can be expected between the imagery produced by the separate establishments. In reconstructing the appearance of a vanished monument or lost work of art scholars examine as many specimens of the coinage as possible in order to assemble a composite image. The same principles should be applied when attempting to reconstruct the appearance of the battle-ships of the later Roman navy.

Secondly, the physical nature of the coin must be considered. In itself the circular area of a coin flan does not lend itself to the accurate representation of the linear features of a ship, while, in certain circumstances, the presence of the legend further circumscribes the area available to the artist, producing a truncated version of the object delineated. We may illustrate this point from the coinage of Allectus who issued ship coins with two reverse

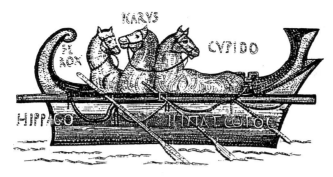

16 Transporting horses by sea in a *hippago*.

egends — *VIRTUS AUG* and *LAETITIA AUG*. The longer inscription fills the flan
and ships on coins with this legend are always represented as short, stubby
vessels (Pl.8, nos 3,5). The former, shorter, legend is normally placed in an
arc around the top of the flan only. On these coins the ships are depicted
as long and racy vessels (Pl.8, no.4), but when the *VIRTUS AUG* legend is
deployed in an extended form around the coin, the ship is depicted as being
a squat craft with an improbably bow-shaped hull (Pl.8, no.5). It follows
that the long, rakish image is nearer to being a true likeness of the
contemporary vessels.

The disposition of the image on the coin also imposes problems where
crucial details of one element of the design would detrimentally impinge
on another. The Arras Medallion shows a warship representative of the fleet
with which Constantius invaded Britain (Pl.7, no.4): the ship is crammed
with soldiers and propelled by oars; there is no mast, sail, cordage or rigging.
The panegyric which celebrates the successful recovery of the island speaks
eloquently about this fleet and its reception by the people of London and
it makes specific mention of the fact that the ships were provided with sails.
Further, the account of Constantius's departure from Boulogne says that he
was delayed by contrary winds, a point which would be valueless were the
ships not dependent as much on sails as oars for their propulsion. The
absence of these features from the medallion is entirely due to the presence
immediately above the boat of the mounted figure of Constantius.

Viewed as a whole the images of ships on coins of the period exhibit a
number of common characteristics. All, when a mast is represented, are
single-masted vessels. On the coins of Carausius and Allectus the mast is
rigged fore and aft with stays; on the single example of a rigged ship in the
coins of Postumus the stays are absent, but the yardarm, with the single sail
reefed up to the yard, is represented (Pl.8, no.7); a vestigial yardarm is also
shown on a coin of Carausius (Pl.2, no.11). Neither yards nor sails are
normally shown on the coins of the British usurpers, though the presence
of the mast ensures that they were in use. These coins also show that the

mast was capped with a truck, which may have housed a pulley-block to assist in raising and lowering the sail. None of the ships displays a bowsprite. This was a feature typical of imperial galleys of the first and second centuries, being provided to carry a small sail which served as an aid to steering. The ships have a high prow which sweeps down to a formidable ram. The prow is occasionally incurved towards the mast but is mostly shown as boldly outcurved, to terminate in a figurehead reminiscent of the dragon prows of later Viking boats. There may have been a change in shipbuilding practices between the middle and end of the third century since all of Postumus's ships are depicted with incurved prows. The stern is higher than the prow with the curve of the timbers terminating in a decorative fantail or *aplustrum*. The exaggerated height and curvature of the stern is probably due to a well-grounded fear of being pooped, a situation in which the sea overwhelms the vessel from the rear. As with all ancient vessels, steering was effected by large steering oars fixed on either side of the stern. These oars were operated by the steersman through a pair of bar helms which transmitted a push–pull motion into a rotational force operating on the steering mechanism.

All of the ships are depicted with a single bank of oars. These are represented in various numbers almost certainly unrelated to the actual provision of the real craft. It is not known whether the oars were operated by a single rower or by a number of men manning the same oar. Ancient warships were rated either by the number of banks of oars or the number of rowers deployed to each oar and confusion can arise as to whether ancient authors were referring to the number of banks of oars or the number of oarsmen (Morrison, 1980). The main visible armament is provided by a ram protruding from the bow. The marine crew, not the rowers, are normally shown lining the bulwarks; on Postumus's coins the marines are shown carrying large round shields (Pl.8, no.8).

An element common to warships of this period, which distinguishes them from merchant ships, is the presence of the *parados*, or side gangway. This created a lateral extension of deck-space to port and starboard which oversailed the hull in the same manner as the deck of an aircraft carrier. This feature is normally shown as a long, box-like object, extending along the gunwales; the oars protrude from the hull below the *parados*. It had a number of functions – first-century sculptures show boarding parties standing on the extension, ready to descend on the enemy – but most importantly the *parados* offered protection to the oars by preventing attacking vessels running alongside and breaking off the blades. The rowers were protected from the enemy missiles by the deck and in action they would have had no visual contact with events outside the hull space of their own vessel. More vulnerable than the oarsmen was the helmsman who occupied a prominent and unprotected position on the deck just in front of the canopied deckhouse accommodating the captain or navigator. Undoubtedly every ship carried a number of trained steersmen in order to maintain a 24-hour watch as well as to replace casualties in action.

The dimensions of the warships of the late third and fourth centuries, the size of their crews and the number of oarsmen employed are all unknown. All illustrations are schematic to a greater or lesser extent and the only archaeological evidence for shipping is derived from merchant vessels. Of these, both the boat from Blackfriars, in London, and that from St Peter's Port, in Guernsey, were about 20m long and about 6m broad at the widest part of the hull. But cargo vessels are designed for their carrying capacity rather than for manoeuvrability and speed, thus they do not give a good impression of the rakish lines of a warship. In any event, we know from later literary sources that the Roman navy employed a number of types of warships which varied in crew complement and function.

A misapprehension as to the height of the warship above the waterline has been perpetuated by modern scholars who have misinterpreted the artistic convention of showing the full depth of the hull above the waterline in order to display the main armament – the ram (Dove, 1971). Since to be effective the ram must have been below or at the waterline the most prominent feature of a warship cannot be shown unless the whole vessel is presented unnaturally high in the water. There is no reason whatsoever for supposing that these ships rode high in the water or that they towered above the surface like eighteenth-century men-of-war. Indeed the episode recounted by Caesar, in which the standard-bearer of the Tenth Legion spurred his reluctant comrades to land on British soil by jumping from a ship to the hostile shore, indicates that Roman warships were low in the water (Caesar, De Bello Gallico, iv. 25). In the case of vessels with single banks of oars, the lower they are in the hull and the nearer parallel to the surface of the sea, the better for energy efficiency. A specific reference to the above-waterline size of Mark Antony's warships at the Battle of Actium mentions that they stood ten feet high in the water; there is reason to believe that this refers to the largest ships engaged in the encounter (Casson, 1971, 117).

Beyond the discussion of Carausius's tactical methods in dealing with the pirates by catching them on their return from raiding in Gaul, we have no specific information regarding the deployment or tactics used by the protagonists in the Carausian episode. For the pirate episode some indication of the sort of Germanic ships of the period can be derived from the burial of a complete vessel at Nydam, in Denmark. This open boat was propelled entirely by rowers with provision for 15 pairs or 30 single oarsmen in its 23m length (Pl. e). The date of the Nydam ship is put by archaeologists into the period AD 350–400, a little later than the Carausian period but none the less a pertinent piece of maritime evidence: the absence of mast and sail makes sense of Carausius's strategy of interception of the enemy when it was fully loaded since, in the long term, the crew of a heavily laden vessel such as the Nydam ship could not outpace a galley equipped with sail and oars. This is especially the case in the Channel where the prevailing wind in the sailing season is from the south west, and it elucidates the tactics for which Carausius was originally condemned.

A little evidence about barbarian shipping can be gleaned from ancien literary sources, including a late Latin translation of Josephus which offer some insights. This translation of the Greek text of Flavius Josephus's *Wa of the Jews* has been attributed to St Ambrose because the manuscript wa preserved in Milan. Actually the translation is the work of Isaac, a Jewis convert to Christianity, who took the baptismal names Hilarius an Gaudentius. Further authorial confusion has arisen because the nam Hegesippus became attached to the manuscript at some stage; this name a Latinized corruption of 'Josephus'. The translation was made in the 37c and is interpolated with a number of anachronistic references to Christianit and to the state of the Roman empire in the age of the emperor Valentinia (368–75).

There are two set-piece orations which are comprehensive reviews of th state and progress of the Roman empire. The occasion for each of th speeches is a fictitious attempt by a member of the Herodian royal hous to dissuade the Jews from rebelling against the Romans. The first is mad before the revolt by Berenice, the sister of Herod Agrippa. The second delivered to the defenders of Jerusalem by Herod Agrippa himself as the await the outcome of the siege being conducted by Titus. Both take th same form: a review of the expansion of the empire and a summary of th fierce peoples brought under Roman subjugation. The author of thes interpolations is very concerned with events in Britain, twice citing th conquest of this remotest of lands as proof of the folly of standing again the might and persistence of the Roman state.

The speeches contain two references to piratical ships operating in norther waters in the fourth century. The first occurs in a discussion of the suppressio of German piracy in which it is observed that the Rhine is no longer fille with '*caupulis Germanorum . . . sed Romanorum liburnis*' (Heg. 11.9,1 *liburni* are the heavier Roman warships of the period. The word *caupuli* cannot be closely defined technically, but is always used in the context c a light craft. The discovery of a number of Roman wrecks in a branch c the Rhine at Mainz included a light war galley, which could have bee adapted from a native prototype. A tentative reconstruction of this vesse which might qualify as being a *caupulus*, shows it with a triangular sail an manned by 26 rowers (Haywood, 1991). The vessel was undoubtedl employed in patrolling the river frontier of the Rhine but was strongl enough constructed to survive inshore seas.

The second reference to barbarian shipping discussed the boats of th Saxons who, because of the success of Roman arms, tremble with fear i their inaccessible marshlands and hidden fortifications from which the formerly conducted stealthy war in their *myoparones*.

Myoparon, and its plural *myoparones*, has a long history in Latin literatur as representing a light craft. The word, of Greek origin and of unknow etymology, came to mean a pirate vessel by the late Roman period. Earlie uses of the word indicate that *myoparones* could be substantial ships, though less formidable than regular warships. Thus Mark Antony in exchange for two legions gave Octavian 100 'bronze beaked galleys' and 26 craft – *myoparonas* (Plutarch, *Antony*, 35). In the Mithradatic wars the Pontic king recruited Cilician pirates in his cause who, after his defeat, continued to ravage the eastern Mediterranean. In the beginning they sailed around with a few small boats' (*skaphesi = scaphae*). But as their success grew they graduated to larger ships. 'They harvested the sea instead of the land, at first with *myoparosi* and *hemiolii*, then with two-banked and three-banked ships [i.e. biremes and triremes]' (Appian, *Mithridates*, 92). From this it is clear that *myoparones* were larger than scout boats (*scaphae*) but smaller than regular naval vessels.

Cicero twice mentions *myoparones*. In the first case he describes the best of the ten vessels built by the city of Miletus as part of their tribute as being *ipse myoparonum pulcherrimum*, 'that handsome vessel'. This ship was sold by the venal Verres to two dubious characters, later declared to be public enemies, who used it to maintain contact between dissidents in Spain and Mithridates of Pontus. This involved voyages between eastern Spain and Sinope, situated half way along the south coast of the Black Sea. While this might suggest a vessel of considerable size and seaworthiness, further consideration would suggest that surreptitious communication by sea would best be accomplished by an inconspicuous boat rather than a fully-fledged warship and that Cicero has overstated his case in seeking the condemnation of Verres (Cicero, *Against Verres*, i. 34, 87). The second appearance of *myparones*, in a very literal sense, is when, due to Verres' neglect of his duties as governor of Sicily, pirates arrived with a few ships (*paucorum . . . myoparonum*) and set fire to the Roman fleet of warships (Cicero, *Against Verres*, ii. iii. 80, 186).

The bulk of references indicate that the vessel in question is associated with pirates, or the word is used to describe ships used by disreputable characters for sinister purposes, but apart from the relative size, no specific details are vouchsafed as to appearance or equipment in the literary accounts. Fortunately, a picture of a Roman *myoparon* is extant which shows it to have been equipped with a mast and sail, as well as oars. The Althibunis mosaic includes a *myoparon* among its array of shipping. It differs from the bulk of vessels by having a distinctive bow which lacks the normal upswept prow (Fig. 17). This suggests that its use was restricted to inshore and river work rather than being suitable for breasting the waves of deep waters. It is probably in this descriptive context that the term is applied to Saxon raiding craft, as well as in the context of their size.

Our specific knowledge of late Roman naval affairs largely depends on a single source – a late fourth-century writer on military tactics, Publius Flavius Vegetius Renatus, whose sources for his *De rei militari* stretched back to the time of the Roman Republic. None the less, we can use his work with some confidence since, unlike land-based warfare and armies,

MYOPARO

17   The Roman *myoparonis*, a light craft favoured by pirates.

naval warfare tactics between technologically equally matched forces did not change between the Hellenistic period, when effective catapult artillery was developed, and the invention of the seaborne flame-thrower by the Byzantines in the seventh century. Several lines of attack were possible, notably ramming, boarding and destruction by bombardment, with catapults hurling stone shot, incendiary material or fire arrows. At close quarters the crews would exchange fire with bows, javelins and slings, and grappling-hooks were thrown, or possibly fired. Ships might also be equipped with a long beam or pole, shod with an iron point at either end, which was hung by ropes from the rigging. This could be swung about in safety by the attacker to disable members of the crew of an enemy vessel held alongside by grapples. Vegetius describes this device, the *asser*, as especially effective in close-quarters actions, being 'a sure method of cutting down and killing enemy marines and sailors' (Veg.46). The *falx*, or sickle, was an alternative version of this contrivance. This weapon was equipped with a sharp, curved iron blade. Vegetius comments that 'It quickly cuts the rigging from which the yard-arm is suspended, and the sails collapse rendering the warship slow and useless' (Veg.46).

Because ships' crews had relatively little space in which to dodge missiles, extra protection in the form of larger shields and heavier armour was issued to marines. A favourite weapon among sailors was the double-ended axe which was especially effective for hand-to-hand fighting in confined spaces and for cutting grapples and rigging; a preferred tactic was to cut away the ropes securing the steering gear.

Vegetius also makes specific allusion to the ships and tactics employed in British waters to defeat piratical attacks in his own day; these tactics may

The Story

OF

CARAUSIUS,

The Dutch Augustus and Emperor of Britain & the Seas;

AND OF

Holland's Mighty Share in the Defeat

OF THE

INVINCIBLE ARMADA:

LIKEWISE,

The Lives of the Dutch Admirals,

FROM THEIR

MONUMENTS AND THE MEDALS

Erected to their Memory and Struck in their Honor

BY THE

"Dierbaar Vaderland,"

COLLECTED, COLLATED AND TRANSLATED

BY A

Descendant of that Race

WHO

ONCE GAVE AN AUGUSTUS TO THE WORLD AND AN EMPEROR TO BRITAIN;

—CARAUSIUS, A. D. 285-'7—292-'4—

TWICE PRESERVED THE RELIGION AND LIBERTY OF ENGLAND;

—IN 1588 AND IN 1688—

THRICE PLAYED A DECISIVE PART IN ALBION'S GREATEST NAVAL TRIUMPHS;

—AT SLUYS, 1340; LA HOGUE, 1692; AND ALGIERS, 1816—

EVER MAINTAINED THE INDEPENDENCE OF THE ANGLO OR

True Saxon Family,

AND

COMPELLED TYRANTS TO RESPECT THE RIGHTS OF MAN;

WHOSE REPRESENTATIVES

The Dutch Nation,

MADE THE WIDE WORLD THE WITNESS OF THEIR GRANDEUR; SPLENDOR WHICH KNEW NO LIMITS BUT THE POLES, THE ZENITH AND THE DEPTH OF THAT ELEMENT

UPON WHICH

THEY

FOUNDED THEIR STATE AND HARVESTED THEIR WEALTH:

A Race to Whom the Ocean was a Friend, an Ally, a Preserver, and a Benefactor;

WON BY THEIR PATIENT VIGOR, AND RETAINED BY THEIR VALOR AND ENTERPRISE.

PLATT & SCHRAM, PRINTERS, POUGHKEEPSIE.
1858.

g The title page of G. Watts de Peyster's work on Carausius.

h   The death of a hero: the eighteenth-century view of the assassination of
Carausius. (E. Barnard, *The new, comprehensive and complete history of
England...*, London, 1783.)

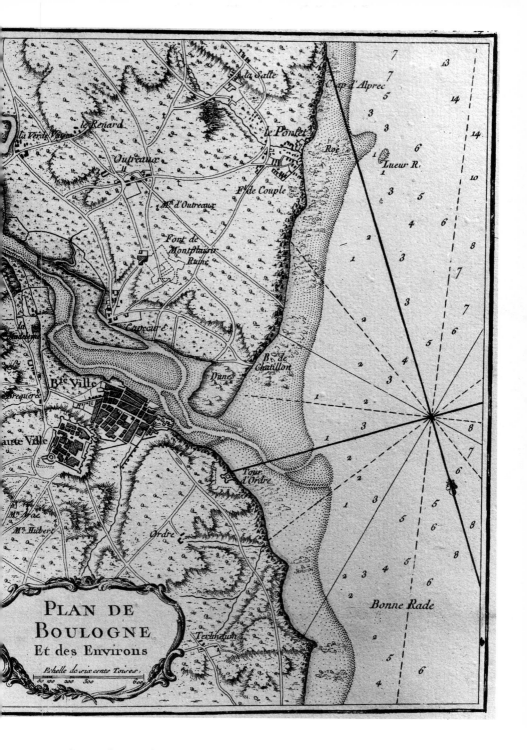

i Boulogne: the port and estuary in the eighteenth century.

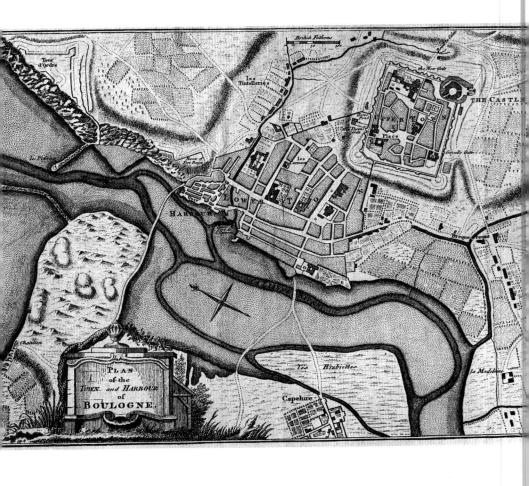

j Boulogne: the port and setting of the Roman fortress.

also be relevant in an earlier period. Having described the classification of warships by the number of ranks of oars, a specification of mere antiquarian interest in his own day, he notes that:

> ...scouting skiffs [*scaphae*] are attached to the large warships, having about twenty oarsmen on each side; these the Britons call *picati*. They are used on occasion to perform descents or to intercept convoys of enemy ships or by studious surveillance to detect their approach or intentions. Lest patrol vessels be betrayed by their brightness, the sails and rigging are dyed Venetian blue, which resembles the ocean waves; the wax used to pay the ships' sides is also dyed. The sailors and marines put on Venetian blue uniforms also, so as to lie hidden with greater ease when scouting by day as by night. (Veg.37)

It is unfortunate that the word *picati* represents a garbled item in the manuscript but most commentators agree to amend the text to *pictae* – painted (boats) – in reference to their being camouflaged. Another name used to designate a class of warships by Vegetius is *liburnae*. In the early imperial period this term was reserved for light, swift warships equipped with two banks of oars but by the late Roman period the *liburna* seems to be any warship larger than a scout craft; a usage probably reflecting the demise of the large battleship of the earlier empire. It seems likely that the vessels depicted on the coins from the time of Postumus to the end of the episode under consideration should be identified as *liburnae*. The scout craft itself may be shown on issues of Allectus in the shape of a small, mastless boat manned by rowers (Pl.8, no.2). Vegetius's description of the relation of the skiffs to the larger ships suggests that the latter normally only went to sea when an enemy had been detected. Ancient warships did not usually stay out at sea or, at best, hugged the coastline.

Even the greatest naval battles before the age of steam took place at walking pace and the ships of antiquity were no greyhounds of the ocean. Recorded speeds of voyages give some indication of their sailing capabilities, but all of the extant references are to voyages in the Mediterranean where conditions are much more favourable than in the North Sea. Even so, with a favourable wind, speeds of about four knots seems to have been regarded as highly satisfactory progress and something in the region of two knots may have been the norm. Possibly warships were capable of slightly higher speeds. The effect of rowing is more difficult to quantify. Reports of the speeds achieved by the replica of a Greek trireme, a vessel specifically designed to ram the enemy at high speed, indicate that seven knots could have been achieved for short periods. It is unlikely that vessels of the Carausian period could match this. Nor would oar power be as effective in the swells of the North Sea as in the calm waters of the Mediterranean, and the fact that ships are normally shown with masts erect probably accurately reflects the primacy of sail power. Rowing would normally be reserved for battle manoeuvres, periods of windless calm and entering and leaving harbour.

A compelling picture of savage and desperate fighting emerges as characteristic of late Roman naval warfare with the deployment of tactics which had been refined by five centuries of development. 'What could be crueller', says Vegetius, 'than a naval battle, where men perish by fire and water' (Veg.35).

· 13 ·

CARAUSIUS II

IN THE MIDDLE OF THE fourth century the Prefecture of the Gauls experienced a dramatic series of events which had a great impact on the economic and political life of the area. One of the results of these events was the production of coins which once again bore the name Carausius. Let us look at the history of the period before turning to this enigmatic coinage.

Following the death of Constantine the Great in May 337 there was an interregnum during which the two halves of the dead emperor's family fought for supremacy. The situation arose from the two marriages of Constantius I – his marriage to Theodora, the emperor Maximian's stepdaughter, meant that Constantine had many half-brothers, and half-sisters, as well as nephews and nieces. Constantine himself was the product of Constantius's marriage to Helena, a marriage which was annulled when union with the families of Maximian and Diocletian became politically expedient. The rejected Helena took every opportunity given by the ascendancy of her doting son to vent her displeasure on the other half of the family. When the time came to make detailed plans for the succession, Constantine allotted parts of the empire to his three sons and to two of his nephews from the Theodora branch of the family. Constantine II was to rule Britain, Gaul and Spain; Constantius II would have the East and Egypt; Italy and the bulk of the Balkan provinces went to Constans. The nephews, Dalmatius and Hannibalianus, were to rule, respectively, Thrace, Dacia and Macedonia and Cappodocia and Pontus. By this Constantine attempted to bring about unity in the warring family. It was not to be. Constantius II in collusion with his brothers instigated the massacre of the other half of the family. Two uncles and seven cousins were killed by troops in Constantinople loyal to the brothers. Two members survived – the half-brothers Constantius Gallus and Julian – the former spared because he was sick, and presumably expected to die, the latter because he was a five-year-old child. Both were detained under conditions of house arrest on imperial estates in the centre of Asia Minor.

Within a couple of years Constantine II and Constans were at war. During an invasion of Italy Constantine was killed, leaving Constans as ruler of the western empire. In 348 the two remaining brothers celebrated the eleven hundredths anniversary of the foundation of Rome and the inception of a new *saeculum*, the third in Rome's history and the last according to the prophecies of the Sybilline oracles. Among the other events heralding the new age was the reform of the lower value coinage system. Three new denominations were issued, two of billon and a third of copper, comprising a unit, its half and its third. All denominations bore the legend FEL TEMP REPARATIO ('The Restoration of the Happiness of the Times') and a variety of symbols of renewal or victory (Pl.9, no.5).

In 350 Constans was overthrown and killed in a coup by Magnentius, a part-British army officer who was acting for Marcellinus, the emperor's *Comes Sacrarum Largitionum*. Magnentius associated his brother Decentius in his rule which, at its furthest extent, included Italy. Magnentius was defeated by Constantius at the battle of Mursa in Illyricum in 351. Retreating to the west he was defeated in Gaul in 353 and both he and his brother committed suicide.

Thus in 353 the empire was again reunited and under the rule of a single emperor, Constantius II. Constantius had no children and an understandably paranoid disposition. Making the best of bad circumstances he brought his cousin Constantius Gallus out of exile, married him to his sister, Constantina, and appointed him regent of the East during his absence in the Magnentian war. For reasons that are confused, Gallus was executed in 354. The remains of the family of Constantine the Great now comprised the emperor Constantius and Julian, who was by now under the protection of the empress Eusebia.

In 355 Julian was recalled from Athens, where he was studying philosophy under the watchful eye of the *agentes in rebus*, the supremely efficient secret police force which had been instituted by Constantine and brought to a peak of perfection by Constantius. Abruptly married to the emperor's sister Helena, he was sent to Gaul where, contrary to every expectation, or imperial intention, he scored a series of brilliant military victories over the Franks and Alemanni, invaded Germany, restored the ravaged cities of the Rhineland and lowered the taxes throughout the prefecture. He was immensely popular with the armies of the West. Inevitably the very situation which Constantius had tried to prevent came about: Julian was proclaimed emperor by his troops who followed him to the East to contest supremacy with Constantius. The clash never came. Constantius died before the armies met and Julian was acknowledged as sole ruler by both East and West.

Two factors contributed to produce a monetary crisis in the West: the need to eradicate all memory of Magnentius; and the need to prevent Julian having access to cash with which to suborn the army (Amm.xxii.7). The first of these was the subject of an imperial enactment which demonetized both the coinage of the usurper and all of the silver-rich Constantinian coins issued before 353, including the reformed FEL TEMP REPARATIO coinage. In the East this coinage had quickly lost any silver content and by the time the empire was reunited the only surviving issue was a very much reduced version of the unit, the production of the half and third having ceased. The main feature of this coin was the reverse type which depicted a Roman soldier spearing a Persian cavalryman who had fallen from his stricken horse. It was this 'Fallen Horseman' coin which was legitimized as the only legal coin in the West by the rescript of 354 (C.Th.9.23). At virtually the same time, Julian arrived in Gaul and supplies of money dried up. Julian himself is recorded as being unable to give a soldier who solicited him for the price of a shave even the few coppers that the barber would have charged. A survey of site finds confirms the virtual absence of official imperial coinage in Britain and northern Gaul during Julian's tenure of office. What is found on sites and in hoards is a substantial quantity of imitations of the coin prescribed as legitimate by the rescript, that is copies of post-353 'Falling Horseman' *FEL TEMP REPARATIO* coinage, often overstruck on demonetized Constantinian coins. The overwhelming bulk of these coins are identifiable as bearing, in some form, no matter how garbled, the name of Constantius II. In this mass have been identified a few, and it is very few indeed, which bear the name Carausius or some recognizable attempt to render that name (Pl.9, no.4).

While the above account encompasses the majority of the 'Carausius II' coins the first specimen to be identified and published is a copy not of the post-353 coinage but of a type issued early in the *FEL TEMP REPARATIO* reform in 348–50. This type features the emperor standing in a galley which is steered by a figure of Victory (Evans, 1887). In discussing the coin, which was found at Richborough, Evans advanced the theory that this Carausius was an otherwise unrecorded fifth-century ruler of southern Britain. Observing the placing of a garbled version of the name Constantius (which he read as 'Constantine') on the reverse, instead of the normal *FEL TEMP REPARATIO* inscription which should have occupied that area, Evans concluded that 'Carausius' was associated with Constantine III, who revolted in Britain in 406, crossed to the Continent and was defeated and killed in Spain in 411. Further, he noted:

> Whether we regard this Carausius as an actual nominee of Constantine at this critical juncture, or whether we regard him as an independent usurper who considered it politic to bid for Constantine's recognition in a Caesarean capacity, we shall not be far wrong...in referring the issue of this...coin to the year 409.

Noting that Constantine was elevated because of his auspicious name, Evans comments that:

> ...the memory of the brave Carausius, who first raised Britain to a position of naval supremacy, may have influenced the choice of this obscure Caesar at a moment when the Romano-British population was about to assert as it had never done before its independence of the Continental Empire.

Evans's paper remained the major contribution to the elucidation of this coinage until the problem was reopened by C.H.V. Sutherland, who drew upon an enlarged corpus of material (Sutherland, 1945). This included not only Evans's coin from Richborough but another from the same site and two other unprovenanced specimens. Where it could be ascertained, a garbled version of the name of Constantius replaced the reverse legend. The new specimens were all of the 'Falling Horseman' variety. A new dimension was added at this stage by the finding, at Richborough, of another 'ruler' making his appearance in this series whose name is read as either Cenceris or Genceris. Sutherland rejected Evans's attribution of this coinage to the fifth century and placed the issue in the general context of other FEL TEMP REPARATIO copies, in the 350s. He remained convinced that they represented issues by actual rulers who, through the inclusion of the name of Constantius on the reverse 'can be seen claiming to be the colleagues – junior, perhaps, but colleagues none the less – of a legitimate emperor, Constantius II, whose name they prudently allow to appear on the reverse, however willingly they may have disowned him'. Sutherland concludes that:

> The temporary emergence of these petty rulers might be attributed to the period of (or just after) the usurpation of Magnentius, when Constantius's grip on Britain must have been weakened. Here was the opportunity for partial autonomy, open to those who had enough enterprise to grasp it: and if this Carausius was the grandson of the third-century emperor, he may well have inherited his grand-father's initiative.

Noting the south-eastern focus of the finds led Sutherland to suggest that a semi-independent *dominium* existed, with Richborough as its administrative centre.

In the following quarter of a century a number of further specimens came to light, including one from Silchester, which led to the suggestion that Carausius II ruled over a wide tract of southern Britain (Boon, 1955). Authors reporting these finds accepted Sutherland's interpretation of their political context (Hill, 1948). A variation on the Sutherland view was offered by C.E. Stevens who proposed that Carausius II was a nominee of Constantius II given the task of detaching Britain from the realms of the usurper Magnentius (Stevens, 1956).

A highly technical review of the problem, and one which is regarded as the definitive study of the coinage, was inspired by the appearance of Stevens's paper (Kent, 1957). In the light of studies of the internal chronology of the FEL TEMP REPARATIO coinage it is possible to isolate the production of the Carausius and Censeris copies to the years 354–8. These were years in which Constantius held undisputed control over the whole empire, indeed this is precisely the period in which his agents were so active extirpating the supporters of Magnentius in Britain. There is no context here for petty insular rulers sharing domain with the legitimate emperor, nor does the date allow credence to Stevens's hypothesis of a nominee created to detach

Britain from Magnentius, who died in 353. Kent meets the problem of the appearance of Constantius's name on the reverse of these coins by pointing out that 'regular' copies occur with a version of the imperial name on both sides. He concludes that it is 'most unlikely that an actual ruler called "Carausius II" ever existed'.

Kent's magisterial survey of the coinage of the mid-fourth century has been persuasive and comment on the Carausius II coins among numismatists has been limited to reiterating his views while observing that specimens of the coins are now known not only from south-east England but from as far north as York and as far west as north Wales (Boon, 1988). This is not the case with ancient historians and an argument has been advanced recently for the re-establishment of Carausius II as a real person, and a rebel in Britain to boot (Thompson, 1990). Such advocacy meets a problem since it must overcome the silence of Ammianus Marcellinus, who gives what appears to be a very full account of events in Britain at the critical period. Thompson dissents from Kent's view that Britain was firmly under imperial control, pointing out that the activities of Constantius's agents, sent to root out the adherents of Magnentius, were actually limited to the year 353 and that the coins in question were not issued before 354. Thompson's view, based on a reading of Ammianus, is that a revolt broke out in Britain in the 350s in which, it is implied, 'Carausius II' was involved. The silence of the historian about the hypothesized Carausius is explained because

... he included only the outstanding events of Roman history and is excluding what he thinks of as details ... Now, Britain was a distant province 'at the extremities of the world', and so its affairs were of less interest than those of other provinces closer to the Mediterranean. Ammianus's silence does not disprove the existence of Carausius II.

This is true to a certain degree but of all the extremities of the empire it is precisely Britain that Ammianus deals with most fully.

For the present, the case for Carausius II remains unproven, and we may note the problem of 'Genseris' has been entirely neglected. The corpus of coinage under review now consists of some twenty specimens, but a close study of *FEL TEMP REPARATIO* copies from hoards and site finds would probably produce more; to date no die-study has been undertaken of the available coins. The questions remain. Why Carausius? Never the easiest of names to reproduce on a coin die, as the bungled efforts of late third-century copyists demonstrate and attempts at the name on the fourth-century coins confirm. Why the imperial name on the reverse and why the use of the titles Dominus and Caesar, in a manner not found in use on the regular *FEL TEMP REPARATIO* prototypes? Uncouth though they may be, there is a degree of originality in these mysterious objects which persuades the sceptic that something, as yet unexplained, lies behind their production. Whether that has any connection with the third-century Carausius or whether we have here a case of what biologists call 'convergent evolution' may never be known.

• 14 •

CARAUSIUS AND ALLECTUS
IN THE POST-ROMAN WORLD

THE EPISODE OF CARAUSIUS AND Allectus made very little impact in the Roman world as a whole. It was soon forgotten and little attention was paid by historians; a revolt in a distant, and not very important, area of the empire was not of much interest to historians in the East. By the time that the Byzantine historian Zonaras completed his universal history in the early twelfth century the memory of events had already become hopelessly distorted: 'The prefect Asclepiodotus destroyed Crassus [sic!] who had held Britain for three years [sic!]' (Zon.xii.31).

In the West we have seen that the short accounts of Aurelius Victor and Eutropius enshrine material from an earlier work, no longer extant, and that Orosius drew his account from Eutropius, offering a paraphrase of his source. In his turn Bede reproduced Orosius word for word (Bede 1.6). There is no reference to the episode or protagonists in Gildas's *De exidio Britanniae*, in itself a startling commentary on his knowledge of Roman Britain.

The post-classical study of Carausius and, to a lesser degree, Allectus made little advance on the statements of the panegyrists and the near-contemporary historians until the development of modern numismatic studies and the advent of large-scale archaeological excavation. On the contrary, the study of the few reasonable records was abandoned in favour of a series of fictions which better suited the historical needs of later ages, as, from time to time, the essential elements of the story attracted the interest of nationalist historians both in Britain and on the Continent.

From the seventeenth century the frequency with which new coins were found and recorded excited a strong collector interest in the subject. The finds were instrumental in creating a body of literary connoisseurship of a generally uninformed nature.

On the whole, each age has created the Carausius it deserved, though there are ages which did not deserve the scholars who did the creating. It is with the *Historia Brittonum*, ascribed to Nennius, that the thread of fantasy which is woven through much of Carausian study was first spun out. The nature of the *Historia Brittonum* deserves, and has received, study in itself. The most apposite description of its nature is that put forward briefly by Alcock:

Internal evidence shows that the Miscellany [Alcock renames the
Historia 'The British Historical Miscellany' for reasons which do not
concern us here] was put together in the second half of the tenth
century . . . The compilation of the Miscellany may reasonably be
attributed to the *scriptorium* of St David's (in Wales) . . . . Nennius is
generally agreed to have had a hand in writing the *Historia*, but it is
disputed whether he merely added fresh material to a pre-existing
Historia . . . or whether he was himself the original author or
compiler . . . . We can readily observe that the Nennian *Historia* is a
hotch-potch of historical material garnered in from various sources . . . .

(Alcock, 1971)

Nennius's most important contribution to the Carausian story is to place
the revolt in the reign of Septimius Severus rather than that of Diocletian.
He lists, in a garbled form, the emperors who personally intervened in
Britain. Thus we have Claudius, Hadrian, Severus, Maximianus and
Constantine of the legitimate emperors and the usurpers, Carausius and
Maximus. There is no mention of Constantine III or his short-lived
predecessors, Gratian and Marcus. The appearance of Maximianus Herculeus,
the colleague of Diocletian, who is not recorded as having visited Britain,
is surprising. The entry may be a garbled scribal duplication of Magnus
Maximus. There is no mention in the list of Constantius who was twice in
Britain. Possibly the name dropped out with the appearance of Maximianus.
The name of Carausius is rendered as Caritius, though whether this
corruption is derived from Nennius's source, is his own creation or a scribal
error cannot be ascertained. The sources of the *Historia Britonnum* are
themselves obscure. The account of Carausius reads:

The fourth [i.e. of the seven emperors resident in Britain] was Caritius,
emperor and tyrant, who on this account was tyrant for the slaying of
Severus. And with him all the leaders of the Roman race who were with
him in Britain, he chastised all the rulers of the Britons and severely
avenged Severus on them and seized the purple in Britain.   (Nen.24)

The association of Carausius with the death of Severus, who actually died
of natural causes at York in 211 while campaigning in Britain, was a theme
which was to be vastly elaborated by Geoffrey of Monmouth in the *Historia
Regum Britanniae* which was completed in 1136. It passed thence into the
chronicle histories of Scotland. These in their turn elaborated the story, for
the benefit of Scottish claims on English territory, and provided a northern
context for Carausian activity which was further elaborated in the eighteenth
century with a wealth of spurious etymological and topographical detail.

Geoffrey claimed that the contents of his work derived from 'a certain
very ancient book written in the British language' which had been given
to him by Walter, the Archdeacon of Oxford. It was claimed that the
information in the book had been handed down orally, generation to

generation, from before the Roman Conquest, until finally committed to written form. Naturally, modern scholars are extremely sceptical of this statement and Geoffrey's work has been described as a pseudo-history of great imaginative power (Wright, 1981). Detailed analysis of the text indicates that a variety of classical works were available from which spurious Roman names could be derived to give a superficial integrity to invented incidents, and that the texts of both Gildas and Nennius were employed.

In any event, the contents of the work have little or no historical value but have been extremely influential in literature and art: the story of King Lear and a great number of the legends of King Arthur derive directly from Geoffrey. The *Historia* is a product of its age. This was an age in which English institutions, and national consciousness, were reasserting themselves after the trauma of the Norman Conquest a century earlier. It has also been described as an age in which writers patronized by the Anglo-Norman aristocracy sought to give a respectable history to the conquered island. Contempt for Anglo-Saxon institutions was widespread, a feeling that an unworthy foe had been overcome was prevalent in intellectual circles. Geoffrey's work supplied a need:

> By re-asserting the Trojan origins of the British, which gave them an
> ancestry as ancient as any European people, Geoffrey was able to
> represent Britain as the equal, and often superior, of Rome. This was a
> history in which the Norman masters of Britain could take pride.
>
> (Wright, 1981)

Thus the work attempts to place Britain and its native institutions in a context preceding the Anglo-Saxon period. Geoffrey was part of the Anglo-Norman ecclesiastical establishment and lived and taught in Oxford; his connection with Monmouth was, at best, simply a matter of geography rather than ancestry. Nevertheless, the condition of Wales is a constant undercurrent in his work, the Welsh of his own day being denigrated as unworthy descendants of the ancestral Britons. Despite this, they are less objectionable than the English, so that in the powerful legend, which makes its first appearance in Geoffrey, that Merlin will rise and call Arthur from his sleep, it is to save Britain, not England. Geoffrey's version of the story of Carausius and Allectus is worth recapitulating *in extenso* since it forms the basis for nearly all pre-modern accounts.

Following the Roman conquest of Britain, the island was returned to the government of British kings. On the death of King Lucius, in the middle of the second century, relations between Britons and Romans broke down. As a result of this the Roman senate sent Severus, with two legions, to restore order. This he did, driving the Britons into Caledonia, confining them there with a wall which he built across the island (i.e. Hadrian's Wall). The British leader, Sulgenius, unable to attack the province, crossed the sea to Scythia where he enrolled the youth of the Picts, returned with a huge fleet and besieged York where Severus was killed. Severus's two sons, Geta nd Bassianus, fought and Geta was killed. At this time a young, humbly orn Carausius, who had shown his bravery in battles in Britain, went to Lome and persuaded the senate to put him in charge of a fleet to defend he coasts of Britain. But he used the fleet to attack the island, eventually orcing the inhabitants to make him king. He then fought Bassianus who, etrayed by the Picts, was killed. In gratitude Carausius gave the Picts land n Albany (i.e. Scotland). When the senate heard of these events they sent Allectus to Britain, who killed Carausius and large numbers of the Britons. The latter turned to the Duke of Cornwall, Asclepiodotus, for help, and lected him King of Britain. Asclepiodotus marched on Allectus, defeating nd killing him. A remnant of Allectus's forces fled to London where they vere besieged and defeated by Asclepiodotus and a confederation of the ribes of Britain. Asclepiodotus then reigned for ten years 'with true justice nd peace'.

Geoffrey's narrative immediately struck root in the vernacular literature f his age, being transcribed into English rhyming couplets in Robert of Gloucester's *Chronicle* which was completed in the first decades of the hirteenth century (Hearne, 1724). The text follows that of the *Historia Regum Britanniae* very closely. The quotation of a few lines will show the loseness to the original:

A stalleworthe young bachiler in this lond was tho,
Caraus was yclepud, that couthe of much wo.
For tho he had in werre y be, & do gret maistrie,
And him much yfond, he thougte do tricherie.
He went and bed leve tho of the empeour of Rome,
And bi het hym, that, gef ther of we avaunced he wer,
To gelde mor god of Rome, than al Breteyne thider bere.

The influence of the *Historia* on the Scottish historians of the medieval period was profound, since it introduced the notion that Carausius had had dealings with the Picts and had assigned land to them in Albany, that is eastern Scotland. Geoffrey is, as far as can be ascertained, the originator of this story. There is no warrant for it in any ancient source and, while it is not impossible that Carausius was active on the northern frontier, it is unlikely in the extreme that Geoffrey would have known of this.

The conjunction of Carausius and the Picts is extraordinary on another count – the first reference to them in Roman literature post-dates the demise of Carausius. They make their appearance, in surviving ancient literature, nine years after the defeat of Allectus when Constantius returned to Britain to campaign against them. We must conjecture that Geoffrey's story is a back formation from the later event and was invented in order to accommodate the presence of Constantius in Britain without the necessity of involving him with the Picts. Geoffrey's version of events is that Constantius came to deal with King Coel, of nursery-rhyme fame, who had risen in revolt against Asclepiodotus and killed him. Subsequently

Constantius marries Coel's daughter, Helena. Constantine the Great is born of this marriage.

It is this narrative thread which is picked up and elaborated by John of Fordun in his *Chronica Gentis Scotorum* (Skene, 1872). Fordun was born in the last years of the thirteenth or the very earliest of the fourteenth century and died in 1385. His early life encompassed that crucial period of Scottish history which culminated in England ceding sovereignty of his native land to the Scottish king Robert the Bruce in 1327. By the terms of this treaty it was agreed:

> that the said kingdom, according to its ancient boundaries observed in the days of Alexander III [1249–86], should remain unto Robert, King of Scots . . . free and divided from England without any subjection, right of service, claim, or demand whatsoever . . .

The later years of Fordun's life saw renewed and steady English encroachment on this territory.

Fordun's purpose in composing the *Chronicle* can be seen as being similar to Geoffrey's in its nationalistic motivation. As Geoffrey sought to establish the distinctiveness of Britain, so Fordun emphasizes the uniqueness of Scotland. Like Geoffrey, he provides the nation with an inspirational version of its own history, in this case stretching back through a line of kings which pre-dates the creation of the English monarchy itself. The sources marshalled for this task were essentially the earlier medieval accounts, with some input from the classical sources. These were supplemented by newly minted stories designed to show that Scotland was able to maintain its independence even when faced by external threat. Characteristic of the nationalist invention is the tale of the intervention of Julius Caesar in Scottish affairs by way of an aggressive letter sent to the Scottish king. Caesar, for his trouble, receives a stirring reply denouncing his threats in terms consonant with the newly established independence of the country from English intervention.

The Carausian episode follow Geoffrey's well-established lines. Fulgentius, the Sulgentius of Geoffrey, the leader of the Britons in Albania, unites the Scots and the Picts to campaign against Septimius Severus but the allies are thwarted when Severus builds Hadrian's Wall. Nevertheless, they circumvent the Wall and launch a naval attack on York which is captured after a siege: Severus is killed. Following this the Picts and Scots fall out, after living in harmony for five hundred years. Evidently the chronicler had forgotten his claim that they had only recently united to deal with the Roman threat.

> . . . in proportion to the earnestness with which they formerly nurtured the friendship between them . . . with bitterness with which their enmity thenceforth grew, from day to day, by rapine, fire, slaughter, treachery, and various tumults and raids . . . However, peace was restored by Carausius, a Briton, whose object . . . was to take them to fight against the Romans . . .

Following his introduction Carausius is defined as a usurper by reference to the ancient sources to which is added that he:

> ... pressingly solicited all the nations of the island, as well as the Scots and Picts, upon whom he had formerly committed the most cruel depredations, to enter into a friendly treaty with him ... [to] join him in driving the Romans out of the island ... he ... conceded to them [i.e. the Picts and Scots] that the possessions they had acquired by the sword, in Nero's time, should ... remain theirs, in their integrity, for ever.

This is simply a confusion of Gildas's account of the attacks by the Picts and Scots on Britain with events in the reign of Nero, when Eutropius mistakenly records that Britain was nearly lost. This itself was a distant memory of Nero's wish to withdraw from Britain in the years immediately following the death of Claudius in 54 (Birley, 1955). In any event, Carausius ratifies the treaty which, like that made with Robert the Bruce, recognized the independent integrity of Scotland. Almost at once a Roman army, sent from overseas, attacked. The leader of this expedition is named as Bassianus who, Fordun specifies, was not the son of Severus, since he knows perfectly well that Caracalla was assassinated while on his way to a campaign against the Parthian empire. Bassianus invaded the island where he:

> ... crushed the Britons by sundry massacres and proscriptions. But he was afterwards, with many of his soldiers, slain in a most hard fought battle, by Carausius, and by the Scots and Picts, who had joined with him.

Having brought together the Picts and Scots, representative of the Highland and Lowland elements of the Scotland of Fordun's day, Carausius succumbs to the treachery of Allectus. With his death the unity of the nation falls apart, stressing that Scotland, because of its devisive tribal structure, can be unified only under charismatic leadership like that of Robert the Bruce:

> Meanwhile, the greater part of the British nation renewed the treaty of alliance they had formerly made with the Scots, and strove, if possible, to put Adlectus to death, or drive him out of Britannia, on account of the death of Carausius, their chief. Adlectus, on the other hand, accompanied by the Picts, who had broken the treaty they had formerly sworn with the Britons, inflicted many injuries on Britannia. At length, a few years after, advancing to battle with them, he himself, after a great slaughter on both sides, fell among the slain, as he well deserved.

The insidious nature of Allectus and his dipomacy is made clear for it has long-term effects on Scotland:

> Afterwards, as often as the Romans made war on the British nation,

the Scots would help the latter, and come faithfully to their rescue; while the Picts would assiduously give their support to the Romans against the Britons. For the cunning of Adlectus had separated the Picts from the Britons, and these two nations thenceforth wasted each other, with mutual massacres, until the time of Maximus, emperor in Gaul [i.e. Magnus Maximus].

Presumably they abruptly stop mutual massacres at this specific time because the evidence of Gildas is that, with the departure of Maximus in 383, the south of Britain was ravaged by the combined attacks of the Picts and the Scots, and it must have been evident to a chronologer, even as inventive as Fordun, that he had a massive evidential discrepancy on his hands.

There is nothing in this text which does not have a place in Scottish history in its medieval context and nothing that has a place in a Roman one. The confusion of easily ascertainable facts indicates that Fordun held no brief with historical accuracy; his aims are not historical in the sense that a modern historian would use the term. His inventions transcend the poverty of his sources to inspire his nation with a sense of place and racial continuity as a buttress against their formidable southern enemy.

The nationalistic theme is continued in the *Scottish Chronicle* of Hector Boethius. Written in the fifteenth century, Boethius's work has been claimed to contain circumstantial detail which may reflect a genuine historical tradition. Webb commented that 'This account is certainly most interesting, and it is difficult to regard it as purely imaginary. Its details are minute and not inconsistent with the accounts of the Roman authors' (Webb, 1906). As we shall see, this optimistic view, expressed in the early twentieth century, had been refuted by a less sanguine editor of Boethius's work as early as 1577.

Boethius adds new inventions to the story, but a glimmer of the historical figure is discernible in the fictional miasma. In Boethius's account Carausius, here named Carantius, is the brother of Findock and uncle of Crathlynt. On being implicated in the murder of Findock, Carantius flees to Italy where he serves in the armies of the successive emperors from Aurelian to Diocletian. Falling foul of Maximian he returns home, settling in the north of Britain. There follows a reconciliation with Crathlynt, who joins Carantius to campaign and fight the Romans. Carantius also reconciles the Picts and Scots. Meanwhile Quintus Bassianus, the Roman governor, marches against Carantius and his allies who have occupied York. A battle in the vicinity of the city results in the death of Bassianus and Hircius, the 'procurator of Caesar'. Carantius then marches to London after rewarding his Caledonian allies:

Hee sent also with them his ambassadors, to render thankes unto bothe the kings [i.e. of the Picts and of the Scots] for theyr ayd in this so prosperous a victorie, assigning unto them as a portion of the conquest, the countreys of Westmorland and Cumberland, with all that region whiche lay betwixt Adrian's walle, and the citie of Yorke, to enjoy as their owne patrimonie for evermore.

Thus, from this tumultuous fiction, the Scots received a patent for the very territory over which their reivers and raiders were ranging at the time of the compilation of the *Chronicle*. Territory in which the Tudor Lords of the Marches were trying to maintain English dominance and peaceful settlement.

Two points in this narrative have excited comment and, among some incautious scholars, the belief in its essential historicity. The first is the naming of the governor of Britain as Quintus Bassianus and the second the reference to a 'procurator of Caesar', Hircius. The former is a further elaboration of the fiction derived from the Nennian confusion of the absolute dates of the emperors whom he lists as having visited or raised revolt in Britain, a confusion which juxtaposed Carausius and Septimius Severus, whose son bore the throne name Marcus Aurelius Antoninus but was originally named Bassianus. Confusingly, history knows him as Caracalla, a nickname which none would have dared use to his face. The procurator has no previous appearance and seems to be an independent invention. None of the chronicle accounts show the least knowledge of the true administrative structure of late-third-century Britain and all persist in the belief that there was a single governor rather than the two officials administering Britannia Superior and Britannia Inferior.

The Scottish sources offer the addition to the Carausian canon of an important topographical detail, the attribution of Arthur's O'on to the usurper. This domed building, erected on the north slope of the Carron Valley, two miles north of Falkirk, stood intact until its demolition in 1743 to provide material to repair a mill-dam. The exact date and function of the building is disputed but it is most likely to have been erected as a mausoleum or shrine during the Antonine occupation of Scotland (Steer, 1958). The fact that the building stood on the banks of the river Carron proved too much of a temptation to early etymologists, and Carron and Carausius became inextricably entwined with the result that the building came to be used as physical proof of the intervention of Carausius in Scotland. Boethius's work first appeared in English as part of Holinshed's *Chronicles* (Holinshed, 1577). Holinshed's translation, quoted above, was not itself a rendition of Boethius's Latin original but an anglicization of a translation 'into the Scottish speech by John Balledon, Archdeacon of Murray'.

Holinshed also contributes a version of the Carausian episode to the history of England, the narrative being similar to that of the Scottish tradition since it is a recapitulation of Geoffrey of Monmouth. But Holinshed includes this version only for completeness for, having toiled through the narrative of Geoffrey, he then cuts the Gordian knot of three centuries of Carausian speculation by reiterating the contemporary Latin sources; he sorts their evidence into order, offers a series of correct dates of events and provides an English translation of the Panegyric of 297. This represents a very considerable scholarly achievement and could have been the point from which an understanding of events, uncluttered by later accretions, might have been launched. In the event, the impact of Geoffrey and the Scottish continuators was too pervasive to be easily dispersed. It is this version which was transmitted by such influential works as that of John Speed who, in his *The History of Greate Britaine* (Speed, 1611) relays Geoffrey of Monmouth to a further generation of English historians.

Geoffrey was also influential in the European historical tradition. While, on the whole, Continental scholarship was always more firmly rooted in the ancient texts than contemporary British scholarship, access to the *Historia*, from Geoffrey's text itself or his Continental medieval assimilators still influenced discussion of Carausius and Allectus. The degree to which the best Continental scholarship exceeded the insular in mastery of source material can be judged by the discussion of Allectus presented by Jean Tristan in his *Commentaires Historiques* (Tristan, 1644). Tristan's concern is with the name Allectus, its derivation and significance. Noting that the word means 'selected' or 'chosen', he deploys a battery of literary and epigraphic evidence to elucidate his thesis, including an inscription from Lyons, the Hymns of Prudentius and three rescripts from the Theodosian Code.

However, Tristan's breadth of classical learning misled him in one important question, the origins of Carausius. As we have seen, the classical sources describe him as a Menapian, that is from the northern coastal area of Gallia Belgica, but Tristan, mulling over all the possible locations of Menapia, came to the conclusion that 'Carausius, duquel nous ne scavons les praenom et nom de famille, estoit Hibernois...' (Carausius, whose forename and family name we do not know, was an Irishman.) The Irish claim to have fostered Carausius was to have a strong advocate in the next century.

While Tristan was producing his history an author of a different complexion was at work in Italy. The result is one of the most extraordinary items in the Carausian canon since the author's object was nothing less than to prove that the Doge of Venice, Giovanni Pesaro (1658–9), was descended from the Roman rebel (Pl.9, no.7). Zabarella derived his narrative of British history from Geoffrey of Monmouth, or the Continental traditions which stemmed from him. On to this he grafted his own inventions in order to bridge the vast gap between the point where Geoffrey's narrative ends and Italian family records begin. Zabarella is plain as to his intentions and the reason for undertaking the work: 'Tutte la famiglie ascritte ne Patrizii delle Serenissima replubicca Veneziana possedono indubitatamente una sublime nobilita' (All of the Patrician families of the Most Serene republic of Venice are, undoubtedly, of the utmost nobility). But none can claim such utmost nobility as the subject of the genealogy since 'Carausio imperatore indubitamente su'il vero stipte Padre et Progenitore di questa Serenissima stirpe, la quale forse lui fu etta detta Carausii, et poi corrotamente de carosii noblissima, et antichissima in Venezia' (The emperor Carausius is undoubtably the true paternal root and progenitor of this most ancient and noble Venetian family, which was, perhaps, called Carausii, and corruptly Carosii).

Zabarella claims that the descendants of Carausius had settled in Venice, under their own name, but had retired in troubled times to Pesaro. On their return to Venice for reasons which are not explained they chose to adopt the name of their place of exile rather than resume the proud name of Carosii/Carausii. Discarding the view that the Pesari were descendants of the mere senatorial Carisii of the late Republic, one of whom, T. Carisius, served as a *quaestor* of Julius Caesar, the genealogist pursues his subject.

His genealogical stemma is ingenious. Sixty-seven generations after the reign of Jove, king of Etruria and emperor of the world, Cunobeline the king of Britain produced a son named Carausius. The latter was the father of a line of three Carausii who are, respectively, his great-, great-great-, and great-great-great-grandsons. The last of these is father of Bonosus, the father of Carausius, the emperor or Britain. Happily for the Pesari, Carausius manages to provide offspring before being assassinated by Allectus. Of the ancestors of Carausius the emperor, the most distinguished was the fourth Carausius, 'The Rhetorician', 'che insegno a gl'Inglesi le buone lettere, la Rhethorica, et li buoni costumi...') (who introduced to the English literature, rhetoric and decent clothes). Thus the origins of the Italian fashion industry in Britain.

Carausius himself is related to King Coel, the seventy-eighth king of Britain, father of Helena, the mother of Constantine the Great. The family reunites legitimacy with imperial rule in the reign of Gratian, after which 15 generations of Carosii are recorded down to the ninth century. The family then gathers strength and under the name Pesaro contributes 24 generations down to the recipient of this extraordinary work.

While it is easy to deride Zabarella's naïve enthusiasm and uncritical methods, a deconstruction of his text points to an important underlying motive for the choice of an ancestor for Giovanni Pesaro. The recipient of the work was in a situation comparable to that of Carausius himself. The parallel will not have escaped Zabarella, since Venice was in a most perilous situation, having recently embarked upon the defence of its most important overseas territory, the island of Crete, which it had gained when the Crusaders sacked Constantinople. The eventual loss of this island was to reduce Venice from being an imperial, to a relatively low-status power on the Italian mainland. At the same time Christian Europe would relinquish its most important strategic bastion against Islam. The Turks invaded in 1645, finally gaining the island in 1669. Pesaro's reign was too short to have had any military importance in the long struggle for mastery of the island, but he did make an important contribution to the outcome of the struggle since he came to the throne because of the vehemence with which he denounced Turkish peace overtures, made during the reign of his predecessor.

The first comprehensive history of Carausius is that of Claude Genebrier, a work which took a fundamentally new approach to the subject, being based on numismatic as well as literary evidence (Genebrier, 1740). Despite this methodological advance on previous work, the execution is less than satisfactory. The patron of this work was John Carteret (1690–1763), 1st Earl of Granville, a prominent politician and diplomat in the reigns of the first two Georges and an outspoken opponent of Walpole. Among other posts held by Carteret was that of Viceroy of Ireland. Genebrier, according to his own account, met Carteret in Paris and discovered that they had a mutual interest in coins, especially those of Carausius. For his part the author, who was a physician at the court of Louis XIV, had visited England in 1713 and had seen and studied the collection of Lord Winchelsea.

The work is entirely partisan and in the preface addressed to the patron Genebrier makes his sympathies entirely clear:

> Mais plus j'avançois dans mes recherches, plus j'y trouvois des difficultés. Cependant, la passion de vous [i.e. Carteret] marquer mon zèle et le désir de mettre la verité dans son jour, l'ont enfin emporté; et Carausius vient aujourd'hui reparoitre dans le monde, non pas sous le déguisement que certains auteurs lui avoient prêté, mais, tel qu'il fut autrefois. Il a fallu chercher des témoignages plus sûrs, les médailles et les autres monumens de ce genre m'ont fait enfin connoître, avec combien d'injustice Mamertin dérobe à notre Heros les louanges que la prévention lui fit prodiguer à Maximien. Mais, dans le dessin de venger Carausius de cette injustice, et de lui assurer à jamais une gloire immortelle; j'ai cru de lui faire revivre sous les auspices de Votre Excellence.

> But the further I progressed with my research, the more difficulties I found. Nevertheless, the desire to show you my zeal and the desire to bring the truth to light finally triumphed and Carausius today reappears in the world not in the guise certain authors have ascribed to him, but as he was in the past. More reliable evidence had to be sought; the coins and other material of that kind finally made me recognize how unjustly Mamertinus [i.e. author of the panegyrics delivered in 289 and 291] withholds from our hero the praise which prejudice made him grace Maximian with. But, with the intention of avenging Carausius for this injustice, and of assuring him an everlasting glory, I believe that I could restore him under the auspices of Your Excellency.

The difficulties encountered appear to have been prolonged since the Royal Censor endorsed the text in 1724, but inscriptions are cited which did not appear until 1726. A permit to publish was given in 1737, three years before the book reached the public. Genebrier also laboured under the difficulty of having no corpus of the coinage, his data base being a random collection of coins noted in cabinets to which he had access. He was unable to put this material into any sort of chronological sequence, with the exception of the EXPECTATE VENI and ADVENTVS AVG types which he reasonably deduced to be early in the reign. In these circumstances Genebrier used his imagination to interpret the coins as revealing a sequence of imperial activities, mostly of a ceremonial nature, which occupied Carausius during his reign. While this investigation results in nothing but fiction it is a pioneering attempt to use the evidence of coinage in a distinctively new manner.

From the literary evidence Genebrier added his own charming but misguided fables to the extant corpus. Typical of the work is the episode of the 'Baths of Carausius'. Having noted that Carausius achieved such fame that 'Après sa mort il y eut des empereurs romains qui se firent honneur de faire porter ce nom à leurs enfans.... Constance [i.e. Constantius II]...avoit une fille entr'autres, qui s'appelloit Carausa...' (After his death there were Roman emperors who did him the honour of giving his name to their children.. Constantius...had a daughter, among others, whom he named Carausa.), Genebrier turns his attention to the *Thermae Carosianae*, an imperial bath-house in Constantinople (Seeck, 1876), which he attributes to this fictitious daughter of Constantius. Carosa was the daughter of the emperor Valens (364–78), not of Constantius, whose only child was Constantia. It was an inconvenience that the baths are in Constantinople but this did not matter. On the contrary, 'Ce qui prouveroit que Carausius auroit étendu les limites de son empire jusque dans l'Orient' ('This proves that Carausius extended the bounds of his empire as far as the Orient'). It is regretted that the *thermae* at Bath could not be equated with this establishment but, after much anguish, Genebrier has to reject the identification. Not merely are the *Thermae Carosianae* firmly located in the eastern capital but those at Bath already have a well-attested name, Aquae Solis (sic! − recte Sulis), the Waters of the Sun.

Nevertheless, Bath has its own claim to fame:

Ces bains sont encore aujourd'hui fort renommés pour la guérison de plusieurs maladies: et c'est la que les Mylords et les autres Seigneurs Anglois vont dans le Printemps et dans l'Automne, tant pour leur propre santé, que pour se délasser du gouvernement de l'état, auquel la plupart s'applique le reste de l'année.

These baths are very famous today for the relief of numerous illnesses; and it is there that the Milords and other noble English go in Spring and Autumn, as much for the sake of their health as to relax from governing the country, which most of them do for the rest of the year.

Presumably the ruling class of Roman Britain used them in the same spirit and we cannot doubt that Carausius genially presided over them in due season.

In deference to his distinguished patron Genebrier, not unexpectedly, endorses the Irish origin of Carausius. From Zabarella he adopts the view that his hero 'Se fut assassiné dans son lit en dormant' (he was assassinated whilst sleeping in his bed). Clearly it paid to keep one's eye open at all times with the likes of Allectus about.

While Genebrier was at work in France, Carausius was not neglected in England. Here the academic world was in one of those doldrums that are all too frequent a feature of the English academic world, cut off as it was by insularity and arrogance. The second half of the seventeenth century had seen the foundation of the Royal Society under the aegis of Newton, Wren and Boyle, by the middle of the next century, the golden age of the Royal Society and that of the recently founded Society of Antiquaries had passed, albeit temporarily, leaving the area clear for the likes of William Stukeley and John Kennedy.

The problem started with a coin of Carausius found at Silchester. This was acquired by Stukeley's patron Dr Richard Mead, a fashionable physician, patron of the arts and confidant of everyone who was anyone in early Georgian society. The coin was presented by Mead to the king of France, thus removing it from close examination. While the obverse was clearly Carausius, the reverse was unusual, featuring the bust of a female figure surrounded by an inscription which was read as ORIUNA. Since the coin is defective and manifestly reads FORTUNA, the vituperative debate which followed the discovery reflects badly on the participants, neither of whom actually saw the coin itself (Boon, 1974). Both agreed on the reading ORIUNA, all that was at dispute was the identification of the lady. Kennedy asserted that she was the patron deity of Carausius, Stukeley that she was his wife. Kennedy got into print first with his *Dissertation upon Oriuna* (Kennedy, 1751).

The arguments are tortuous but, in brief, the name *Oriuna* is derived from *Oriens* and identified with the female form of either Mithras or Orion. The latter identification has particular weight and merit because 'this constellation was of the highest veneration amongst the antients...' and since Carausius was a sailor 'so if he honoured, or shewed a more special regard and respect to this Constellation, can no way seem strange'.

Stukeley replied with a paper entitled *Oriuna wife of Carausius, Emperor of Britain* (Stukeley, 1752). In this he asserts his confidence in his own eccentric views: 'Tho' I never saw the real coin, yet I always entertained an opinion that Carausius had a family... Therefore on seeing a drawing of the coin, I was induced to think, that it exhibited to us, the picture of Oriuna his wife'.

Though there have been 'some doubts roused' about the coin (notably by Stukeley himself, who acknowledged that the best interpretation of the legend was indeed FORTUNA) he decides that 'I myself, in my own mind, have no great doubt, in thinking it to exhibit Oriuna, the emperors wife'.

His proof involved postulating a son for Carausius, named Silvanus, whom he adopts from the fictions of Zabarella, though he confesses that he is a little bemused that that author 'informs us not whence his intelligence is derived'. None the less, a son, even without supporting evidence, is a great convenience since his existence presupposes a mother. More than fifty pages of eccentric learning are devoted to the son who, among other duties, presides over horse-races held annually at York on 25 December to honour the Sun and denigrate Christianity. This extraordinary invention can be traced back to the discovery of a Mithraic sculpture found at Micklegate, York, in 1747 which depicts Sol mounting his chariot.

Dr Kennedy, not discountenanced by this weight of learning, published his riposte four years later (Kennedy, 1756). This work, which sets out to 'Answer those trifling objects made to the former discourse', was a vigorous reply, full of acid politeness, which reasserts the author's former position. Stukeley is hard hit:

> The different, idle, simple criticisms, or ill-founded objections, which
> have been advanced by some, are in reality scarce worthy of public
> notice. As to the Rev. Dr. St – y's Letter or Dissertation . . . to prove
> Oriuna to be the wife of Carausius, I do verily believe he scarce
> believes it himself, but did in reality only mean it, as a high puff, to
>   his patron's [i.e. Dr Mead] present to the Most Chr. Majesty . . .

Despite this, it was Stukeley who triumphed with the publication of *The Medallic History of Marcus Aurelius Carausius, Emperor in Britain* (Stukeley, 1757, 1759). Though Kennedy was to produce two further pamphlets it was Stukeley's work which was to be the base of Carausian studies into the nineteenth century.

Stukeley's study bears a very close relationship to that of Genebrier although he claims not to have read Genebrier, lest he borrow anything from him. Nevertheless he did obtain Genebrier's plates, including the frontispieces, and reprinted these in his own work. Further he adopts exactly the same methodology as had been adopted by the French author. This consisted of identifying reverse legends with religious or public festivals in the Roman calendar, sometimes by false etymologies or parallelisms made with Biblical events, and claiming that the alleged event was the occasion for the production of coin. The order in which the coins were placed depended entirely upon Stukeley's interpretation of events during the reign; most of these he invented. In this he followed Genebrier so closely that the claim not to have read his rival's work stretches belief.

A number of points are to his credit, notably that he recognized mintmarks for what they are, though the attribution to mint is, with the exception of London, mistaken in every case. The C mint is attributed to Catteractonum (sic!) (Catterick) in Yorkshire, the RSR series to Rutupiae (Richborough); the Unmarked mint is not noticed. The observation that Clausentum (Bitterne) was also a mint which has received praise from such an authority as Mattingly, who observed that 'it was one of the few cases where his intuition was triumphantly right'. Alas, the years have dealt severely with this judgement and there are no longer any grounds for ascribing minting to Clausentum in the reign of Carausius or in any other period.

The work appeared in two parts, with a production interval of two years between them. Little changed in the interim and the second volume merely reiterates the fallacies of the first, while extending the theory that coin issues can be dated by recognition of the festivals to which they allude, however obliquely and however much the allusion is in the mind of the beholder. In the area of narrative, Stukeley is firmly wedded to that of Geoffrey of Monmouth, or that transmitted by the Scottish chroniclers whenever it suits his case. Thus Arthur's O'on, about which he had formerly written a good account and published excellent drawings before its destruction, becomes a symbol of the treaty with the Scots and Picts, which had been invented in the medieval tradition. Oriuna appears but there is no extended comment on her. The ridicule which had been heaped on both Stukeley and Kennedy may have had its effect.

Throughout his work Stukeley depended heavily on the evidence of a notorious forgery which had been foisted on him by Charles Julius Bertram, an Englishman resident in Copenhagen. Bertram faked a chronicle purporting to be the work of a fourteenth-century monk of Westminster named Richard of Cirencester, which incorporated an account of Roman Britain from hitherto unknown sources. The manuscript also boasted a road guide, or itinerary, from which could be reconstructed a map of the island in Roman times. It was from the latter that Stukeley drew his conclusion that Menapia was St Davids, in Pembrokeshire. Thus was created the Welsh Carausius to compete with the Irish one.

A recent biographer fairly sums up the Carausian contributions of Stukeley; 'there is little to his credit in the voluminous books of notes and drafts of Histories of Carausius that he so laboriously compiled in the later years of his life' (Piggott, 1985).

The Stukeley–Kennedy debates had a number of spin-offs, both academic and literary. The Oriuna controversy had evidently achieved public notice to the extent that her coinage became the subject of a play, by Samuel Foote, which was performed at the Drury Lane Theatre in the year in which Stukeley first made a claim that she was the wife of Carausius (Foote, 1745).

The plot of this lively comedy hinges on the activities of Messrs Puff and Carmine, the latter a painter of fashionable portraits of ugly women, who had run out of commissions. This pair, as well as faking old master paintings, are dealers in antiquities, all of which are the product of their own hands. Among their victims are Mr Novice and Lord Dupe; the former is the proud owner of a coin of Oriuna:

NOVICE: But where are your Busts; Here, here, Gentlemen, here's a curiosity; a Medal of Oriuna, got me by Dr Mummy; the only one in the visible World; there may be some underground.

DUPE: Fine indeed! Will you permit to taste it? It has the relish.

NOVICE: The Relish! Zooks it cost me a hundred Guineas.

PUFF: By Gar, it is a dear Bit tho'.

NOVICE: So you may think; but three times the Money should not purchase it.

DUPE: Pray Sir, whose Bust is it that dignifies this Coin?

NOVICE: The Empress Oriuna, my Lord.

DUPE: And who, Sir, might she be? I don't recollect to have heard of the Lady.

NOVICE: She, my Lord? Oh, she was a kind of what d'ye call'em – a sort of Queen, or Wife, or Something or other to Somebody, that lived a damn'd while ago – Mummy told me the whole Story; but before gad I've forgotten it....

Finally both Puff and Carmine are unmasked and in the denunciations which follow poor Novice is disabused of the value of his coin.

PUFF: What, my sprightly Squire! Pray favour me with a sight of your Oriuna. – It has the Relish; an indisputable Antique; being a Bristol Farthing, coined by a Soap-Broiler to pay his Journeymen in the Scarcity of Cash, and purchased for two Pence of a travelling Tinker by, Sir, your humble Servant, Timothy Puff. Ha, ha, ha!

NOVICE: My Oriuna a Bristol Farthing!

PUFF: Most assuredly.

The year that this play appeared also saw the appearance of Thomas Amory's *Memoirs of Several Ladies of Great Britain* (Amory, 1745). This work purports to contain the journal of a certain Mrs Marrisa Benlow, a formidable Northumbrian blue-stocking. The lady is encountered by the author while he is on a walking tour; amazingly she turns out to be a daughter of his best friend. Mrs Benlow is not only thoroughly proficient in classical languages and an impressive Shakespearian scholar, but she conducts literary duels on theological topics with bishops and on mathematical ones with scientists. This paragon also does the milking.

It is alleged that in 1741 Mrs Benlow set out on a Hebridean tour, during which she had a number of intellectual adventures. A notable event in her itinerary was her visit to a nunnery in which all the nuns confessed themselves to be, secretly, strict Anglicans. On the Isle of Lewis she met a certain Mr Bannerman. True to the spirit of the age this good man passed his days in the compilation of religious treatises on the nature of the Holy Ghost. He also turns his hand to digging up Roman remains in which the island is extraordinarily rich. His haul of antiquities is remarkable and includes a Flavian tombstone, an altar dedicated by Pertinax, an urn containing the ashes of the daughter of Virius Lupus and, best of all, an altar inscribed: *FORTVNAE CONSERVATRICI/PRO SALVTE/IMP CARAVSII PF AVG/ET/ORIVNAE AVG* ('To Fortune the Preserver, for the welfare of the Emperor Carausius Pius Fortunate Augustus and Oriuna the Augusta'). But there was more:

> ... Near the altar I have described, there was found an extraordinary fine urn of speckled marble, full of ashes, but had no inscription on it. That in this are contained the ashes of Carausius cannot be affirmed; tho' it is probable enough; as this emperor was often in Scotland, and in league with the chief of the Picts, Scots and Western Islands. They had a great regard for him, while living; and lamented him greatly, when dead. His ashes might be brought to this country, to save them from the destroying Allectus. This is no more than fancy, however.

This uncharacteristically modest disclaimer may serve as an epitaph for the work as a whole, which can be shown to have been confected from Stukeley's Oriuna pamphlet.

Of a very different character is the literary hoax perpetrated by James Macpherson, whose claims to have discovered Gaelic manuscripts of bardic verses dating to the pre- and Roman period took literary Britain by storm (Macpherson, 1762). These epic poems claim to be the work of Ossian but are, in reality, a confection drawn from the literary imagination of the author and authentic medieval Scottish ballads (Thomson, 1952). Macpherson's prose 'translation' was quite quickly exposed but his work has merit as an example of the new romanticism which started to permeate literature in the middle of the eighteenth century. He also had a declared social and political motive for his literary production, being distressed by the disintegration of traditional Scottish culture after the Act of Union and the failure of the two Jacobite invasions (Bysveen, 1982).

An entire poem, 'The War of Caros', is devoted to Carausius who is cast in an unfavourable light. The delineation owes nothing to the Scottish medieval tradition, in which he is depicted as mediator between warring factions of the Picts and Scots. On the contrary he is an aggressor who must be resisted as being potentially destructive of Scottish culture. Some geographical elements are derived from contemporary topographical studies, especially those of Stukeley, since the setting of the action is on the banks of the river Carron and Arthur's O'on is described. According to the disingenuous footnote provided by Macpherson the occasion for the conflict was when:

> He [i.e. Caros/Carausius] repaired Agricola's wall, in order to obstruct the incursions of the Caledonians; and when he was employed in that work, it appears he was attacked by a party under the command of Oscar the son of Ossian. The battle is the foundation of the present poem ...

Given the location of the fictitious battle one must assume that Macpherson believed that the Antonine Wall was the creation of Gnaeus Iulius Agricola.

The action seems to be centred on Arthur's O'on:

> A green vale surrounded the tomb which rose in the times of old.
> Little hills lift their heads at a distance; and stretch their old trees to the
> wind. The warriors of Caros sat there, for they had passed the stream
> at night. They appeared, like the trunks of aged pines, to the pale light
> of the morning.

In the event the entire Roman army is routed, single-handedly, by Oscar,
who is fortified and encouraged to feats of heroism by the assembled spirits
of his warrior ancestors.

A sole, sensible, well-informed and scholarly voice was raised against the
inventions of the likes of Stukeley; it passed unnoticed in the clamour. This
voice was that of Richard Gough, the editor of the magisterial edition of
Camden's *Britannia*. His work was published anonymously and the targets
of his criticism were Genebrier and Stukeley (Gough, 1762).

There is no beating about the academic burning bush: Stukeley is roasted
in a line-by-line dissection of his work, little of the *Medallic History* or of
Genebrier's work remains intact under his onslaught. Gough was a master
of both acid derision and the classical sources. Of Stukeley he wrote:

> None that have perused his former Compositions can be Strangers to
> the lively Invention with which he is blest for elucidating Obscurities
> and enodating Difficulties. By the proper Application of this much to
> be envied Faculty, Persons, Places and Things which none had ever
> supposed had an Existence, and some are still absurd enough to doubt
> of, have been brought into being: the long and hard-fought Wars of
> the Critics of several Ages have been decided in an instant: the
> Receptacles of the vilest Miscreants have risen into the Retirements of
> illustrious Devotees: the contested Originals of eminent Cities and
> Towns have been broken from the Fetters of Tradition, and boasted
> irrefragable Certainty: and the best-founded Hypotheses have vanished
> like the subterraneous Vapours before the instantaneous force of
> Electricity.

The Oxford historian cannot deny himself fun at the expense of Stukeley's
attempts to associate Carausius, literally by way of the Car Dyke, the
digging of which he had credited to his hero, with his own university city:

> Dr S. positively affirms him [Carausius] 'sprung of the old British
> Blood-Royal', to which Assertion he is, to be sure, authorised by some
> MS. in his Possession; for we have seen all other Evidences fail him.
> And so much for the Birth and Parentage of Carausius. It would be
> hard if a Person with all these Advantages joined to that of 'a fine
> understanding' should not have had a good Education. But it is very
> hard on us to be left in the dark about the Particulars of it: if we could
> depend on Ages next after the destruction of Troy, or to King
> Arviragus about seventy Years after Christ, we might conclude that

Carausius was beholden to this venerable Seminary for the first
Rudiments of it: But the Circumstance of his own founding first a
Temple, and afterwards a Town at Granta, now Cambridge, so largely
insisted on by his Historian, makes it more than probable that he was
directed thereto by some heavenly Vision predicting the Establishment
of Learning and the Muses in this happy Spot, to make up the
Deficiencies of this Sort which the Island then laboured under, amply
forwarded by the many grateful Sons of Almer Mater, not one of
whom have had the Grace or Gratitude to acknowledge their first
Founder; nay have even treated him with Scorn and Derision.

The most scholarly work on Carausius and Allectus since Holinshed's
pioneering restoration of the primacy of the contemporary historians passed
unremarked.

The reason for this lies in the nature of the national myth which Stukeley
was instrumental in creating at a time when naval heroism was in the
forefront of the nation's consciousness. We have seen that Carausius was re-
created to meet the needs of different ages. The Anglo-Norman, the Welsh,
the Scottish and even the Venetian versions of the reign were now to give
way to Carausius the British Naval Hero. Whereas the land frontier with
Scotland had preoccupied the creators of the Carausian myth hitherto, the
defeat of the Stuart cause in 1745 and the growth of an overseas empire
was now to place the emphasis of the tale on its naval aspects.

Since Britain was more or less constantly at war in the eighteenth century,
the reformulation of a national myth, albeit a minor one, took place in the
light of contemporary events. Stukeley, himself, was conscious of this:
'What I here propose, is an important instance, of the power of Brittain
[sic!], under proper counsel, and the favor of Providence; as to its natural
and naval strength.'

The theme was taken up immediately. Captain George Berkley's influential naval history claimed to be ' . . . a just Account of the Rise and Progress
of the Naval Power of Britain . . . to its present full Perfection, and Meridien
Glory' (Berkley, 1756). Carausius cuts a large figure in this work since
' . . . he taught the Britons what they should have done long before. He
placed his Strength and Dependence on a Navy'. In doing this he acted just
as an ideal captain of the British navy of the period would have done,
knowing that:

> . . . his Designs . . . must all depend on the Fidelity and Affection of his
> Sailors. Two Things he knew commanded that, Success and
> Liberality . . . he was indefatigable in the Search after Prizes. None but
> himself knew what he gained by his Captures: when he had laid by a
> Sufficiency, enough still remain'd for all the Purposes of an abundant
> Generosity. This he distributed freely and by that Beneficence, and by
> his prudent Conduct, he kept the Hearts of his Sailors while he
> preserved the most strict Discipline.

Furthermore this version of Carausius anticipated the tactics of the Royal Navy against their traditional enemies, the French:

> Carausius, who himself commanded, was continually out: not content with defensive Strength, he acted on the offensive, plundering all along the Coasts of Gaul. This British Navy acted on British Principles; sparing no Roman Settlement where it could be destroyed.

This work received a critical drubbing from an anonymous reviewer in the Monthly Review (xvii, 1757, 481–8), where it was pointed out that the book had been compiled, allegedly from Berkley's posthumous papers, by John Hill, a notorious literary hack. The account of Carausius received particularly unfavourable attention:

> Carausius . . . makes his appearance; and the ingenious Doctor [i.e. Hill] very quaintly styles him. A Signal Commander in the British Navy. Here we have a pompous subject of declamation. A British navy acting on British principles ! – The Romans fearing to face the power of Britain now disjointed from them! – And the navy of our country giving a presage of what it has since arrived at, conquering all the sea! – who would have imagined that this swelling and boasting only implied that Carausius, a Roman admiral, brought, from the coasts of Gaul, the fleet under his command, composed of various nations, and prevailed on the Roman forces in Britain to support him in his independency! – a practice then very frequent in every province throughout the empire.

Even Gibbon succumbed to the prevailing mood:

> His fleets rode triumphant in the Channel, commanded the mouths of the Columns of Hercules, with the terror of his name. Under his command, Britain, destined in a future age to obtain the empire of the sea, already assumed its natural and respected station of a maritime nation.

Curiously Gibbon seems to have been ignorant of Gough's work and depended on Stukeley, though he used him with caution: 'Dr. Stukeley in particular has devoted a large volume to the British emperor. I have used his materials, and rejected most of his fanciful conjectures.' Most but not all.

Less disenchanted with earlier sources was the standard and popular naval history of the later eighteenth century: Campbell's *Lives of the British Admirals* (Campbell, 1742–4). This work appeared in no less than five editions between its introduction and the end of the Napoleonic Wars, as a succession of naval victories brought new officers to prominence. The treatment of Carausius follows the Stukeley narrative in all essentials though a note of caution is introduced in the 1779 edition regarding the legitimacy of his actions in taking Britain away from the Empire. Contemporary events in the American Colonies imposed a certain circumspection which moderates the normal adulation for the subject:

> In the succeeding distractions of the Roman Empire, Britain, like the rest of its provinces, fell into the hands of various masters, styled by their adherents, emperors, and by the rest of the world tyrants. Amongst these, there is one who deserves to be remembered in this history; since, how bad soever he might be, he made a good prince of the Britons, and, which is still more to our purpose, carried the maritime power of this country so high, as not only to vindicate his own independency, but also to strike terror into the whole Roman Empire: it is true, many historians treat him as a usurper, a thing that appears a little hard; since those they style emperors had no other title than what they derived from fighting on land, which seems to afford him some colour of right, in virtue of his power by sea.

and

> This certainly is a transaction worthy of being recorded in our naval history, unless we have so far lost the spirit of our ancestors, as to be proud rather of being slaves to Rome, than of contesting the sovereignty of the sea with that haughty people.

Allectus gets short shrift in this. Since he commands the same excellent fleet as Carausius, and maintained his regime for three years, it is difficult to find grounds for his condemnation. But these are at hand:

> He was for some time superior in power at sea, but he employed that superiority rather as a pirate than a prince, sending out his squadrons to spoil the adjacent coasts of Gaul, and to interrupt the trade of all of the Roman provinces.

No longer is this a British fleet acting on British principles.

The nineteenth century saw the abandonment of the excesses of the previous century in most fields of scholarship – German academic research had unravelled the Roman past from its skein of medieval accretions and good texts of classical authors became widely available. Numismatics, too, began to benefit from this more rigorous attitude. By the time that John Yonge Akerman, who had been instrumental in founding what was to become the Royal Numismatic Society, published his *Coins of the Romans relating to Britain*, he could say that in his work '...there is little room for fancy or ornament...'. Of Stukeley he remarks: '...his absurd reveries...have rendered his name ridiculous to the really sensible and enquiring antiquary' (Akerman, 1844). The steady publication, from an increasing body of excavated material, of coins with provenances was to be the main contribution of the century to the study. This phase culminated in the publications of Percy H. Webb on the reigns and coinage of Carausius and Allectus. These have remained the standard references up to the present day, though now sadly in need of revision (Webb, 1906, 1907). These papers, and Webb's later treatment in the relevant volume of *Roman Imperial Coinage* (Webb, 1933) are the starting point for all modern consideration of the reigns. Webb himself acknowledged that the study of the usurpers had peculiar resonances in British history. He published his studies at the height of the naval race between Britain and Germany, when the cry of 'We want eight [i.e. battleships] and we won't wait' shook the government. 'It may be', he says, 'that the following pages will serve not entirely without interest to the general reader, at a time... when the sufficiency of the sea power of Britain is of the most vital importance.'

Webb's comments may have been inspired by the appearance of one of the most influential works of fiction in the present century, Erskine Childers *Riddle of the Sands* (Childers, 1903). In this work two amateur yachtsmen discover a German invasion fleet lurking among the sandbanks off the Frisian Islands, poised to descend on Britain. This was, of course, the very area from which emerged the German pirates who were pursued and defeated by Carausius.

No survey of the literature of the study of Carausius and Allectus can conclude without mention being made of the American writer (the use of the word scholar is inappropriate in this instance), John Watts de Peyster (de Peyster, 1858). The flavour of his work is best judged from the briefest of the three separate, and increasingly fulsome, title pages with which the work is furnished (Pl. g):

> The history of Carausius, the Dutch augustus and emperor of Britain, with which is interwoven an historical and ethnological account of the Menapii, the ancient Zeelanders and Dutch Flemings. Compiled from upwards of two hundred ancient, mediaeval and modern authorities.

De Peyster, of Dutch extraction and bearing the name of one of the foremost families of the original settlement of New Amsterdam, was a very prolific author. Among his many works are to be counted a large number of pamphlets on military affairs, including a bloodthirsty treatise on the employment of the bayonet, a dissertation on fire brigades and volumes on Dutch history, including a book entitled *The Dutch at the North Pole*. His enthusiastic pursuit of an amateur military career in the New York Militia did not extend to participation in the American Civil War, rather he was struck with a 'strange debilitating illness' in 1861 which did not clear up until the cessation of hostilities in 1865. This curious illness, coinciding as it did with the outbreak and end of the war, was not of such a nature as to inhibit the production of a stream of advice to the Union generals, nor did it stop de Peyster soliciting promotion to the rank of Brigadier-General.

While it is easy to see de Peyster as a sham scholar and pusillanimous soldier, there is an underlying seriousness to his work on Carausius and his other volumes of Dutch history. The sub-text to his work is reaction against the failing influence of the descendants of the original Dutch settlers in New

England. In this he inhabits an intellectual milieu similar to that of Macpherson in the previous century, or even of the medieval chroniclers. Significantly, de Peyster's work appeared just as the mass migrations were changing the political climate of the United States and influence was draining away from the traditional holders of political power.

De Peyster's version of Carausius is derived almost entirely from Stukeley, and thus from Geoffrey of Monmouth, augmented with exhilarating inventions of his own. A flavour of the scholarship of this breathless work may be had from the discussion of the name of his hero:

> It is scarcely possible that Carausius was the real name of our Menapian (Hollandish) hero, any more than Caractacus was the actual patronymic of Caradoc or Cradoc – signifying 'The Warrior' – (who, having lost his kingdom by the victory of Ostorius Scapula, won it again by his undaunted demeanour and spirit in his interview with the Emperor Claudius) – or Arminius that of Hermann, the German or Saxon hero, the conqueror of Varus, and victor of the fifth 'Decisive Battle of the World'. After examining the matter with earnest attention we must arrive at the conclusion that it is at least very reasonable to believe that name was Karel (Hollandish) (Charles, English – Carl, German) which means, A (Valiant) Man. To Carolus, the Latin for Karel, the AVSVS, (whence OUSADO, Portuguese; OSADO, Spanish; both of which, particularly the former, are said – in some cases – to resemble the Latin more closely than even the Italian) – The 'Bold', 'He that dareth, or is not afraid', the 'Fearless One' – together, CAROLVS-AVSVS, abbreviated, corrupted and euphonized in Carausius.

Apart from the intellectual problems set by this work, which reads like Tristram Shandy without the benefit of Sterne's sublime artistry, we must sympathize with the provincial typesetter who laboured on our author's behalf, not least because throughout the work whenever the sacred name of Carausius appears it is set in Gothic type. The book ends with an act-by-act outline of a projected melodrama, blessedly never written, featuring Carausius as the hero and Allectus as the unredeemed villain. Watts de Peyster brought the study of Carausius and Allectus back through a full circle to where it began in the post-Roman period.

The theme is not at an end, new discoveries of coins are made daily refinements in the excavation of sites of the period may be anticipated undreamed of new techniques of study will be developed if interest in the topic is maintained in the future for as long as it has been studied in the past. Geoffrey of Monmouth could not have conceived of television or rockets to Saturn, nor can we conceive of what techniques or apparatus will be available at the same distance in the future to answer the problems which we have striven to cast light upon here. What is certain is that *this* version of Carausius and Allectus will prove to be nothing more than an interim stage in the process of what Genebrier called 'bringing him to life again'.

APPENDIX:

The Literary Sources

Translated by R.S.O. Tomlin

MAMERTINI PANEGYRICVS MAXIMIANO AVGVSTO DICTVS
(Mamertinus's Panegyric in Honour of the Emperor Maximian)
The author of this work, who also delivered the Panegyric of 291, is known only
by his writings which contain virtually no biographical details. Gaul was famed
throughout the empire in the third and fourth centuries for the eloquence of orators
trained at the University of Bordeaux. Mamertinus was probably a product of this
school. His concern with peasant revolts, a constant problem in Gaul and a
preoccupation of the Gallic aristocracy, probably indicates that he was a native of
Gaul. The speech was delivered at Trier, the year of delivery not clear from the
text itself but circumstantial evidence points to 21 April 289, the traditional birthday
of the City of Rome and the occasion of celebrations at the imperial court.

The panegyric takes the traditional form, outlining the reason for the speech, the
modest attainments of the orator and the virtues and achievements of the recipient.
In this case Maximian is praised for his successful campaigns against the Bagaudae
in 285–6, the Germans in 287–8 while his forthcoming success against the rebellious
Carausius is confidently forecast.

Pan. Lat. x(ii)

(11.7) It is proof of your good fortune, your success, Your Majesty, that your
soldiers have already reached the Ocean in victory, that the tides have
swallowed the blood of enemies slaughtered on that shore. (12) That pirate
must now lose heart, when he sees that your armies have almost entered those
straits which alone have postponed his death until the present, that his men
have abandoned their ships and have followed the retreating sea. Is there any
more distant island he can now hope for, any other Ocean? How can he
escape punishment for treason, without being swallowed by an earthquake, or
swept by a hurricane on to lonely reefs? Splendid fleets were built and
equipped, which would head for Ocean simultaneously by every river; men
not only competed in their labours to complete them, the rivers suddenly rose
to receive them. For almost a whole year, Your Majesty, when you needed
good weather to build shipyards, to fell timber, to invigorate the workers, to
keep their hands from idleness, hardly a day has been spoiled by rain. Even
winter copied the mildness of spring. Now we thought we were not living in
the north; we felt the clemency of a southern sky as if stars or countries had
changed places. This river of ours, having for a long time lacked a supply of
rain, could not carry the ships; it only brought down the timber for your
shipyards. But suddenly, when the warships had to be launched, the earth

produced abundant springs for you, Jupiter poured out masses of rain, and Ocean flooded whole river beds. And so the ships attacked the waters that came beneath them of their own accord, ships moved by the slightest effort of their crews: the happiest of beginnings that needed a sailor's shanty more than his hard work. Anyone can easily understand, therefore, Your Majesty, how prosperous an outcome will follow you upon the sea, when even the weather obeys you at the right moment.

(13) (Diocletian and Maximian will visit Rome together, more harmonious than Romulus and Remus. Rome envisages their presence by invoking the gods Iuppiter Stator and Hercules Victor.) For this was the title given the latter god by the man who defeated pirates with a cargo boat, and heard from Hercules himself that it was by his help that he had gained the victory. And thus after many ages, Most Holy Emperor, it is one of the duties of your divinity to overcome pirates.

(14) Certainly that day will soon dawn, when Rome sees you victorious . . .

MAMERTINI PANEGYRICVS GENETHLIACVS MAXIMIANO AVGVSTO DICTVS

(Mamertinus's Birthday speech in Honour of the Emperor Maximian)
Like the previous speech, that of 291 was delivered at Trier, probably on 21 July 291. According to the panegyric, little had happened since the delivery of the first speech except that Diocletian had travelled west and Maximian east in order to confer in Milan. The conference is the central theme of the panegyric. No mention is made of Carausius or of affairs in Britain. This deafening silence is highly significant.

PANEGYRICVS CONSTANTIO CAESARI DICTVS

(Panegyric for Constantius Caesar)
The author of this work is not known but internal evidence suggests that he had held a post at the imperial court, participated in Maximian's campaign against the Alamanni in 287, and had previously delivered a speech to the emperor. He retired to the vicinity of Autun, perhaps in or after 293. This background suggests that the anonymous author had first-hand knowledge of events in Britain. The speech was delivered on 1 March 297, not to commemorate the reconquest of Britain the year before but to celebrate the day on which Constantius had been elevated to the rank of Caesar in 293. It was delivered at Trier, where the celebrations were held. The panegyric follows the usual form and after extolling the joint virtues and achievements of the emperors settles down to a detailed account of the defeat of Carausius on the Continent and the recovery of Britain from Allectus.

Pan. Lat. viii(v)
(6) By coming to Gaul, your Gaul, Caesar, you immediately conquered it: for the speed with which you outran all news of your accession and arrival caught and penned within the walls of Boulogne an obstinate, deluded band of piratical rebels, and took the Ocean that washed its gates away from men who had depended on the sea. This displayed your godlike forethought and an outcome the equal of your strategy: you made the whole of that tide-swept harbour inaccessible to ships by driving piles into the entrance and dumping stones over them, and by this wonderful method overcame the very

nature of the place, for the futile returning of the sea seemed to mock them for being cut off from retreat, and was no more use to these prisoners than if it had given up returning altogether. What fort walls will ever be a surprise to us, after this new wall in the sea? Why should it be surprising if walls remain firm against a battering-ram, or their heights look down on siege engines, when Ocean itself, hurled with such impetus, surging in such a mass, whether it is thrown back from lands beyond, as men say, or is lifted by the vapour of its own breath, whatever the force that moves it, when Ocean itself, Caesar, never broke through your barrier nor tore it down at all in so many days and nights of ebb and flow? Meanwhile it was eroding coasts and bursting banks as it flowed round the world, but in the one place this was needed, was either inferior to your majesty in power, or merciful out of the respect it owed you.

(7) Xerxes, I have heard, a most powerful Persian king, threw golden fetters into the deep, asserting that he was chaining Neptune because of his wild waves: a stupid boast, and blasphemous vanity. But your godlike forethought, Caesar, adopted an effective plan by not insulting the element, so as to earn its obedience rather than provoke its hatred. What other explanation can there be for the fact that, as soon as dire straits and a trust in your mercy had ended the siege, the first tide to fall upon the barrier broke through; and that whole line of tree-trunks, which had resisted the waves as long as it was needed, broke up like an army when the signal is given and its duty is over? There can be no doubt that the harbour, which had been blocked to stop the pirate bringing his men help, opened of its own accord to bring us victory. For with the momentum of your courage and success, unconquered Caesar, you could have finished the whole war at once, if circumstances had not insisted that time was needed to build ships. And yet there was no pause in the total overthrow of those enemies who could be approached by land.

(8) (A successful campaign between Rhine and Scheldt, despite the treacherous swamps, with the barbarians being forced to migrate with their families and cultivate deserted land.) (9) We saw barbarian prisoners waiting to be drafted; and now Chamavi and Frisii are peasants in Gaul, are even conscripted into the army.)

(9.5) What am I to do, Caesar? Forgive me if I linger; forgive me if I hurry on, for I am passing over many of your wonderful achievements in the period when the preparations were made for the crossing to Britain, so eager am I to reach the unique victory that finally recovered the whole Empire....

(10) (The loss of Britain in the reign of Gallienus was less painful because most of the Empire had been lost besides; whereas now, its loss was an affront to all our victories. (11) Moreover it was a major province, another world according to Julius Caesar whose invasion met with no naval resistance.)

(12) In that criminal usurpation first the fleet that used to protect Gaul was stolen by a pirate on the run, then many ships were built in our style, a Roman legion was seized, several units of non-Roman soldiers were secured, Gallic merchants were recruited, considerable forces of barbarians were seduced by the loot of the very provinces, all of these being trained in

seamanship by the authors of the crime, and we heard that our armies with their lack of naval experience, for all their indomitable courage, were faced with a wicked great war as a result of that shameful usurpation; and yet we were confident of the outcome. A protracted impunity for their crime had swollen the desperate creatures' audacity, making them claim that the sea's harshness which had inevitably postponed your victory was a cover for your fear of them, and making them believe that war had been abandoned in despair, instead of interrupted on purpose; and so the henchman killed his pirate chief, no longer afraid of a punishment they would both share, and thought his crime would be rewarded by imperial power.

(13) This was the war, so inevitable, so inaccessible, so deep-seated, so well prepared, on which you thus embarked, Caesar, that immediately you poised the baleful thunderbolt of your majesty it seemed as good as finished. First of all, the prime need to ensure that the barbarian peoples did not try to rebel when your divinity turned towards it, you provided for by invoking the majesty of your father. Lord Maximian, eternal Emperor, you deigned to speed the arrival of your divinity by a new short-cut and suddenly appeared on the Rhine, guarding the whole of that frontier not by forces of cavalry or infantry, but by your formidable presence: the bank where Maximian is equivalent to an army. And you, unconquered Caesar, by equipping and deploying several fleets so bewildered and baffled the enemy that he finally felt surrounded, not protected, by Ocean.

(14) At this point it occurs to me how delightful was the good fortune in public administration and prestige of those emperors who gained triumphs and titles from peoples defeated by their generals, without leaving Rome. Fronto, for example, the other (not the second) glory of Roman eloquence, when praising the emperor Antoninus for finishing the war in Britain, declared that although he had remained in the palace at Rome and delegated command, he was like the steersman of a warship and deserved the credit for its sailing and course. But you, unconquered Caesar, not only directed that voyage or war by virtue of being emperor, you were also its immediate inspiration by the example you gave of determination. For you embarked first on Ocean, rough as it was, from the coast of Boulogne, and inspired your army after its sail down the river Seine with such irresistible enthusiasm that it spontaneously demanded the signal to sail, even though its generals were still hesitating, sky and sea being stormy; and although the signs looked threatening, the army ignored them, set sail on a day of rain, and because the wind was not right, used it at an angle. However hostile the sea, who would not trust themselves to it with you sailing? When they heard you were sailing, everyone, it is said, with a single voice cried encouragement: 'Why do we hesitate? Why delay? He has already started, he is on his way, perhaps he has arrived already. Let us try everything, whatever the waves. What is there to fear? We are following Caesar.'

(15) Nor did their belief in your good fortune let them down, for, as we learned from their own report, at that moment such a fog touched the surface of the sea that the hostile fleet, which was posted on watch in ambush off Vectis [the Isle of Wight], was by-passed without the enemy's knowledge, and

was unable to delay, let alone resist, the invasion. As for the fact that the army, unconquered under your leadership, burnt all its own ships as soon as it landed in Britain, what other prompting can have inspired them but that of your godhead? What other reason persuaded them not to keep a means of escape, not to fear the chances of war, not to believe that Mars is 'common to all', unless it was that their thought of you made any doubt of victory impossible? They considered then, not force, not human strength, but your divinities. To be sure of success whatever the battle that faces them, is the good fortune of emperors rather than the self-confidence of their soldiers. Why did the very standard-bearer of the criminal rebellion abandon the shore he was holding, why did he desert fleet and harbour, unless the sight of your looming sails, unconquered Caesar, made him fear that you were coming yourself at any moment? At any rate he chose to risk your generals rather than face the actual thunderbolt of your majesty, madman not to know that, wherever he fled, the force of your godhead was present wherever your features, your statues, were worshipped.

(16) Fleeing from you none the less, he fell into the hands of your men; conquered by you, he was destroyed by your armies. In fact he was terrified by the sight of you behind him; dazed as a madman, he rushed to his death without forming a line of battle or organizing all the forces he led; he forgot all his resources and plunged into ruin with only the old ringleaders of the conspiracy and groups of barbarian mercenaries. And so your good fortune, Caesar, contributed even this to Rome, that hardly a single Roman died in the victory of the Roman empire. All those plains and hills, I hear, were covered by none but the fallen bodies of the foulest enemies. Barbarian, or imitating barbarism in the clothes they wore and their long, reddened hair, they lay filthy with dust and blood in the various postures dictated by the agony of their wounds; and among them was the flag-bearer of the usurpation himself, who had cast off the costume he had dishonoured when alive, with hardly a single garment by which he could be identified. Just before he died he must have told himself to make his body unrecognizable.

(17) The favour of the immortal gods granted you, unconquered Caesar, the destruction of all the enemies you attacked, the Franks in particular; those of your soldiers who lost their way in the sea-fog, as I have just said, reached the town of London independently and finished off the survivors from the battle of that horde of barbarian mercenaries, all over the city which they were intending to loot before they took to flight; and in slaughtering the enemy they gave your provincials the pleasure of the sight, as well as saving their lives. What a manifold victory of countless triumphs, which restored Britain, annihilated the power of the Franks, imposed obedience upon many peoples involved in the criminal conspiracy, and swept the seas and made them peaceful for ever! You may boast, unconquered Caesar, of discovering another world, by restoring its naval glory to Roman power and adding to the Empire an element greater than all the land. Unconquered Caesar, you have finished a war which loomed over every province, since it could range and flare up wherever they were washed by the whole ocean and its inlets.

(18) (Constantius's victory had saved more than Britain, it had saved the

whole Mediterranean from the possibility of attack by pirates.)

(19) You were the avenger, the liberator long prayed-for, and the moment you reached the shore, a triumphant procession met Your Majesty as you deserved; the Britons, jumping for joy, with their wives and children presented themselves, not merely falling down to worship you yourself, whom they regarded as come down from heaven, but even the sails and the oars of that ship which had brought to them your divinity, and they were quite ready to throw themselves upon the ground and thus feel your coming. And no wonder they were elated with such joy, if, after that helpless captivity of theirs for so many years, after the outrages committed upon their wives, after the degrading servitude of their children they were at length free, at length Roman, at length refreshed by the true light of the empire. For over and above that reputation for piety and mercy, belonging to your colleague [i.e. Maximian], which is celebrated by the voice of the people, they saw in your face, Caesar, the outward and visible signs of all the virtues. On your forehead signs of dignity, in your eyes signs of gentleness, in your blushing signs of modesty, in your address signs of justice. When they had marked each of these characteristics and had observed them, they sang together with shouts of joy. They devoted themselves and their children to you both, to your children they devoted all their posterity.

PANEGYRICUS CONSTANTINO AUGUSTO DICTUS
(Panegyric for the Emperor Constantine)
This work is by an unknown author who may have had career connections with the imperial court. The discourse was delivered at Trier in the summer of 310 following the death of the emperor Maximian. Maximian had retired, together with his senior colleague Diocletian, in 305. Uneasy in retirement he re-emerged in late 306. Constantine sought him as an ally but in 310 they were engaged in a civil war in which Constantine, by now Maximian's son-in-law, was the winner. Maximian's death, either by suicide, or more probably execution at the hands of Constantine, left the panegyricist with a delicate task of flattery. Happily he recounts the reconquest of Britain by his father, Constantius, in order to bolster the legitimacy of Constantine's thoroughly illegal regime.

Pan. Lat. vi(vii)

[Speaking of Constantine's father Constantius:]
(5) Who does not, I do not say remembers, but who does not still see how greatly he increased and adorned the Empire? After being appointed emperor, he came and at once shut out the ocean which was seething with an infinite fleet of enemies, and isolated by land and sea the army which had occupied the coast of Boulogne. He did this by driving piles through the waves and cutting off the ebb and flow of that element, to deny the sea they used to touch, to men whose gates the sea had washed. His valour captured that army, his clemency preserved it, and while he prepared to recover Britain by building fleets, he cleared Batavia entirely of enemies, after its occupation by various Frankish tribes under a sometime inhabitant; and not content with conquering them, he converted them into Roman peoples, to make them surrender their savage ways as well as their weapons. And what need I say of the recovery of Britain? The sea was so calm when he sailed there that the

ocean seemed to have been stunned by its passenger's greatness into losing all motion: his journey was such that victory did not escort him, but was already awaiting him.

(6) What need I say of his mercy towards the conquered? What of the justice with which he restored to the victims what they had lost? What of the vision with which he attached subjects to himself, presenting himself as a ruler to make the recovery of freedom attractive to men who had suffered slavery, to call the consciously guilty to repentance by remitting their punishment?

THE HISTORIANS

Three surviving ancient historians retain versions of the revolt of Carausius. Aurelius Victor's *Liber De Caesaribus* (*The Caesars*) is the earliest of these sources, being composed in the middle years of the fourth century, probably in 360. It is a brief history of the Roman empire divided by the reigns of emperors (or 'Caesars'), beginning with Augustus. The *Breviarium* of Eutropius was composed as an aide memoire of Roman history for the emperor Valens (364–78). It is thought that like Aurelius Victor, Eutropius derived his information from a lost imperial history composed in the Constantinian period. Orosius's *Historiarum adversus paganos libri VII*, or 'Seven Books of History against the Pagans', was written in 417 to argue that the collapse of Roman military power had nothing to do with the adoption of Christianity. His work is a catalogue of setbacks suffered by the Roman state throughout her long history under pagan rule. His account of affairs in the reign of Diocletian derives from Eutropius and has no independent evidential value.

Aurelius Victor, *The Caesars*, Ch. 39

[Diocletian sent his colleague Maximian to restore order in Gaul where there had been an uprising of Bagaudae after Carinus had left.] (20) Carausius, a Menapian, distinguished himself in this war, and because he was also thought to be an experienced sailor, having earned his living in this way as a young man, they commissioned him to put together a fleet and fight off the Germans who were infesting the seas. This turned his head. He killed many of the barbarians, but did not pay all the booty into the treasury; because he was afraid of Maximian therefore who (he learnt) had ordered his execution, he usurped the imperial power and seized Britain. [War with Persia and rebellions in Africa and Egypt prompted the creation of two Caesars, Constantius and Galerius, with whose help the Persians and the rebels were defeated.] (39) Only Carausius was left with imperial power, over the island, after being thought amenable to orders and to protect the island's inhabitants from warlike peoples. And even he was overthrown six years later, by the treachery of someone called Allectus. Carausius had made him his chief minister of finance, but fear of his own crimes and of execution for them made Allectus usurp the imperial power. He had only enjoyed it for a short time when Constantius sent Asclepiodotus, whom he had made praetorian prefect, ahead with part of his fleet and legions, and destroyed him.

Eutropius, *Breviarium*, Bk IX

(13) [Diocletian sent Maximian to suppress the uprising of the Bagaudae in Gaul.] At this time also Carausius, a man of very humble birth, had gained a great reputation in a command on active service: he had been commissioned

at Boulogne to bring peace to the sea infested by Franks and Saxons, along the Belgica–Armorica sector, and he had often captured many barbarians, but had not returned all the booty to the provincials or sent it to the emperors; the suspicion had arisen that he allowed the barbarians in on purpose, to catch them as they passed with their booty, and thus to enrich himself; and when Maximian ordered his execution, he usurped the purple and seized the British provinces.

(14) Because of the disorders throughout the world, Carausius's rebellion in Britain [etc., Diocletian made Maximian Augustus, and Constantius and Galerius Caesars]. Peace was finally made with Carausius, since wars were waged in vain against a man of great military experience. After seven years his own ally Allectus killed him, and himself held the British provinces for three years; he was crushed by the agency of Asclepiodotus, the praetorian prefect. Thus the British provinces were recovered after ten years.

Orosius, *Historiae*, vii.25, 3–6
This is a close paraphrase of Eutropius, a little more self-consciously stylish and pointed (e.g. 'Carausius, a man of humble birth, but ready in plan and action'), and a little less informative ('Boulogne' and 'the Belgica–Armorica sector' became 'the shores of Ocean'). His statements of time have no independent value. Carausius held Britain 'for seven years' (*per septem annos*), Allectus 'for a period of three years' (*per triennium*); Britain was recovered 'after ten years' (*post decem annos*) – this last statement is more explicit than Eutropius', but is in fact only a paraphrase of his '*decimo anno*'.

Bibliography and Abbreviations

AA 1922   *L'année épigraphic*
Abad, M. 1991   'Una moneda de Carausio aparecida en la peninsula
                               Iberica. "Lancia", Villasabariego (Leon)', *Gaceta
                               Numismatica* 102, 55–9
Adams, J.N. 1982   *The Latin sexual vocabulary*, London
Akerman, J.V. 1844   *Coins of the Romans relating to Britain*, London
Alcock, L. 1971   *Arthur's Britain: history and archaeology AD 367–634*,
                               London
Ammianus Marcellinus   *The Works*, Ed. & trans. J.C. Rolfe, London, 1935–9
Appian   *Roman history*. Ed. & trans. H. White, London, 1912
Aurelius Victor   *Liber de caesaribus*, Ed. F. Pichmayr & R. Gruendel,
                               Leipzig, 1961

Bailey, C.J. 1981   'Some notes on the coinage of Carausius' *N. Circ.*
                               LXXXIX. 10, 321–2
Barnes, T.D. 1982   *The new empire of Diocletian and Constantine*,
                               London
Bastien, P.E. 1977   *Le trésor de Beaurains (dites Arras)*, Wettern
—, 1978   'Multiples d'or, adventus et panegyriques de Constance
                               Chlore', *B.C.E.N.* 15.1, 1–6
—, 1980   'The Iantinum mint', *A.N.S. Mus. Notes*, 77–85
Beaujard, B. and   'Le trésor de Rouen et l'occupation de la Gaule par
   Huvelin, H. 1980   Carausius', *C.A.N.* 12, 63–87
Bede   *Ecclesiastical History*, Ed. B. Colgrave & B. Mynors,
                               Oxford, 1969

Berkley, G. 1756   *The naval history of Britain, from the earliest periods
                               of which there are accounts in history, to the
                               conclusion of the year M.DCC.L.VI.*, London
Bidwell, P.T. 1985   *The Roman fort of Vindolanda at Chesterholm,
                               Northumberland*, London
Birley, A.R. 1981   *The fasti of Roman Britain*, Oxford
Birley, E. 1936   'An altar from Bankshead, and the Imperium
                               Galliarum', *T.C.W.A.A.S.* XXXVI, 1–7
—, 1952   'Britain under Nero: the significance of Quintus
                               Veranius', *Durham Univ. Jnl.*, 88–92
Bland, R. and   The Normanby, Lincolnshire (hoard), *The Normanby*

Burnett, A. (eds) 1988   *hoard and other Roman coin hoards*, London

Boethius, H.   *The chronicles of Scotland*, Ed. J. Bellenden *et al.* Edinburgh, 1941

Boon, G.C. 1955   'A coin of the "second Carausius" from Silchester', *N.C.* 235

—, 1967   'The Penard Roman imperial hoard: an interim report and list of Roman hoards in Wales', *B.B.C.S.* 22, 306

—, 1974   'Oriuna again', *N. Circ.* 428

—, 1987   'The legionary fortress of Caerleon-Isca', Caerleon

—, 1988   'Counterfeit coins in Roman Britain', in P.J. Casey and R. Reece (eds) *Coins and the archaeologist* (2nd edition), London

Breeze, D. and Dobson, B. 1987   *Hadrian's Wall* (3rd edition), Harmondsworth

Brenot, C. and Loriot, X. 1992   *L'or monnaye III. Trouvailles de monnaies d'or dans l'occident roman*, Paris

Brewer, R. 1980   'A hoard of Roman coins from Pen-y-Corddyn hillfort, Clwyd', *B.B.C.S.* XXVIII, 747–50

Brulet, R. 1989   'The continental Litus Saxonicum', in V. Maxfield (ed.) *The Saxon Shore: a handbook*, Exeter

—, 1991   'Le Litus Saxonicum continental', in V. Maxfield and (M.J. Dobson) (eds) *Roman frontier studies 1989*, Exeter

Burnett, A. 1984   'The coinage of Allectus: chronology and interpretation', *B.N.J.* 54, 21–41

Burnett, A. and Casey, P.J. 1984   'A Carausian hoard from Croydon, Surrey, and a note on Carausius' continental possessions', *B.N.J.* 54, 10–21

Bushe-Fox, J.P. 1932   'Some notes on Roman coastal defences', *J.R.S.* 22, 60–71

Bysveen, J. 1982   *Epic tradition and innovation in James Macpherson's Fingal*, Uppsala

Campbell, J. 1742–44   *Lives of the Admirals, and other eminent British seamen. Containing their personal histories, and a detail of all their public services. Including a new and accurate naval history from the earliest account of time...* (4 vols.), London

Carr, E.H. 1987   *What is history?* (2nd edition), Harmondsworth

Carson, R.A.G. 1959   'The mints and coinage of Carausius and Allectus', *J.B.A.A.* XXII, 33–40

—, (ed.) 1971   'The sequence-marks on the coinage of Carausius and Allectus', *Mints, dies and currency*, 57–65, London

—, 1973   'Bronze medallions of Carausius', *B.M.Q.* XXXVII. 1–2, 1–4

—, 1987   'Carausius et fratres sui... again', in H. Huvelin *et al.* (eds) *Mélanges numismatiques offerts à Pierre Bastien*, 145–48, Wettern

—, 1982   'Carausius et fratres sui: a reconsideration', in S. Scheers

	(ed.) *Studio Paulo Naster oblata. I. Numismatica antiqua*, 245–58, Louvain
Carson, R.A.G. and Kent, J.P.C. 1956	'Constantinian hoards and other studies in the later Roman bronze coinage', *N.C.* 83–161
—, 1971	'A hoard from fourth-century bronze coins from Heslington, Yorkshire', *N.C.* 207–25
Carson, R.A.G., Hill, P.V. and Kent, J.P.C. 1960	*Late Roman bronze coinage. Pt. II.* London
Casey, P.J. 1971	'Excavations at Brecon Gaer', 1970, *Arch. Camb.* CXX, 91–101
—, 1977	'Tradition and innovation in the coinage of Carausius and Allectus', in J. Munby and M. Henig (eds) *Roman life and art in Britain: a celebration in honour of the eightieth birthday of Jocelyn Toynbee*, 217–31, Oxford
—, 1977	'Carusius and Allectus – rulers in Gaul?', *Brit.* 8, 283–301
—, 1978	'Constantine the Great in Britain: the evidence of the London mint . . .', in J. Bird *et al.* (eds) *Collectanea Londiniensia: studies . . . presented to Ralph Merrifield*, 181ff., London
—, 1980	'The coins from the excavations at High Rochester in 1852 and 1855', *A.A.* VIII, 75–89
—, 1982	'Soldier and civilian: friends, Romans, countrymen?', in P. Clack and S. Haselgrove (eds) *Rural settlement in the Roman north*, Durham
—, 1984	*Roman coinage in Britain*, Princes Risborough
—, 1986	*Understanding ancient coins*, London
—, 1987	'The coinage of Alexandria and the chronology of Hadrian', *Mélanges de numismatique offerts à Pierre Bastien*, Wettern
—, 1989	'Coin evidence and the end of Roman Wales', *Arch. J.* 146, 320–30
—, 1990	*The legions in the later Roman world*, Cardiff
—, 1992	'The Coins', in P. Austin (ed.) *Excavations at Bewcastle and Old Penrith*, Carlisle
—, forthcoming	'The coinage of the Roman fort and vicus at Piercebridge', in P.R. Scott, *Excavations at Piercebridge, Co. Durham*
—, forthcoming	*Excavations in the vicus of the Roman fort at Greta Bridge, Co. Durham*
Casey, P.J. and Davies, J.L. 1993	*Excavations at Caernarfon (Segontium)*, London
Casey, P.J. and Noel, M. 1992	'A geophysical survey of the fort at Lanchester, Co. Durham and a note on the garrison', *Arch. J.* 149
Casson, L. 1971	*Ships and seamanship in the ancient world*, Princeton
Childers, E. 1903	*The riddle of the sands*, London
CIL	*Corpus Inscriptionum Latinarum*

Cicero — *Against Verres*, Ed. & trans. L.H.G. Greenwood, London, 1928

Codex Theodosianus — Ed. & trans. E. Phaar, New York, 1952

Cope, L.H. 1974 — 'The metallurgical development of the Roman imperial coinage during the first five centuries A.D.', unpublished Ph.D.

—, 1977 — 'Diocletian's Price Edict and second coinage reform in the light of recent discoveries', *N.C.* 220–6

Cunliffe, B. 1976 — *Excavations at Portchester castle 1*, London

—, 1977 — 'The Saxon Shore: some problems and misconceptions', in D.E. Johnson (ed.) *The Saxon Shore*, London

Curteis, M. 1988 — *The coinage of the Roman fort at Housesteads*, unpublished M.A. thesis, Durham University

Degrassi, A. 1952 — *I fasti consolari dell'impero Romano*, Rome

de Peyster, J.W. 1858 — *The history of Carausius, the Dutch augustus and emperor of Britain, with which is interwoven an historical and ethnological account of the Menapii, the ancient Zeelanders and Dutch Flemings. Compiled from upwards of two hundred ancient, mediaeval and modern authorities*, Poughkeepsie (NY)

Delamaire, R. 1982 — 'Monnaies d'or romaines isolée dans le Nord et le Pas-de-Calais (inventaire provisoire)', *B.S.F.N.* 37.5, 175–80

Dio Cassius — *Historiae Romae*, Ed. E. Cary, London, 1914–27

Donaldson, G.H. 1990 — 'A reinterpretation of RIB 1912 from Birdoswald', *Brit.* 21, 207–14

Dove, C.E. 1971 — 'The first British navy', *Antiquity*, 45, 15–20

Drinkwater, J. 1987 — *The Gallic Empire: separatism and continuity in the north-western provinces of the Roman empire A.D. 260–274*, Stuttgart

—, 1992 — 'The Bacaudae of fifth-century Gaul', in J. Drinkwater and H. Elton (eds) *Fifth-century Gaul: a crisis identity?*, Cambridge

Eicholz, D.E. 1953 — 'Constantius Chorus' invasion of Britain', *J.R.S.* XLII, 41–6

Ekrim, K. *et al.*, 1971 — Diocletian's currency reform: a new inscription, *JRS*, 61, 171–7

Eutropius — *Breviarum ab urbe condita*. Ed. C. Santini, Leipsig, 1979

Evans, A.J. 1887 — 'On a coin of a second Carausius, caesar in Britain in the fifth century', *N.C.* 191–219

Evans, J. 1886 — 'On some rare and unpublished Roman coins', *N.C.* 265–84

—, 1890 — 'On a small hoard of Roman coins found at Amiens', *N.C.* 267–72

Evans, D.R. and Metcalf, V.M. 1992 — *Roman Gates, Caerleon: the 'Roman gates' site in the fortress of the Second Augustan Legion at Caerleon, Gwent*, Oxford

Evans, E. *et al.* 1985 — 'A third-century maritime establishment at Cold

Knapp, Barry, South Glamorgan', *Brit.* 16, 57–125

Fink, R.O. *et al.*, 1940   *The Feriale Duranum*, Yale Classical Studies, VII.

Foote, S. 1752   *Taste: a comedy in two acts*, London

Fordun, John of,   *Chronicle of the Scottish nation*, W.F. Skene (ed.), Edinburgh, 1872

Frere, S.S. 1987   *Britannia: a history of Roman Britain* (3rd edition), London

Frere, S.S. *et al.* 1982   *The excavations of the Roman and medieval defences of Canterbury*, Maidstone

Fulford, M. 1985   'Excavations on the sites of the amphitheatre and forum-basilica at Silchester, Hampshire: an interim report', *Ant. Jnl.* LXV, 39–81

Garnsey, P. (ed.) 1983   *Trade in the ancient economy*, London

Gauckler, P. 1905   'Un catalogue figuré de a batellerie Greco-Romaine: la mosaique d'Althiburus', *Fondation Eugène Piot Monuments et Memoires*, 12, 113–54

Gauld, W.W. 1990   'Vegetius on Roman scout boats', *Antiquity*, 64, 402–6

Genebrier, C. 1740   *Histoire de Carausius, Empereur de la Grande-Bretagne ... prouvé par les médailles*, Paris

Giacchero, M. (ed.) 1974   *Edictum Diocletiani et collegarum de pretiis rerum venalium*, Genoa

Giard, J-B. 1969   'La monnaie locale en Gaule à la fin du IIIe siècle, réflet de la vie économique', *Jnl. des Savants* (Jan–March), 5–35

Gibbon, E. 1775–88   *The decline and fall of the Roman empire*, London

Gough, R. 1762   *The history of Carausius or, an examination of what has been advanced on the subject by Genebrier and Stukeley, in which the many errors and inaccuracies of both writers are pointed out and corrected, with an appendix, containing observations on their method of explaining medals*, London

Gricourt, J. 1967   'Les événements de 289–292 en Gaul d'aprés les trésors de monnaies', *R.E.A.* IX, 366–76

—, 1969   'Trésor de monnaies romaines de Noyelles-Godault (Pas de Calais)', *R.E.A.* LXIX, 228–54

Grueber, H.A. 1900   'Find of Roman coins and gold rings at Sully, near Cardiff', *N.C.* 27–65

Hanson, W. and Keppie, L. (eds) 1980   *Roman frontier studies, 1979*, Oxford

Hassall, M. and Tomlin, R.S.O. 1977   Inscriptions, *Brit.* 8

Haywood, J. 1991   *Dark Age naval power: a re-assessment of Frankish and Anglo-Saxon seafaring activity*, London

Hearne, T. (ed.) 1724   *Robert of Gloucester's chronicle*, London

Hegesippus   Ed. V. Ussai. *Corpus Scriptorum Ecclesiasticorum*, 36. Vienna, 1932

Hendy, M.F. 1985   *Studies in the Byzantine monetary economy, c. 300–1450*, Cambridge

Herodian   *Ab excessu divi Marci.* Ed. C.R. Whittaker, London, 1969–70

Hill, P.V. 1948   'Three new 'Carausius II' coins', *N.C.* 91–92

Hinchcliffe, J. and Green, C.J.S. 1985   'Excavations at Brancaster 1974 and 1977', *E.A.A.* 23

Hodius-Crone, A. 1955   *The temple of Nehalennia at Domburg,* Amsterdam

Holinshed, R. 1577   *The firste volume of the chronicles of England, Scotlande, and Irelande, conteyning the description and chronicles of England, from the first inhabiting unto the Conquest. The description and chronicles of Scotland, from the first originall of the Scottes nation till the yeare 1571. The description and chronicles of Yrelande, from the first originall, untill the yeare 1547,* London

Huelson, C. 1904   'Neue Inschriften', *Mitteilungen des Kaiserlichen Deutsches Archaeologischen Institut, Romische Abteilung,* 19

Huvelin, H. 1983   'Deux nouveaux antoniniani de Carausius frappés a l'atelier de Rouen', *B.S.F.N.* 38.8 381–83

—, 1985   'Classement et chronologie du monnayage d'or de Carausius', *Rev. Num.* XXVII

—, 1992   'Note sur le monnayage de Carausius à la marque RSR', in M. Christol *et al.* (eds) *Institutions, société et vie politique dans l'empire romain au IVe siècle ap. J.-C.,* 171–81, Rome

Huvelin, H. and Loriot, X. 1983   'Quelques arguments nouveaux en faveur de la localisation de l'atelier "continental" de Carausius a Rouen', *B.C.E.N.* 20.4, 65–74

ILS   H. Dessau (ed.) *Inscriptiones Latinae selectae,* Berlin, 1892–1916

Johnson, S. 1970   'The construction of the Saxon Shore fort at Richborough', *Brit.* 1 240–48

—, 1979   *The Roman forts of the Saxon Shore,* London

—, 1983   'Burgh Castle: excavations by Charles Green, 1958–61', *E.A.A.* 20

Jones, A.H.M. 1956   'Numismatics and history', in R.A.G. Carson and C.H.V. Sutherland (eds) *Essays in Roman coinage presented to Harold Mattingly,* Oxford

—, 1964   *The later Roman empire,* Oxford

Jones, M. and Casey, P.J., 1988   'The Gallic Chronicle restored; a chronology for the Anglo-Saxon invasions and the end of Roman Britain', *Brit.* 19, 367–98

Julian   *The works of the emperor Julian.* Ed. W.C. Wright, London, 1913

Kennedy, J. 1751   *Dissertation upon Oriuna, said to be empress or queen of England, the supposed wife of Carausius, monarch and emperor of Britain, who reigned in the time of Diocletian the great persecutor of Christians, whom he was at war with for many years, until received as colleague with him in the Roman Empire. Illustrated with the coin of Oriuna, and several others most remarkable of Carausius, hitherto not made public; this coin of her's being lately sent to France to his Most Christian Majesty*, London

—, 1756   *Further observations on Carausius, emperor of Britain, and Oriuna, supposed by some to be real person. With answers to those trifling objections made to the former discourse*, London

Kent, J.P.C. 1961   'The Comes Sacrarum Largitionum' in E.C. Dodd, *Byzantine silver stamps*, Washington, D.C., 35–45

—, 1957   'Carausius II – fact or fiction?' *N.C.*, 345–49

Kienast, D. 1990   *Romische Kaisertabelle*, Darmstadt

King, A. 1991   'The date of the stone defences of Roman Bitterne', in V. Maxfield and M.J. Dobson, *Roman frontier studies 1989*, 108–16, Exeter

King, C. 1985   'The Unmarked coins of Carausius', *B.N.J.* 54, 1–9

Kolb, F. 1987   *Diocletian und die Erste Tetrarchie*, Berlin

Lactantius   *De mortibus persecutorum*. Ed. & trans. J.L. Creed, Oxford, 1984

Leeds, E.T. 1946   *A hoard of Roman folles from Diocletian's reform to Constantine Caesar found at Fyfield, Berks*, Oxford

Loriot, X 1979   'Monnaies de Carausius en Haute-Normandie', *B.S.F.N.* 34.5, 521–23

—, 1979   'Trouvailles de monnaies de Carausius sur le continent', *B.S.F.N.* 34.8, 576–83

—, 1980   'Antoninien de Carausius au Musée de Moulins', *B.S.F.N.* 5, 697–98

—, 1981   'Les aurei de Dioclétien et Maximien à la marque IAN', *B.S.F.N.* 36.7, 88–92

—, 1992   'La carriere d'Allectus jusqu'à son elevation à la pourpre', in M. Christol *et al.* (eds) *Institutions, societé et vie politique dans l'empire romaine au IVe siècle apres J.-C.*, 161–69, Rome

Loriot, X & Delaporte, J. 1978   *Trésors de monnaies romaines découverts dans le Départment de la Seine-Maritime*, Paris

Macpherson, J. 1762   *Fingal, an ancient epic poem, in six books: together with several poems, composed by Ossian the son of Fingal. Translated from the Galic language by James Macpherson*, London

Mann, J.C. 1977   'The Reculver inscription - a note', in D.E. Johnson (ed.) *The Saxon Shore*, London

—, 1977   'Duces and Comites in the 4th century', in D.E. Johnston (ed.) *The Saxon Shore*, 11–15, London

—, 1989   'The historical development of the Saxon shore', in V. Maxfield (ed.) *The Saxon Shore: a handbook*, Exeter

Marsden, P. 1990   'A re-assessment of Blackfriars 1', in S. McGrail (ed.) *Maritime Celts, Frisians and Saxons*, 66–74, London

Maxfield, V. (ed.) 1991   *The Saxon Shore: a handbook*, Exeter

McCormick, M. 1988   *Eternal victory: triumphal rulership in late antiquity, Byzantium and the early mediaeval West*, Cambridge

Milne, G. 1985   *The port of Roman London*, London

—, (ed.) 1992   *From Roman basilica to medieval market: archaeology in action in the City of London*, London

Mitard, P.H. 1980   'Trouvailles de monnaies de Carausius dans le Vexin français (Val d'Oise)', *B.S.F.N.* 35.4, 675–6

Mitchell, S. and Waelkens, M. 1987   'Sagalassus and Cremna 1986', *A.S.* XXXVII, 37–48

—, 1988   'Cremna and Sagalassus 1987', *A.S.* XXXVIII, 53–65

Mossup, J.C. 1958   'A hoard of folles from Market Stainton', *N.C.* 59–72

N.D.   *Notitia dignitatum*. Ed. O. Seeck, Berlin, 1876

Nash-Williams, V.E. 1950   *The early Christian monuments of Wales*, Cardiff

—, 1969   *The Roman frontier in Wales* (2nd edition), Cardiff

Nemesianus   *Cynegetica*, J.W. & A.M. Duff, eds *Minor Latin poets*, London, 1968

Nennius   *The British history and Welsh Annals*, Ed. & trans. J. Morris, London, 1980

Ottoway, P. 1993   *Roman York*, London

Orosius   *Historia adversum paganos*. Ed. C. Zangmeister, Leipsig, 1889

Pan. Lat.   *XII panegyrici latini*. Ed. R.A.B. Mynors, Oxford, 1964

Peacock, D. 1973   'Forged brick-stamps from Pevensey', *Ant.* XLVII, 138–40

Perring, D. 1991   *Roman London*, London

Philp, B. 1981   *The excavation of the Roman forts of the Classis Britannica at Dover, 1970–77*, Dover

Piggott, S. 1985   *William Stukeley: an eighteenth century antiquary*, London

Reece, R. 1976   'The coins', in B. Cunliffe (ed.) *Excavations at Porchester Castle*, 188–97, Oxford

—, 1978   'The Roman coins', in B. Cunliffe (ed.) *Fifth report on the excavation of the Roman fort at Richborough, Kent*, 188–216, Oxford

Rhodes, M. 1991   'The Roman coinage from London Bridge and the development of the City and Southwark', *Brit.* 22, 179–90

RIB   R.G. Collingwood & R.P. Wright, *The Roman inscriptions of Britain. 1. Inscriptions on stone*, Oxford, 1965

Richmond, I.A. 1945   'The Sarmatae, Bremetennacum Veteranorum and the Regio Bremetennacensis', *J.R.S.* XXXV, 15–29

Rule, M. 1990   'The Romano-Celtic ship excavated at St Peter Guernsey', in S. McGrail (ed.) *Maritime Celts, Frisians and Saxons*, 49–56, London

St Joseph, J.K. 1936   'The Roman fort at Brancaster', *Ant. J.* 16, 444–60

Salzman, L.F. 1907   'Excavations at Pevensey; 1906–07', *Sus. Arch. Col.* 53, 83–95

Seaby, H.A. 1956   'A find of coins of Carausius from the Little Orme's Head', *N.C.* 205–46

Seeck, 1876   *Notitia urbis Constantinopolitanae,* Berlin

Serres, J.T. 1802   *The little sea torch; or, a true guide for the coasting pilots,* London

SHA   *Scriptores historiae augustae.* Ed. & trans. D. Magie, London, 1922–32

Shiel, N. 1974   'Un aureus de Carausius conservé au Cabinet des Medailles de Paris', *R.N.,* XVI, 163–6

—, 1975   'The Blackmoor hoard of third century Roman bronze coins' (*Sale catalogue Christie, Manson and Woods Ltd.*), London

—, 1976   'An aureus of Carausius from Hertfordshire', *N. Circ.* LXXXIV, 7/8, 274

—, 1977   *The episode of Carausius and Allectus,* Oxford

—, 1979   'Another BRI coin of Carausius', *N. Circ.* LXVII, 336–7

—, 1980   'Carausius et fratras sui', *B.N.J.* 48, 7–11

Skeat, 1964   *Papyri from Panopolis in the Chester Beatty Library, Dublin,* Dublin

Smith, D.J. 1969   'The mosaic pavements', in A.L.F. Rivet (ed.) *The Roman villa in Britain,* 71–126, London

Speed, J. 1611   *Historie of Greate Britaine under the conquest of the Romans, Saxons, Danes and Normans,* London

Steer, K. 1958   'Arthur's O'on: a lost shrine of Roman Britain', *Arch. J.* CXV, 100–10

Stevens, C.E. 1956   'Some thoughts on "second Carausius"', *N.C.* 345–49

—, 1957   'Marcus, Gratian and Constantine', *Athenaeum* 35

Stuart, P. and Bogaers, J.E. 1971   *Deae Nehalenniae,* Leiden

Stukeley, W. 1752   'Oriuna wife of Carausius, Emperor of Britain', *Palaeographia Britannica* III

—, 1757–59   *The medallic history of Marcus Aurelius Carausius Emperor in Britain,* London

Sutherland, C.H.V. 1945   'Carusius II, "Censeris", and the barbarous Fel. Temp. Reparatio overstrikes', *N.C.* 125–33

—, 1954   'A hoard of Roman folles from Wroxton Heath near Banbury', Oxon, *N.C.* 62ff.

Tatlock, J.S.P. 1950   *The legendary history of Britain: Geoffrey of Monmouth's Historia Regum Britanniae and its early vernacular versions,* Los Angeles

Thoen, H. 1981   'The third century Roman occupation in Belgium: the evidence of the coastal plain', in A. King and M. Hening (eds) *The Roman west in the third century,* Oxford

Thomas, J.D. 1976   'The date of the revolt of Domitius Domitianus', *Z.P.E.* 22, 253–79

—, 1977   'A family dispute from Karanis and the revolt of Domitius Domitianus', *Z.P.E.* 24, 231–40

Thompson, D.S. 1952   *The Gaelic sources of Macpherson's 'Ossian'*, London

Thompson, E.A., 1974   'Peasant revolts in late Roman Gaul and Spain', in M. Finley (Ed.) *Studies in ancient society*, London

—, 1990   'Ammianus Marcellinus and Britain', *N.M.S.* XXXIV, 1–15

Tristan, J. 1644   *Commentaires historiques. Contens l'histoire génerale des empereurs, imperatrices, caesars, et tyrans de l'émpire romain*, Paris

Vegetius   *De rei militari*. Trans. N.P. Miller, Liverpool, 1993

Wade, W.W. 1953   'Carausius, restorer of Britain', *N.C.* 131–4

Walker, D.R. 1988   'Roman coins from the sacred spring at Bath', Oxford

Webb, P.H. 1906   'The coinage of Allectus', *N.C.* 127ff.

—, 1907   'The reign and coinage of Carausius', *N.C.* 1ff.

—, 1933   *The Roman imperial coinage. Vol. V. Pt. 2*, London

White, D.A. 1961   *Litus Saxonicum: the British Saxon Shore in scholarship and history*, Madison (Wisconsin)

Wightman, E. 1985   *Gallia Belgica*, London

Williams, T. 1989   'Allectus' building campaign in London: implications for the Saxon Shore', in V. Maxfield and M.J. Dobson (eds) *Roman frontier studies, 1989*, Exeter

—, 1993   *Public buildings in the south-west quarter of Roman London*, London

Wright, N. (ed.) 1981   *The Historia Regum Britanniae of Geoffrey of Monmouth. I. Bern. Burgerbibliothek, Ms. 568*, Cambridge

Zabarella, G. 1659   *Il Carosio overo origine regia et augusta della serenissima famiglia*, Padua

Zonaras   *Corpus Scriptores Byzantinae*, Bonn, 1987

Zosimus   *The new history*, trans. R.T. Ridley, Canberra, 1982

Index